T0330442

The New Global Political Economy

NEW DIRECTIONS IN MODERN ECONOMICS

Series Editor: Malcolm C. Sawyer, *Professor of Economics, University of Leeds, UK*

New Directions in Modern Economics presents a challenge to orthodox economic thinking. It focuses on new ideas emanating from radical traditions including post-Keynesian, Kaleckian, neo-Ricardian and Marxian. The books in the series do not adhere rigidly to any single school of thought but attempt to present a positive alternative to the conventional wisdom.

For a full list of Edward Elgar published titles, including the titles in this series, visit our website at www.e-elgar.com

The New Global Political Economy

From Crisis to Supranational Integration

Riccardo Fiorentini

Professor of International Economics, University of Verona, Italy

Guido Montani

Professor of International Political Economy, University of Pavia, Italy

NEW DIRECTIONS IN MODERN ECONOMICS

Edward Elgar

Cheltenham, UK • Northampton, MA, USA

Published by
Edward Elgar Publishing Limited
The Lypiatts
15 Lansdown Road
Cheltenham
Glos GL50 2JA
UK

Edward Elgar Publishing, Inc.
William Pratt House
9 Dewey Court
Northampton
Massachusetts 01060
USA

A catalogue record for this book
is available from the British Library

Library of Congress Control Number: 2012935293

MIX
Paper from
responsible sources
FSC
www.fsc.org FSC® C018575

ISBN 978 0 85793 404 8

Typeset by Servis Filmsetting Ltd, Stockport, Cheshire
Printed and bound by MPG Books Group, UK

Contents

Figures

Tables

Preface

Why publish a new book on the 2008 financial crisis? The basic reason is that, during these dramatic years, we became aware of the fact that the first global crisis will have a similar impact on the international economic and political systems as the 1929 crisis between the two world wars had. Not only did the Great Depression mark the end of the gold standard, the old economic order of the nineteenth century, it also marked the beginning of the transition to a new political order, after World War II, based on the hegemonic power of the US and, to a lesser extent, the USSR.

The main features of our study are analyses of the causes of the crisis and the measures of political economy required to build a safer and more stable international order. We try to show that the deep roots of the financial crisis are to be found in the flaws of the dollar standard. The heart of the crisis was in the US, but the turmoil immediately spread all over the world because of the deep integration of all national economies in the global financial market. The crucial vehicle for global economic integration is the dollar, but the dollar is the sovereign currency of the US, a tool at the disposal of the US government for its policy aims. The dollar as an international currency has no government and no central bank. Of course, this problem is not new – it has been discussed since the heyday of the Bretton Woods system – but the financial crisis shows how urgent it is to face a new organization of the world economy. Parts I and II aim to explain why the dollar and globalization should be considered together in order to understand the present challenges. For instance, global imbalances and income inequalities, within and between countries, can be considered by-products of the present international monetary and financial order. Moreover, regional unions reveal a tendency towards supranational integration and the development of a multipolar global economy.

Part III explains why it is necessary to reform the international order. The political background in which we planned these reforms is characterized by the transition from a monopolar system, led by the US, to a multipolar international system where, next to the old superpowers of the Cold War, new emerging countries – such as China, India, Brazil and South Africa – are quickly falling into place. The European Union, with the euro carried away by the devastating sovereign debt crisis, cannot yet be considered a new global player, but its model for the integration of different national peoples, once fierce enemies, has inspired the institutional reforms presented here. The novelty of the European method of integration is the building of supranational institutions. In 1950, the European Coal and Steel Community was shaped according to the federal model, though with powers limited to the management of two sectors, coal and steel, crucial to avoid a new war between France and Germany. The fact that European integration developed solely along an economic pathway blurred the political meaning of the European project. Likewise, today it is not plain that the lack of a European political government is the real cause of the sovereign debt crisis. But whatever the outcome of this crisis, the history of European integration is full of useful teachings for the architecture of a new multipolar world.

Today supranational institutions in the global economy are necessary to provide global public goods to national peoples, such as a world currency and a policy for sustainable development, to overcome the divide between rich and poor people, and to stop the insane race of humankind towards an irreversible ecological crisis. Supranational institutions are required to overcome a double failure: the failure of the market and the failure of cooperation among national governments. Supranational institutions must have limited but effective power to foster policies that are essential for the provision of global public goods. To face this problem a part of this book is devoted to clarifying the relationship between monetary and fiscal policy among different national governments in a multitier system of governments, that is a federal union.

Monetary policy and fiscal policy are the core of macroeconomic theory, but international economics examines this relationship assuming the existence of national sovereign governments without supranational institutions. Indeed, economists study international monetary relations as a choice between fixed and flexible rates of exchange. Likewise fiscal policy is hardly ever considered a competence of international institutions: for international economics the only substantial problem is the impact of national fiscal policy on national welfare: the impact on the rest of the world is seldom considered.

The state-centric point of view is also the explicit assumption of international political economy, an academic branch developed after the breakdown of the Bretton Woods system. International political economy is an attempt to melt international economics and the theory of international relations. Some say that it studies the struggle for power and wealth among sovereign states. Indeed, this approach can help to overcome the restricted point of view of international economics. But after the accomplishment of globalization, there is a growing uneasiness among its scholars. Susan Strange (2002) resolutely protested against its incapacity to understand the mechanism of the new global framework, and some scholars tried to found a 'heterodox' international political economy (Pogatsa, 2011).

Adopting the supranational point of view we were able to overcome the shortcomings of international economics and international political economy. But we realized that our analytical framework was – if the individual members of a political community are considered the final subjects of a policy – hanging in the air. A national government acts for the wellbeing of its national citizens. The so-called international community is only a coalition of nation states, when they have some common interest to manage, such as the G20. Nevertheless a summation of national peoples is not a political community.

The ambiguous meaning of internationalism can be explained. Internationalism – basically a simple propensity to negotiate problems among national governments – is also an ideology embedded in liberal, democratic and socialist thinking. The positive side of internationalism claims that peaceful and cooperative relationships can be established among liberal, democratic and socialist governments. But this claim very often fails because national interest prevails over the interest of other national peoples.

To sum up, our effort to overcome the shortcomings of international cooperation required the identification of a new political community, a new political subject. We had to answer the question: a policy for whom? Thanks to a debate already under way among many political scientists, the solution to our problem was not difficult: we were working out policies for a cosmopolitan community. According to Brown and Held: 'In its basic form, cosmopolitanism maintains that there are moral obligations owed to all human beings based solely on our humanity alone, without reference to race, gender, nationality, ethnicity, culture, religion, political affiliation, state citizenship, or other communal particularities' (Brown and Held, 2010: 1). The logical outcome of our research was a more precise terminology: we prefer to speak of a 'global political economy' or 'supranational political economy.' Although, if the political values are taken into account, the correct terminology should be 'cosmopolitan political economy.'

No concluding chapter is necessary for this book. Our conclusions are two proposals: one for a World Monetary Union (WMU) and, following this, a World Eco-Monetary Union[1] (WEMU). We are fully aware that the realist school of international politics and economics will criticize these proposals. Reforming the international political and economic order is the most difficult task for all policy makers. The social scientists should be aware that their work risks being disregarded and left to gather dust in some library. In 1949, Professor Rappart, after Robert Triffin's presentation of his project for the *European Payments Union*, commented: 'You are far too optimistic . . . such proposals cannot be agreed to in a negotiation involving so many governments and contradictory national interests.' To this remark Triffin's answer was: 'If my main concern were to make safe forecasts, I would agree with you and be proven right nine times out of ten. But I prefer to be wrong nine times out of ten, if I can contribute once in ten times to divert us from catastrophy, and help build a better future' (Triffin, 1981).

Our chances to be heard are much lower than Triffin's even if the overhanging catastrophes of our day are not less dreadful of those of the 1940s. We are aware that our task is difficult but not hopeless. The limit of our proposals is that we worked out a cosmopolitan design starting from a European point of view. We cannot overcome this hurdle: we were born and we live in Europe. Nevertheless there is a way out. Our work will be useful – and governments will think over bold reforms of the international order – if people living in other continents enrich and widen the debate with their points of view on the future of the cosmopolitan community.[2]

December 2011
Riccardo Fiorentini
Guido Montani

NOTES

1. 'Eco' is an abbreviation of 'economic' and 'ecological' union.
2. The authors take joint responsibility for the full content of the book, but they specify that Riccardo Fiorentini wrote Part II and Guido Montani Parts I and III. They wish to thank Deirdre Kantz for revising the English draft of Parts I and III, and Marcus Perryman for revising Part II.

PART I

Why a supranational political economy?

1.   The invisible Leviathan

1.1   THE FINANCIAL CRISIS AND THE DECAY OF THE OLD INTERNATIONAL ORDER

Like the world crisis of 1929, the financial crisis of 2007–8 triggered dramatic economic damage and a sharp awareness of the irreversible decay of the international order established after the Second World War. From the US, the financial turmoil spread to Europe and other industrialized countries, bringing on bank failures and unemployment. A great number of emerging economies suffered a sudden stop of foreign financial funds; international trade and output collapsed. But the political reaction was very different from what happened after the 1929 crisis, when all national governments tried to save themselves without considering the negative effects of their policies on other countries. Promptly the G20 was set up and the response of the industrialized and the emerging countries, in the spring of 2009, was a global plan for the recovery of the world economy. This plan was to some extent effective. International cooperation rather than self-sufficiency was the main political difference between the present financial crisis and the 1929 world crisis.

During the 1930s in Europe and the US, many governments launched national recovery plans, raised high custom duties to protect national industry and employment, and implemented competitive devaluations among national currencies. Keynes' *General Theory* offered the best theoretical explanations of the 'national self-sufficiency' policy, whose aim is to 'minimize, rather than . . . maximize economic entanglement between nations.' (Keynes, 1933). Today, the world's economic recovery and development cannot be built on the same political assumptions. Global interdependence of peoples, ideas, technologies, commodities and financial capitals is a reality recognized and accepted by a great number of political parties and governments, in all continents. Every national government supports international cooperation in public statements, even if in practice their behaviour is not always coherent with the official stance. In effect, international cooperation is based more on occasional goodwill than solid institutions. We continue to live in a precarious, unstable and risky world. The international institutions built after World War II are under stress.

In order to understand why the old international order cannot work today and requires fundamental reform, it is necessary to recall its historical background and some of its main features. Even before the declaration of war, the Roosevelt administration was aware that the US had to plan a post-war order capable of guaranteeing stability, peace and prosperity for the international community. The failure of the League of Nations was a lesson to be considered: a victory is not a guarantee of lasting peace. Therefore, the Roosevelt administration worked promptly during the conflict in order to prepare the institutional framework for the post-war international order (Gardner, 1969). The United Nations, the Bretton Woods institutions and the General Agreement on Tariffs and Trade (GATT) (today World Trade Organization, WTO) were built on the initiative of the US government in order to facilitate international political and economic cooperation at the end of warfare. The United Nations went beyond the defects of the League of Nations because only five big powers entered the Security Council, whose role was to keep order in their continent. The International Monetary Fund (IMF) and the World Bank had the task of building a stable international monetary system. The GATT worked effectively to create an international free trade area among the member countries. Of course, none of the international institutions could work without the active support of the US. Indeed, the US government was well aware that its isolationist policy after World War II was one of the causes of the League of Nations' failure and that its full commitment in world affairs was crucial to foster peace and prosperity.

This universal project – today we can call it global – was implemented only partially, because in February 1945 (before the end of the war) the Big Three (Churchill, Roosevelt and Stalin) met in Yalta to shape the post-war political order. Europe and the world were divided into two zones of influence. In Yalta, though not declared officially, the concept of the superpower was created. The old idea of great European powers, unceasingly fighting for supremacy, was not suitable to describe the new reality of world politics. Now the US and the Soviet Union, two continental powers, took the lead. The old European system of nation-states was substituted by a bipolar world system, ruled by two continental superpowers. The Cold War was the inevitable outcome of World War II and bipolarism.

One of the features of the Cold War was ideological confrontation. The US was considered the champion of democracy and free market economy. The Soviet Union was considered the champion of communism and social planned economy. But, for political theorists, the real novelty and importance of the post-war international system was certainly its political stability. Rightly, John Gaddis calls the Cold War the 'long peace', where, because of the 'overall stability of the [two] basic alliance systems, defections from both the American and Soviet coalitions – China, Cuba, Vietnam, Iran, and Nicaragua, in the case of Americans; Yugoslavia, Albania, Egypt, Somalia and China again in the case of Russians – have been tolerated without the major disruption that might have attended such changes in a more delicately balanced multipolar system' (Gaddis, 1987: 222). Furthermore, if we look for the main causes of the long peace we have to take into consideration the military factor: that is the possession of nuclear weapons. After the Hiroshima and Nagasaki bombings, the American government was extremely wary about using the atomic bomb again, even when the Soviet Union did not have nuclear weapons. It is reasonable to say that 'the development of nuclear weapons has had, on balance, a stabilizing effect on the post-war international system. They have served to discourage the process of escalation that has, in other eras, too casually led to war' (Gaddis, 1987: 231).

During the years of the Cold War and the balance of terror, the United Nations worked more as a confrontation arena than as a forum for peace settlements. Nevertheless, the US government was able to promote its project to build a free international market in the Western zones of influence. Thanks to the Marshall Plan, the gold-exchange standard – based on the Bretton Woods institutions – and the series of GATT rounds for tariff reductions, the European states were able to recover from the war catastrophe and to build the first supranational institutions to integrate their economies and societies. And when Japan took the lead of Asian development, it became clear that the original American project of a world integrated economy, at least in the Western hemisphere, was being achieved. The demise of the Bretton Woods system, after Nixon's declaration of the inconvertibility of the dollar into gold, in 1971, was only a serious accident along the road of an increasingly freer and thriving global economy. Between 1989 and 1991 the Soviet Union collapsed, in the attempt to reform their command economy to keep pace with Western economic performances, because of internal political and nationalistic rivalries. But the US too was obliged to face new international challenges. Before the fall of the Berlin Wall, Paul Kennedy, after a long and thorough historical analysis of the interplay of military, financial and economic factors in the world balance of power, came to the conclusion that the relative decline of the US's power was inevitable. This decline was only 'masked by the country's enormous military capabilities at present, and also by its success in "internationalizing" American capitalism and culture' (Kennedy, 1988: 533), but the bipolar system was doomed to become a multipolar system, according to Kennedy a 'pentarchy', which included the US, the USSR, China, Japan and the European Community.

Kennedy's structural analysis of the evolution of the international order was completely forgotten after the fall of the Berlin Wall and the disruption of the USSR. Many political analysts welcomed the dawn of a new age ruled by the US, the only surviving superpower. The approaching twenty-first century was called the American century and monopolarism was considered the main feature of the new international order. Francis Fukuyama provided the ideological framework for this new political outlook: after the failure of the communist ideology the way was already open for the success of democracy as a universal political regime. In all countries, many people could embrace the American democratic model. This does not mean that all the problems of humanity had been solved: mass poverty, wars, religious and ethnic rivalries will stay with us for a long time, said Fukuyama. But as democracy spreads in every country, international cooperation will become a permanent feature of the international community. Therefore, Fukuyama (1992) could affirm that the 'end of history' was coming, because the liberal-democratic ideology was the final stage in the development of human political thinking. Unfortunately, history did not follow this idealistic course. In the following years many wars took place in the Middle East, Africa and Asia; and in 1997 the Asian economic crisis provoked a dramatic fall in income and employment in many countries. After the terrorist attack upon the World Trade Center on September 11 2001, the US responded with two wars: in Afghanistan and in Iraq. We should not be surprised that, after Fukuyama's idealistic outlook, some years later, Robert Kagan (2008) reaffirmed the political realist stance. According to Kagan, international politics is firmly based on nation-states and the balance of power, as in the last centuries. The present international system is unipolar, according to Kagan, and the US remains the only superpower. The American economic and military power is indispensable for winning the hegemonic struggle of liberalism against autocracy, that is the Russian and Chinese regimes.

Nevertheless, not all political analysts accept Kagan's point of view. The debate on the main features of the new international order after the end of the Cold War is still open. For instance, Richard Haass (2008), President of the American Council on Foreign Relations, maintains that nation-states have lost their monopoly on power, because they are challenged by regional and global organizations, such as NGOs and multinational corporations. International politics, in the age of globalization, is becoming more and more multipolar. But a multipolar system is not necessarily a world of perpetual wars of great powers; it can be cooperative. We live in the age of 'nonpolarity,' Haass affirms.

Here, we presented a short summary of the debate on the new international order preceding the financial crisis of 2007–8. This crisis opened new perspectives on the state of the world and its future.

1.2 THE FINANCIAL CRISIS: ITS CAUSES

In economics, as in all social sciences, ascertaining facts is not an intellectual activity independent of interpreting them. This general rule can be easily verified with the example of the financial crisis of 2007–8. As a matter of fact, even its name is in doubt; some prefer to speak of the 'great recession.' But nobody disputes the fact that the epicentre of the crisis was the US economy, especially its monetary and financial system, and that from the US the crises spread all over the world. Here, we maintain the label 'financial crisis' because the crisis erupted in the US financial and banking sector and because cross-border financial investments are the salient feature of the global economy. According to some estimates, global financial assets rose from US$123 trillion in 1980 to US$196 trillion in 2007 (for the IMF the latter figure is US$241 trillion). Moreover, this trend is soaring: in 2000 only 11 countries had financial assets of more than 350 per cent of their GDP; in 2007 these countries added up to 25 (Blankenburg and Palma, 2009: 531). The 2007–8 crisis is the symbol of a new stage of development of the international economy.

Since our aim is to show that the financial crisis had its roots in the malfunctioning of the old international monetary system and that, in order to avoid future calamities, it is necessary to create supranational institutions for the new multipolar world, we begin our inquiry by considering four explanations for the financial crisis. These explanations are not necessarily in conflict with one another; each explanation – which is also an interpretation of the market-state relationship – points out some interesting aspect and all of them agree on the fact that the cure cannot be found solely inside the US but that some reform of the international order is required.

In a slim booklet, John Taylor (2009) shows, by means of quantitative research, how the Federal Reserve purposefully deviated from the 'regular' interest rate based on the usual macroeconomic variable, that is the inflation rate and the output gap (the Taylor rule). In the years 2002–03 the interest rate was held at a very low level and was raised only in 2004–06, as a reaction to the exaggerated increase in housing prices. During the period of low short-term interest rates the price of adjustable-rate mortgages (ARMs) rose to a very high level and 'this made borrowing attractive and brought more people into the housing markets, further bidding up housing prices' (Taylor, 2009: 11). There was an 'interaction between the monetary excesses and the risk-taking excesses' (Taylor, 2009: 13). Following this boom, most adjustable-rate sub-primes were packed into mortgage-backed securities (MBSs) and sold on the financial market. When the crises began, it was impossible for many financial institutions to know the real risk stored in their balance sheets.

The Federal Reserve monetary policy explains why the housing boom began; the intervention of the federal government explains why the crisis deepened. Taylor maintains that neither the Fed nor the federal government understood the real nature of the trouble. At the beginning, it was considered a liquidity crisis, but in fact it was a systemic or counterparty risk crisis, which became acute in August 2007. In December 2007 the term auction facility (TAF) of the federal government was introduced in order to make it easier for banks to borrow from the Fed. But the crisis did not end there. In February 2008, the federal government proposed $100 billion to spur household consumption. But personal consumption expenditure did not increase significantly. Finally, in April 2008 the Fed reduced the interest rate sharply, causing a depreciation of the dollar. But the result was an increase in the price of oil (on the international and the internal markets), which hindered economic recovery. The crisis accelerated dramatically with the decision, on 15 September 2008, to let the Lehman Brothers go bankrupt. Financial markets feared that the government would not prevent the financial institution from failing. Only when the Troubled Asset Relief Program (TARP), whose aim was to support commercial papers and restore confidence among financial institutions, was announced on 13 October 2008, did the crisis come to an end. Taylor's conclusion is: 'during the Great Depression, a crisis to which the current one is often compared, there was a liquidity shortage, and the Fed did not provide liquidity . . . In this crisis the Fed did provide liquidity, but the problem was not a shortage of liquidity' (Taylor, 2009: 46).

Taylor is convinced that the best option for monetary policy is to moderate the inflation rate. During the 1970s, the breakdown of the Bretton Woods system caused the lack of a framework for monetary policy, floating exchange rates, fluctuations in the demand for money, an increased inflation rate and GDP volatilities in all Western countries. Only the Fed policy of the following decades – called the Great Moderation – aimed at reducing inflation and output volatility, and this was able to restore market stability and stimulate growth. This policy was crucial not only for the US economy but for Europe, Japan and the emerging economies too. The eight-year crisis for developing countries – from Mexico in 1994–5, Argentina in 1995–6, the Asian contagion in 1997–8, the Russian contagion in 1998–2001, and Uruguay in 2002 – ended thanks to the IMF introducing a predictable framework of operation, called exceptional access framework (EAF). This stated clear rules for intervention and defined the exceptions. The aim of the EAF was 'to increase predictability and reduce uncertainty about official policy actions in the emerging markets.' Thanks to this clear framework of operation the emerging economies were able to find a sustainable path of development. Taylor's general conclusion is in agreement with Milton Friedman's teaching: 'policy makers should rethink the idea that frequent and large government actions and interventions are the only answer to our current economic problems' (Taylor, 2009: 62).

Raghuram Rajan (2010) widens the political and economic framework in which the financial crisis burst. He uses the metaphor of fault lines to show that the financial crisis has many different causes: in geology, fault lines are breaks caused by the movements of tectonic plates. In the US the financial crisis was caused by a flow of money coming from inside and outside the national economy. Global imbalances, mainly between China and the US, cannot be ignored. Moreover, the crisis was also caused by rising inequalities in income distribution in the US and the attempt by the federal government to smooth them with a specific housing policy. Therefore, to understand the US financial crisis one needs a worldwide explanation of the fault lines of international economy.

Nevertheless, the starting point of this analysis is the US economy. Rajan observes that, in the US, income inequalities are increasing. The 90th percentile earner – people who earn a higher income – increased their income by 65 per cent in the 1975–2005 period more than the 10th percentile earners. There are many explanations for this trend. The first is that technical changes favour people with high school and university diplomas; that is people born into families and social environments which value human capital and can afford expensive education for their children. A second reason behind income inequalities is the deregulation of the 1980s and the associated increased competition in the market, where firms can choose talented people in a more volatile labour market. Moreover, international deregulation favoured immigration and competition in the labour market of people looking for low wages. A third and more general explanation lies in the American ideology of a society according to which the ordinary people can attain success and great fortune. This explains why the American welfare system is less effective and generous than the European one. Taxation on higher incomes is considered a punishment for the effort, not a means to redistribute income.

In the American political system, we can understand why different governments, especially the Clinton and Bush administrations, tried to improve the conditions of poor families by means of the housing policy. Since the 1930s, the years of the New Deal, the federal government set up a special agency – the Federal National Mortgage Association (FNMA, later Fannie Mae) – to help people get long term financing to buy their houses. Today, Fannie Mae and Freddie Mac (Federal Home Loan Mortgage Corporation) are considered government-sponsored enterprises (GSEs). They have private shareholders, but they receive government benefits and have government appointees on their boards. Therefore, when the federal government decided to launch a policy to allow poor people to buy their homes, the two agencies became the obvious instrument. They, says Rajan, 'bought mortgages that conformed to certain size limits and credit standards they had set out, thus allowing the banks they bought from to go out and make more mortgage loans.' Moreover, they 'packaged pools of loans together and issued mortgage-backed securities underwritten by other banks. Because the mortgages were sound, these were fairly safe and extremely profitable activities' (Rajan, 2010: 34). Eventually, in June 2008, the amount of sub-prime and Alt-A loans from the federal agencies was 'approximately 59 per cent of total loans to these categories. It is very difficult to reach any other conclusion than that this was a market driven largely by government, or government-influenced, money' (Rajan, 2010: 38).

At their outset, the housing policies sponsored by the Clinton and Bush administrations could have been considered a reasonable way to achieve some important social goals. But the private financial sector soon understood that sub-prime mortgages, supported by a semi-public agency, could become a good investment. 'Low risk and high return – what more could the private sector desire?' (Rajan, 2010: 39). In this fertile soil, the rush to the housing boom and the final bust were inevitable. Even if the intent of the American government was sound, the ultimate result was not. The state of income inequality pushed the government to distort lending in the financial sector. Easy credit, says Rajan, proved an extremely costly way to redistribute. 'Too many poor families who should never have been lured into buying a house have been evicted after losing their meagre savings and are now homeless'. Moreover, we must also consider the negative impact on public finance as a social loss: 'too many financial institutions have incurred enormous losses that the taxpayer will have to absorb for years to come' (Rajan, 2010: 44).

Not all economists agree on the connection between the financial crisis and the federal government's housing policy. Krugman and Wells (2010), for instance, disagree with largely blaming the Democrats for being behind the big push to make loans to the poor. Some other economists disagree on the link between the crisis and government aid; others on the size of the mortgages allowed. But, in a survey of the debate on the Rajan thesis, *The Economist* (January 22 2011) convincingly concludes: 'ultimately it may be hard to prove a causal connection between inequality, sub-prime lending and the Wall Street boom. Even so, most economists at the annual American Economic Association meeting agreed that the three forces combined in the American economy in an unsustainable and unhealthy way.'

Joseph Stiglitz (2010) considers the financial crisis to be a case study of market failure. The US political system adopted the ideology of market fundamentalism, that is that the markets, especially the financial ones, work better if the government reduces regulations to a minimum. The history of deregulation started, according to Stiglitz, with the Reagan administration in the US and the Thatcher government in the UK. After the two-digit inflation of the 1970s, Paul Volker, the President of the Fed, was able to bring the inflation rate to 3.6 per cent in 1987, at the end of his chairmanship. Normally, says Stiglitz, 'such an accomplishment would have earned automatic reappointment. But Volker understood the importance of regulations, and Reagan wanted someone who work to strip them away' (Stiglitz, 2010: XVII). Therefore Reagan appointed Greenspan, who sided with deregulation policies.

The deregulation of the financial sector raises several risks, eventually heading to market failure. Modern financial markets have two features, which should be taken into account by regulators: agency, that is people (agents) who make decisions on behalf of others; and externalities, that is costs and benefits shifted onto others. In developed economies, savings come from people, – workers, clerks, public servants and so on – who do not invest their money directly in business but entrust it to some 'agent', for instance banks, hedge funds or pension funds. Usually people look for long term returns, and agents look for short term returns. Therefore, financial agents have the chance to 'innovate' the investment vehicles and to sell the new products to other agents. The agency chain extends and the link between lenders and borrowers becomes invisible.

Securitization is a good example of this kind of innovation. A bank once negotiated a home mortgage with a certain house owner; afterwards the bank kept the issued mortgage, bearing the risk of insolvency. Since the 1990s banks have packaged a certain number of mortgages with different risks and sold the package to some other agent. But the new investor had no idea of the people and town where the house in question was located. So it happened, that a mortgage originally made in Illinois was sold to a European or an Asian investor. This created problems of information asymmetries: 'the buyer of the security typically knew less than the bank or firm that had originated the mortgage.' This financial innovation soon became a danger not only for the American economy but also for the world. 'The whole securitization process depends on the greater fool theory – that there were fools who could be sold the toxic mortgages . . . Globalization had opened up a whole world of fools; many investors abroad did not understand America's peculiar mortgage market' (Stiglitz, 2010: 91).

The failure of the American financial market is proof that the markets are not efficient when they are not regulated effectively by a public authority. The inefficiency depends not only on the agency problem, but also on the externalities, which are not taken into account by the agents. Likewise, a major problem was created by the repeal in 1999 of the Glass-Steagal Act, which was approved during the New Deal in order to separate the activities of the investment banks and commercial banks. The outcome was the creation of very big banks, aware that they were too big to fail. The regulator has thus created a situation of moral hazard; an incentive for excessive risk taking. The inner mechanism that triggered the crisis was so-called 'financial engineering': basing the calculation of the risk of a single investment or a package of investments on sophisticated mathematical models. Private investors, financial institutions and rating agencies used these models. In spite of their mathematical accuracy, these models suffered a fundamental flaw: they did not assume the possibility of a correlation of risks, as happens in the case of a systemic crisis. As Stiglitz says, 'the premise of securitization was diversification, but diversification only works if the loans that make up the security are not correlated. Their thinking ignored the common elements creating the housing bubble throughout the economy: low interest rates, lax regulations, and close to full employment' (Stiglitz, 2010: 93). To this inner mechanism of miscalculated investment risks, one should add the fact that the American regulation provided 'positive' incentives for further miscalculations. The rating agencies, which in theory should have recognized the risk and pointed it out to the investors, had a clear conflict of interest with the financial agents. 'They were being paid by the banks that originated the securities they were asked to rate. They had an incentive to please those who were paying them.' (Stiglitz, 2010: 92).

In the last resort, the crisis came not by chance or by accident, but because the market was badly regulated or not regulated at all. Low interest rates are often considered one of the causes of the crisis, but they are not the main cause. 'Cheap money can lead to an investment boom in plants and equipment, strong growth, and sustained prosperity', affirms Stiglitz. On the contrary, in the US cheap money led to a housing bubble. 'That's not the way the market is *supposed* to behave. Markets are *supposed* to allocate capital to its most productive use' (Stiglitz, 2010: 80). Misallocation of resources was a result of bad regulation. Note that better regulation is possible. In Denmark, for more than two centuries, the mortgage market worked well with low default rates. The reason is 'strict regulations – borrowers can borrow at most 80 per cent of the value of the house – and the originator has to bear the first losses. America's system . . . encourages speculative gambling' (Stiglitz, 2010: 106). Bankers and financial investors are not especially greedy: they look for profits, if possible very high profits, like every other manager. The problem is not in the men, but in the institutions. Bankers and central bankers, 'like all humans, are fallible. Some observers argue for simple, rule-based approaches to policy (like monetarism and inflation targeting) because they reduce the potential for human fallibility.' For instance, this is the theoretical background of John Taylor's analysis of the crisis. But 'the belief that markets can take care of themselves and therefore government should not intrude has resulted in the largest intervention in the market by government in history; the result of following excessively simple rules was that the Fed had to take discretionary actions beyond those taken by any central bank in history' (Stiglitz, 2010: 145). The general guideline, according to Stiglitz, is that 'enhancing economic performance requires improving both markets and government. There is no basis to the argument that because governments sometimes fail, they should not intervene in markets when the markets fail – just as there is no basis to the converse argument, that because markets sometimes fail they should be abandoned' (Stiglitz, 2010: 245).

José Gabriel Palma (2009a, 2009b) provides a fourth interesting explanation of the financial crisis. According to Palma, the financial crisis is the outcome of a structural factor: the 'attempt to use neo-liberalism (or, in US terms, neo-conservatism) as a new technology of power to help transform capitalism into a rentiers' delight' (Palma, 2009a: 13). Indeed, in his analysis, based on social critical theory, Palma shows how the power of financial capital has increased in the last 30 years in the US political system and in the world economy. 'For example, in the upswing (1980–2007), in real terms the four components of the stock of global financial assets (equity, public and private bonds and bank assets) jumped 9-fold, increasing from US\$ 27 to US\$ 241 trillion (US\$ at 2007 value). As a result, the multiple of the stock of financial assets to world output augmented nearly four-fold (from just 1.2 to 4.4)' (Palma, 2009a: 2–3). Compared with this impressive increase, we can understand why the problem of the so called 'global saving glut' is almost immaterial: 'by 2007 the overall Asian 'saving glut' was equivalent to less than 1 per cent of the global stock of financial assets' (Palma, 2009a: 5).

If we consider the distribution of income between the richest 1 per cent of the US population and the bottom 90 per cent there is a clear 'reversal of fortune' at the beginning of the 1970s. The end of the Keynesian cycle was marked by full employment, rising real wages, improving distribution and limited cross-borders capital movements. Since then the share of the small group increased from 8.9 to 22.8 per cent in 2006; the bottom 90 per cent received only the remaining 50 per cent. Nevertheless, the growing inequality in income distribution in US society did not spur investments and productivity growth. Says Palma, 'Contrary to what was widely predicted by the 'supply-siders' of the Washington consensus in this new neo-liberal-type capitalism a remarkable fall in corporate taxation led to a decline in corporate saving as share of corporate profits (as opposed to what had happened for most of the 'financially repressed' Keynesian period) (Palma, 2009a: 36). According to Palma, the popular belief that the growth of the financial sector is crucial for the development of the economy is groundless. In the US economy, 'during the period of so-called "financial repression" that followed the Bretton Woods agreement in 1944, total financial assets remained relatively stable as shares of GDP for about three decades (at the level of about 500 per cent), while private investment experienced some acceleration.' But in the following period of financial liberalization, 'a period of huge asset inflation (that more than doubled the value of total financial assets as a share of GDP) was accompanied by a slowdown of the rate of private investment (from 28.5 per cent of GDP in 1979 to 15.5 per cent in 2007)' (Palma, 2009a: 38–9). Moreover, the relative share of financial profits in total profits increased substantially during the phase of international liberalization. 'The share of the financial sector in overall corporate profits increased from 10 per cent to about one-third between 1986 and 2006' (Palma, 2009a: 39). This achievement was possible because of the great increase in private indebtedness, mainly through the policy of mortgages and low interest rates, as we have already seen in the analysis of Raghuram Rajan.

The increasing power of the rentiers in the US economic and political systems can be easily checked if only one considers the composition of the US governments when the crisis opened: Henry Paulson, the Treasury Minister, rescued AIG but refused to rescue Lehman Brothers, a Goldman Sachs rival. Let us not forget that Paulson was previously CEO of Goldman Sachs. (Palma, 2009a: 56). The boundary between financial and public affairs is rather blurred in the US system. Therefore, this is Palma's conclusion, the neo-liberal ideology is in fact a 'technology of dispossession' not only of poor people and the middle class, but also of the industrial system. The roots of the crisis 'can be found mostly in a rent-seeking and politically unchallenged capitalist élite transforming neo-liberalism into a toxic ideology capable of generating a monsoon of toxic assets' (Palma, 2009a: 66).

The four analyses of the 2007–8 financial crisis, here summarized, explain some crucial aspects of the American economic and political system. According to Taylor, the crisis was caused by some Fed monetary policy mistakes; according to Rajan the crisis was mainly caused by the inappropriate welfare system in the US; for Stiglitz the main faults lie in the doctrine of efficient and unregulated markets; and finally, Palma underlies the detrimental link between politics and finance. Nobody denies that the origin of the crisis was located in the US. But all these authors also consider, at the conclusion of their analyses, the need for some reforms of the international economic order. It is true that, since we live in a global market, the crisis provoked severe impacts in all continents. But it is also true that the financial crisis in the US can be considered a by-product of globalization: the growth of the financial sector in the US would be unthinkable without the existence of the global market, where important countries like China, India and Brazil, are increasingly integrated in the international economy. Therefore, it seems reasonable to inquire whether the deep roots of the financial crisis should not be found outside the US, in the functioning (or malfunctioning) of the world economy. In other words, the old international order might contain the seeds of its own decay.

1.3 THE FINANCIAL CRISIS: ITS AFTERMATH IN EUROPE

The aftermath of the US financial crisis on the world economy was impressive, showing that the financial system was truly becoming an integrated sector of the world economy. The world trade in volume dropped by 11 per cent in 2009, compared to 2008, and the world output fell by 0.6 per cent. In 2009, the growth rate of some emerging economies, like China and India, simply slowed down, but the crisis provoked the loss of 6.5 per cent of Mexico's GDP and 7.9 per cent of Russia's GDP. It had a major impact on the European economy: the euro area's GDP suffered a loss of 4.1 per cent (Germany 4.7; France 2.5; Italy 5; Spain 3.7 per cent). Among the advanced economies, Japan's GDP dropped by 5.2 per cent and the UK's by 4.9 per cent (data from IMF, 2010; table 1.1).

Europe was especially hit by the crisis, due to the inadequate construction of the Economic and Monetary Union (EMU). In 1991, at Maastricht, only a monetary union was really established. The economic union was agreed as a future project, but at the same time the budget of the European Union was not increased from the very low level of 1 per cent (or a little more) of the EU's GDP. Therefore, the present condition of the European Union, after the Lisbon Treaty (2009), is that there is a monetary union but not a fiscal nor an economic union.

In 2008 the financial crisis struck Europe because many banks had large investment positions in innovative instruments (toxic bonds). After the failure of Lehman Brothers, liquidity became scarce because of a sudden lack of confidence in each other's financial institutions, inter-bank interest rates rose and the ECB was obliged to launch non-conventional interventions, increasing open market operations and overnight borrowing. On

October 8 2008 the ECB, in a coordinated action with the central banks of the US, Canada, Switzerland and Sweden, cut the interest rate by 50 basis points, bringing it to 1.5 per cent in March 2009 (ECB, 2010a). In order to react to the credit crunch, the fall of effective demand and rising unemployment, the European Commission launched, in November 2008, a European Economic Recovery Plan to provide budgetary support to effective demand. The total package of the plan amounted to 200 billion euros – 1.5 per cent of EU GDP – of which only 0.3 per cent of EU GDP (30 billion euros) was provided by the European Commission, the most important share (1.2 per cent of EU GDP) was supplied by member states. Given the limited size of the EU budget, the effort of the European Commission was modest and not enough to promote a real coordination among the national recovery plans. Only some countries, such as Germany, the Netherlands, Spain, Austria and Finland, were able to stimulate their economy. The most indebted countries, such as Italy and Greece, were unable to provide any stimulus. Indeed the result of the European Plan was limited: according to European Commission calculations, the fiscal stimulus package amounted to almost 2.0 per cent of EU GDP in two years: 1.1 per cent in 2009 and 0.8 per cent in 2010 (ECB, 2010b, table 4).

Of course, the financial efforts of the European governments worsened the debt to GDP ratio. The euro area had a debt/GDP ratio of 66 per cent in 2007, but this ratio increased to 70 per cent in 2008 and 85.4 per cent in 2011. Italy and Greece had a ratio higher than 120 per cent in 2010. At this point, the state of European public finance opened the way for a further step in the international financial crisis: the attack on sovereign debts. This happened at the beginning of 2010, when the Greek government was discovered to have falsified its national accounts for years and the rating agencies lowered their mark on Greek public debt. The spreads between ten-year Greek bonds and German bonds started to increase. The financial markets nourished increasing doubts on the sustainability of Greek indebtedness. The euro area governments announced, on 9 May, a package of measures, including the European Financial Stability Facility (EFSF) of 750 billion euros, of which 60 billion were administered by the European Commission, 440 billion euros by member countries and 250 billion by the IMF. The aim of the EFSF was to preserve financial stability in Europe providing financial assistance to member states. Soon the ECB started to purchase government bonds in the secondary market to help the sovereign debts under attack. In the following months these interventions were required to support Ireland, Portugal and Spain's bonds too. In August 2011 the crisis of the sovereign debt spread out to Italy. These measures are only provisional. It is not clear if the size of the EFSF is big enough and if there is a political will to support a medium member state (such as Spain or Italy) seriously in distress.

We can understand the EMU's leaks better if we compare what happened in the euro area during the crisis with what happened in the US. In Europe, the reaction of financial markets to the deterioration of public finance was a flight to safety, with investors moving from risky private financial assets into government bonds. But there was also a flight to quality towards safer public bonds and away from countries with high government deficits and high ratio of debt to GDP, for instance towards German bonds and US Treasury bonds. For the same reasons, during the crisis, the dollar strengthened against the euro, because many investors preferred to put their money in the American financial market. Moreover, the euro area was perceived as a politically weak construction, if compared to the US. In 2010, the US had a debt/GDP of 94.3 per cent; the euro area 84.2 per cent. The ratio of public deficit/GDP was 9 per cent for the US and 6.35 per cent for the euro area. In spite of that, international finance attacked some European indebted states, not the American states and the federal government.

From this short summary of the impact of the financial crisis on Europe we can learn two lessons. The first is that the European governments reacted to the speculative attack to euro area sovereign debt without a comprehensive plan, but with incidental measures, suggested mainly by the most important country, Germany. The reason for this inability of the European Union to face global challenges is its inadequate construction. Notwithstanding the existence of a European Parliament, elected by the European people, some powers like public finance are not entrusted, at least to some extent, to the European Union, but are preserved in the hands of national governments. Therefore, when in the US the federal government can act, pooling financial resources from the federal budget, in the European Union, national governments start a discussion about who should pay, and how much, for a certain common emergency.

The second lesson concerns the relative powers of public and private finance. For the first time, since the birth of an integrated international economy, we must take note of the increasing and arrogant power of international finance. It is true, as Reinhart and Rogoff (2008: 29) observed, that Greece, since its independence in the nineteenth century, 'has lived in a perpetual state of default', but Ireland, Portugal, Spain and Italy were also, in a different way, under the pressure of international finance. At a certain point, it seems that the same European Monetary Union was on the brink of collapsing. This means that even the most important industrial states, such as the United States, are not safe from the attack of international finance if their public finance is not in order. The banking system was saved by the taxpayers' money: yesterday's private debts are today's public debts. This is a major problem for post-crisis recovery. A study on the future of public debt (Cecchetti et al, 2010: 9) shows that, if the increasing burden of age-related spending is taken into account:

> by 2020 the primary deficit/GDP ratio will rise to 13 per cent in Ireland; 8–10 per cent in Japan, Spain, the United Kingdom and the United States; and 3–7 per cent in Austria, Germany, Greece, the Netherlands and Portugal' [moreover] debt/GDP ratios rise rapidly in the next decade, exceeding 300 per cent of GDP in Japan; 200 per cent in the United Kingdom and 150 per cent in Belgium, France, Ireland, Greece, Italy and the United States.'

If sovereign public finance will survive – and this is essential for the survival of the economy – important reforms should be made at the supranational level, not only in Europe, to check the increasing power of private international finance.

1.4   THE FINANCIAL CRISIS: ITS POLITICAL AFTERMATH

The financial crisis opened another controversy, which started in the nineteenth century, on the decline of Western civilization. According to Niall Ferguson (2011) the Western dominance of the world, which began in the sixteenth century, is doomed not only to fall into decay but also to collapse, because the rest of the world, mainly Asia, is going to rise to dominance. In the US, this debate among historians has taken on the form of a political debate on US global leadership. The political analyst Fareed Zakaria (2011) thinks that the US can avoid decline only with a radical change of their internal policy:

> We think of America as a global society because it has been the center of the forces of globalization. But actually, the American economy is quite insular . . . We spend vast amounts of money on subsidies for housing, agriculture and health, many of which distort the economy and do little for long-term growth. We spend too little on science, technology, innovation and infrastructures, which will produce growth and jobs in the future. (Zakaria, 2011)

Joseph Nye (2011), who says that Zakaria has painted a 'too gloomy picture of American decline', criticizes this 'declinism' point of view. American history has experimented other 'cycles of declinism', says Nye. One reason for concern is certainly the US debt, that will be equal to its GDP in a decade, and that will undermine confidence in the dollar. But, Nye suggests, 'some aspects of the current mood are probably cyclical and related to unemployment, while others represent discontent with the bickering and deadlock in today's political process. . . The greatest danger to America is not debt, political paralysis, or China: it is parochialism.'

This exchange of different points of view on the role of the US in the present world political system is interesting, not only because it closes the debate on the 'American century', but also because it places economic factors at the core of the political analysis. Indeed it is impossible to avoid the increasing economic power – and, as a consequence, military power too – of emerging countries, in Asia and in Latin America. Let's explore this assumption more profoundly. In Section 1.2 we took into account the main explanations of the direct causes of the crisis. But the exploration of the more general economic background in which the crisis burst can help us to explain the turning point of the present international order better; and the monetary system is a pillar of the political international order.

In a recent reconstruction of the 'rise and fall of the dollar', Barry Eichengreen admits: 'financial excesses would not have spread so quickly to such destructive effect had the Fed not poured fuel on the fire' (Eichengreen, 2011: 109). But the Fed did not act in an economic space disconnected from the global economy. In 2005, Alan Greenspan talked about a 'conundrum' he was unable to explain: the persistence of low long-term interest rates, even when the Fed allowed the funds rate to rise in 2004. Ben Bernanke tried to give a reply to this conundrum with its supposition of the 'global saving glut,' that is the excess of Asian saving invested in the United States. In any case, the persistence of low interest rates encouraged investors to assume more risks and it seems reasonable to affirm that 'foreign purchases of US debt securities were largely, even wholly, responsible for Greenspan's conundrum. This was the dollar's exorbitant privilege in yet another guise' (Eichengreen, 2011: 118).

In the next chapter, we will present an extensive analysis of the present international monetary order and global imbalances. Here we would like to note that today's problems have deep roots and are not new. The main link between the American monetary policy and the international monetary system was clearly analyzed and denounced by Robert Triffin, the economist who was able to see, in 1959 (a decade in advance) the intrinsic contradiction of the gold exchange standard founded on a fixed rate of exchange between the dollar and gold. According to Triffin the issuing country of the international reserve currency must face an unavoidable dilemma: national monetary policy goals conflict with international monetary goals and, usually, the national central bank favours national goals, creating in this way the conditions for a major international crisis. This dilemma did not disappear after the break down of the gold exchange standard in 1971 and the subsequent development of the dollar standard.

In his last paper of 1992, on the 'IMS or International Monetary Scandal', Triffin clearly explains the main shortcomings of what is today called the dollar standard. The 'disastrous results of the use of a few national currencies as the major, or sole, instrument of international monetary reserves' is that, first, 'the deficits of a reserve-centre country may be financed mostly – or even over-financed – by an increase of world exchange reserves, with little or no decline of gross reserves for that reserve-centre country and, therefore, no imperative pressure for the readjustment of inflationary policies' (Triffin, 1992: 13–14). Secondly, 'this process may easily degenerate into a self-feeding spiral of inflationary reserve increases, since these are reinvested in the reserve centres and increase the ability of their leaders – official and private – to pursue inflationary policies.' Finally, the third shortcoming is the stimulation 'of lending by poorer and less adequately capitalized countries to richer countries, far less dependent on foreign capital for their economic development.' It is easy to read in these short statements of twenty years ago a fairly accurate picture of the roots of the recent financial crisis. Lately another economist, Richard Duncan (2003), developing an analysis similar to Triffin's theoretical background, was able to forecast in a more precise way, including the sub-prime crisis in the United States, what really happened in 2007–8.

Scholars aware of the serious shortcomings of the dollar standard were not surprised when, on the eve of the G20 London summit of April 2009, the Governor of China's central bank raised the issue of substituting the dollar with a new 'international reserve currency' in order to secure global financial stability and facilitate world economic growth. According to Zhou Xiaochuan (2009a):

> issuing countries of reserve currencies are constantly confronted with the dilemma between achieving their domestic monetary policy goals and meeting other countries' demand for reserve currencies. . . . The Triffin Dilemma, i.e., the issuing countries of reserve currencies cannot maintain the value of the reserve currencies while providing liquidity to the world, still exists.

The solution to the Triffin Dilemma, says Zhou Xiaochuan, can be found in the IMF issuing a 'super-sovereign reserve currency' in order to eliminate the burden for a single national country to issue a reserve currency and make it possible to manage global liquidity. The Special Drawing Rights (SDR), a basket of national currencies issued by the IMF, can be a first step on the road of a super-sovereign reserve currency. 'The SDR – says Zhou Xiaochuan – which is now only used between governments and international institutions, could become a widely accepted means of payment in international trade and financial transactions.'

The proposal for 'a super-sovereign reserve currency' opened a worldwide debate on the future of the dollar and the international monetary system. This time the proposal did not come from some visionary economist, but from the governor of China's central bank, the emerging economy that in a decade can surpass the US and that is actively working to make the yuan convertible, in order to compete with the dollar as a reserve currency. At the time of writing, the American government had not taken a position on the Chinese proposal, but a number of international organizations started to study the problems, sketching out plans to reform the international monetary system. Here, it is enough to quote two studies of the IMF (2011a and 2001b), a report sponsored by the French Government, called the Palais-Royal Initiative (2011), a series of papers by Chatham House (2010) and the study on multipolarity by the World Bank (2011).

The issue of the reform of the international monetary system is on the agenda of international politics and cannot be avoided as happened during the second half of the twentieth century. Nevertheless, there is a common awareness that a second Bretton Woods is not possible, for the simple reason that the US is not the same overwhelming power it was in 1944. The Bretton Woods system was a hegemonic construction. Today, the new monetary international order will be shaped by the contribution of many countries, which have the choice between cooperating or non-cooperating among each other. Of course, the final result will be very different according to the issue singled out. Therefore, the next section is devoted to the exploration of the general political framework of which the monetary problem is only one of the issues, though a very important one.

1.5 THE INTERNATIONAL ORDER AND THE FAILURES OF THE NATION-STATE

The so-called international community is inhabited by nation-states. Political realism and international political economy scholars (for instance, Gilpin, 2001) consider the sovereign nation-state as the major subject of international relations. Therefore, in order to explore the possibility – and the necessity – of supranational institutions and of cooperation among nation-states today it is necessary to clarify what a nation-state is.

In a scholarly essay on the public/private relationship, Norberto Bobbio (1985) states that Roman law originated the 'great dichotomy', which today is adopted not only by modern law scholars but also by all social sciences, such as political science and economics. Bobbio talks of a dichotomy because the two concepts are opposed; therefore a certain body, authority or institution belonging to one pole of the dichotomy cannot belong to the other pole. Since Roman times this dichotomy produced countless debates because of the historical moving line of division between the two poles. During the Middle Ages the dichotomy was blurred due the difficulties in using Roman law to regulate relationships between the Church, the Emperor and the Vassals, but in modern times the great dichotomy became crucial once again. Since the seventeenth century it fed the theoretical and practical debate on the relationships between the state and the market. Since then two main streams of thought can be singled out. The first is the primacy of private over public, which was especially invoked by supporters of private property and human rights, including the classical economists. The idea that there is a sphere of individual autonomy, which must be protected against the public power sphere, is one of 'the cornerstones of the liberal conception of the state' (Bobbio, 1985). The second stream includes the supporters of the primacy of public sphere, whose main idea is that the common good cannot be traced back to the summation of private goods. This second political and economic way of thinking, which granted increasing power to the state, was adopted by socialist and communist ideologies in the nineteenth century, and by the fascist and Nazi ideology in the twentieth century, which developed the extreme notion of total state, a pure public community, in which private relationships are only tolerated – sometimes forbidden – by the ruling class. Today the common notion of the state, in Western countries, is a balanced mixture of the two streams, where private doesn't rule over public, nor public rule over private. The state is an organization where the conflict between private and public spheres of human life is solved and the two spheres live together peacefully.

The notion of the state as a place in which public and private meet and cohabit leaves out two important features of the modern state: sovereignty and nationality. Since the Westphalia Treaty every state is considered a sovereign political community in the sense that the sovereign – the king or the government – does not recognize any superior power and, at the same time, the sovereign is the internal highest authority enacting and enforcing the laws that the subjects (later on, citizens) must obey. Therefore, the international community is made up of exclusive sovereign states, whose relationships are not regulated by an enforceable law – because a world government and a world police force do not exist – but only by the so-called international law, more similar to a voluntary pact among equals than to domestic legislation. In the last resort, when two or more states disagree, war is inevitable. The second feature of today's state is that the ruling class adopts the ideology of nationalism in order to maintain the cohesion and obedience of the citizens. The nation-state is based on the principle that the nation and the state coincide. But when we try to understand what a nation is, some say it is sharing a language, some say it is having history in common, and others believe it is everyday consensus. The reality is that such a state does not exist. There are some states with different languages (Switzerland, Canada); many states, especially in Europe, have a common history only because some ancient local powerful sovereign was able to conquer external provinces by force and, finally, if a share of the people belonging to a nation-state aim at independence, the national government usually does not hesitate to convince them not to leave the state, even with military means. Indeed, the nation is a myth or a political ideology a certain ruling class exploits to obtain the citizens' consensus and obedience (Albertini, 1960; Gellner, 1985; Hobsbawn, 1990)

Johann G. Fichte's *Die Geschlossene Handelstaadt*, published in 1800, outlines the ideal type of nation-state, a political community which closes off all trade with neighbouring communities in order to be entirely sovereign. If we compare Fichte's nation-state with the reality of today we should come to the conclusion that nation-states are surviving only nominally, but the reality is quite different. Every nation-state, even those of continental size like the US, China, India, Russia and Brazil, are open to international trade. According to OCDE (Factbook 2010), in 2008, trade in goods and services as a percentage of GDP was 15.2 per cent for the US; 17.4 for Japan; 30.4 for the UK; 85.3 for Belgium; 72.6 for the Netherlands; 44.1 for Germany; 78.3 for Ireland and 50.5 for Sweden. As far as financial transactions are concerned, the IMF (2011b: 23) states: 'total external assets and liabilities of the largest economies rose sevenfold between 1971 and 2009, to about 2.5 times global GDP. This was driven by an explosion of cross-border financial relationships between advanced countries . . . whose average total external assets and liabilities rose from 60 per cent of own GDP to close to 500 per cent.' Today integration of the nation-state with the international economy is not a political choice, it is a necessity. If some national government refuses to integrate its economy into the global economy, it condemns its citizens to poverty. But the other aspect of integration into the global economy is that the nation-state loses some crucial sovereign powers. Afterwards, we can list four areas of externalities to national sovereign powers.

Military and Civil Security

As we have already mentioned, today the technology available to produce weapons of mass destruction compels national governments to negotiate – or to accept as a matter of fact – agreements not to provoke a war with countries empowered with weapons of the same might. Of course, this state of affairs does not exclude war from the horizon of international politics, but strongly pushes governments to accept a peaceful coexistence as the history of the Cold War testifies. After the end of the Cold War, many regional conflicts burst out in Africa and Asia, but they were mainly brought about by a civil society not yet capable of regulating its controversies peacefully. National armies are deployed for police interventions by a coalition of states in peacekeeping operations. And, since national borders are today porous, the turmoil in a region spurts risks – effective or imagined – all over the world. Security is no longer an affair that a single national government can guarantee to its citizens.

Monetary Stability and Free Trade

The IMF, the GATT and, more recently, the WTO, were created in order to guarantee a stable international economy, at least in the Western hemisphere. The reality behind these international institutions was that they worked insofar as the US had an interest in their effectiveness and the power to support their policies. In fact, in the second half of the twentieth century, the interest of the US for a stable international monetary system and for a world free trade matched the interest of the Western countries and, after the fall of the Berlin Wall, also the rest of the world, since China and Russia were willing to get into these international institutions. But the transition to a multipolar international system requires radical reforms of the old economic order. Today the control levers of world economic governance should be shared among all the subjects contributing to world production and wealth. The global economy compels all nation-states to cooperate with each other in order to promote the international division of labour, which is the real source of the wealth of nations. No nation-state can do without external trade and global interdependence. National self-sufficiency is a wreckage of the past.

Poverty and International Justice

The nation-state was a powerful framework to integrate all citizens in the political community, whatever their original social status. Today, in rich countries, democracy and social rights are more or less warranted, even if some marked pockets of poverty survive in the US and Europe. But, after the end of World War II and colonialism, the line of division between rich and poor was perceived as a dramatic issue no longer only among the social classes of the same nation but also between rich and poor nations: today the fight against poverty is a crucial international problem. Of course, international solidarity among different national peoples is not so strong as solidarity among citizens of the same nation. Nevertheless, global interdependence shows that, on occasions of dramatic calamities (tsunamis, genocides and so on), an international wave of solidarity appears. Large areas of extreme poverty exist in Asia and Latin America, but are endemic in Africa. Poverty generates negative externalities such as political instability, civil wars, international terrorism and mass migrations towards rich countries. Rich countries not only have the duty, but also the interest, to help poor countries to develop, industrialize and reach a decent standard of living. The fight against world poverty cannot be fought and won by any single nation.

The Ecological Challenge

Humankind – not some national people – is more and more aware that its future on Planet Earth is at risk. This risk does not come from natural – or extraterrestrial – forces, but from humankind itself, destroying all living animal species and depleting natural resources. The present industrial model of development is not sustainable. Several UN conferences on climate change and the conservation of biological diversity have convinced the public of the urgency of action, but national governments are not able to agree on a radical change in favour of an environmental friendly system of production and consumption. It is crystal clear that the ecological problem is a global issue and that a single nation-state cannot hope to solve the problem by itself, nor to avoid a global catastrophe. Cooperation with other nation-states is not a choice; it is a duty. The real national interest is to agree to an effective global policy for the survival of humankind.

When we talk of the failures of the nation-state we do not mean that the historical experience of the nation-state was a complete failure. The nation-state was crucial to spread democracy among citizens, to consolidate the rule of law and human rights and to build the welfare state. But today national sovereignty is a tenet, which prevents complete supranational cooperation. Let us clarify this problem by recalling a theoretical debate. The 'public choice' school has elaborated a doctrine aiming at containing the power of the modern Leviathan, national governments. According to James Buchanan 'we can summarize public choice as a theory of "government failure" . . . here in the precisely analogous sense that theoretical welfare economics has been a theory of "market failure"' (Buchanan, 1979: 178). Indeed, public choice scholars provide a theoretical framework (Buchanan and Tullock, 1965) to analyze the essential functions of the modern state pinpointing some essential constitutional rules, according to them, to limit exorbitant public expenditure, such as the balanced budget rule (however, for a critique of the narrow concept of state/market relationships in public choice school see Musgrave, 1981). One of the main tenets of the public choice school is the critique of Keynesian economic policy of deficit spending, which is considered an implicit abrogation of the more sound fiscal austerity rules established during the gold standard age (Buchanan and Wagner, 1978). In general this school fosters the critique of rent-seeking niches in public administration and excessive public expenditure. Today to slim down the big state is a popular policy supported especially in Anglo-Saxon countries after the financial crisis, which compelled many governments, maybe grudgingly, to increase the public deficit to save the economy from collapsing. For instance, *The Economist* (2011a), in its survey *Taming Leviathan*, observes that in Western countries (Europe and US) government spending as a proportion of GDP was only 10.4 per cent in 1870; 23.8 in 1937; 44.1 in 2005; and 47.7 in 2009, after the financial crisis. Therefore, according to *The Economist*, 'the state everywhere is big, inefficient and broke.'

Of course, to look for inefficiency and rent-seeking niches in public administration is a legitimate policy: the national government may sometimes fail. But that is not the meaning we want to give to our idea of nation-state failures. Nation-states may fail because they are too small and weak to face global challenges such as the four problems just mentioned. As local governments are not able to face national problems, so national governments are not able to face global problems. Economists and political scientists find it hard to detect the problem because their theory of international relations is founded on the dogma of national sovereignty. A supranational government or a supranational state (Montani, 2010) is unthinkable for political realists and scholars of international political economy. Nevertheless a global market cannot function really without some form of government, which can be a hegemonic one (as was the Western system, with the US hegemony, during the Cold War) or a more or less democratic government, as the European Union is now. This point of view is not new. It was clearly stated by Lionel Robbins after the Great Depression (Robbins, 1937) and later on in his study on classical political economy. Robbins (1952: 56) says that 'the invisible hand which guides men to promote ends which were no part of their intention, is not the hand of some god or some natural agency independent of human effort; it is the hand of the law giver, the hand which withdraws from the sphere of the pursuit of self-interest those possibilities which do not harmonize with the public good.' Market and state are not two opposing and conflicting polarities: they are complementary polarities both in the national and the international sphere.[1] As a matter of fact the experience of the European Union shows that the Single European Market cannot work effectively without the regulations enforced by the European Court of Justice and the supervision of the Commission, which oversees when national governments grant aid to national industries. Likewise the euro is today the common currency of 17 nation-states because a supranational agency, the ECB, has the 'sovereign' power of issuing a currency and managing a certain monetary policy according to the rules established in the Lisbon Treaty. The invisible European hand is the supranational power of the EU. In Europe the supranational Leviathan is visible (even if it is so weak that to think of the EU as a Leviathan seems a mockery). But in the global economy and the international political system, which is becoming increasingly multipolar, a world power 'which withdraws from the sphere of the pursuit of self-interest those possibilities which do not harmonize with the public good' does not exist. And since the world Leviathan, enforcing the rules agreed upon by all the peoples taking part in the international community, does not exist, it may happen that the unruled global market itself becomes a Leviathan, as the recent financial crisis has shown. Of course, each one of the four problems previously discussed can cause a serious international crisis. After the 2007–8 crisis, the financial market is so strong that even the US's international position, due to its big national debt, is threatened; but the most dangerous threat is likely to be the ecological challenge, which can cause an irreversible global catastrophe. In any case, it seems correct to affirm that the international political system and the global economy are today out of control. The invisible Leviathan is like the Roman Janus: one face, the public face, is invisible to social scientists and politicians convinced that supranational government is utopian thinking; the other face, the private one, is a global society inhabited by individuals, multinational firms, NGOs, religious communities, secret societies, mafia, international terrorists and so on, which live together in a unstable spontaneous order, easily worsening into a global crisis which can sweep away the so-called 'sovereign' nation-states, the visible Leviathans.

1.6 NATIONAL MARKET, INTERNATIONAL MARKET AND INTERNATIONAL INTEGRATION

Our inquiry aims at giving a visible face to the supranational Leviathan. As we said, the problem has an economic aspect and a political aspect, because new rules and new international (or supranational) institutions are at stake. The first step is to examine the relationships between national and international markets, a problem studied at length by economists.

In many textbooks on international economics, the starting chapter is devoted to Ricardo's theory of comparative costs. In his *Principles of Political Economy* he explains how the prices of two commodities, for instance wine and cloth, depends on the quantity of labour employed in the production of each commodity: indeed, if we assume (as Ricardo does at the beginning of his inquiry) that the means of production are made up only of advanced wages and that, thanks to competition, the rate of wages and the rate of profit are the same in every industry; the relative price of the two commodities is equal to the relative quantity of the labour employed in their production. This result is possible in the national market because of the customs and laws regulating the circulation of workers and capital from country to towns, from different towns and from different provinces. Competition, or free trade, is highly beneficial to consumers because they can acquire the commodities they need at the lowest price; at the same time, competition obliges the manufacturers to employ the available means of production in the most efficient way. The same benefits can be obtained by free trade among nations. 'Under a system of perfectly free commerce, each country naturally devotes its capital and labour to such employments as are most beneficial to each', says Ricardo (1966: 133). Free trade spurs the most beneficial international division of labour for humankind.

> 'By stimulating industry, by rewarding ingenuity, and by using most effica-ciously the peculiar powers bestowed by nature, it distributes labour most effectively and most economically: while, by increasing the general mass of productions, it diffuses general benefit, and binds together by one common tie of interest and intercourse, the universal society of nations throughout the civilized world'. (Ricardo, 1966: 134)

In spite of the great advantages of free trade, Ricardo notices: 'the same rule which regulates the relative value of commodities in one country, does not regulate the relative value of the commodities exchanged between two or more countries' (Ricardo, 1966: 133). The reason for that is that capital and labour do not move from one country to another as happens in the national market. Here, Ricardo brings in the famous example of England and Portugal. Both countries produce wine and cloth, but the absolute costs, measured in hours worked, are higher in England. At a first glance, international trade should not be convenient for Portugal: English wine and cloth are more expensive. But Ricardo observes that if the interna-tional price is one quantity of wine for one quantity of cloth, international trade becomes convenient for both countries. However, in such a case 'the quantity of wine which [Portugal] shall give in exchange for the cloth of England, is not determined by the respective quantities of labour devoted to the production of each, as it would be, if both commodities were manufactured in England, or both in Portugal' (Ricardo, 1966: 134–5).

Ricardo is very clear about the distinction between a theory of national values and a theory of international values. Let us imagine that England and Portugal belong to the same economic union, for instance the European Union.

> It would undoubtedly be advantageous to the capitalists of England, and to the consumers in both countries, that under such circumstances, the wine and cloth should both be made in Portugal, and therefore that the capital and labour of England employed in making cloth, should be removed to Portugal for that purpose. In that case, the relative value of these commodities would be regulated by the same principle, as if one were produce of Yorkshire, and the other of London [and in such a case] if capital freely flowed towards those countries where it could be most profitably employed, there could be no difference in the rate of profit, and no other difference in the real or labour price of commodities. (Ricardo, 1966: 136)

If we consider the Ricardian theory of international trade on the basis of today's experience, especially in the light of the development of the European Union after World War II, we can say that we can single out three stages of international integration. The first one can be defined as 'mercantilist' in which Portugal and England are closed markets and do not exchange any commodities; the second one can be defined as a 'free trade stage' in which England and Portugal exchange their products and specialize in producing the commodity where their labour productivity is relatively greater, but capital and labour do not cross the border of the national market; the third stage can be defined as an 'economic union', where capital and labour move freely from one country to the other, and where both commodities are produced according to their lower cost. If we measure the wellbeing of humankind (the sum of the Portuguese and English populations) in terms of labour productivity, we can say that it increases from stage one to stage two and from stage two to stage three, a full economic union, with free trade and free mobility of the factors of production (for an analytical discussion of the three stages see Montani, 2008: 87–94 and Montani, 2011a).

Ricardo's distinction between a theory of national values and a theory of international values is fully adopted by Alfred Marshall in his early formulation of the neoclassical theory of value. In the twin essays *The Pure Theory of Foreign Trade* and *The Pure Theory of Domestic Values*, privately printed and circulated among the main economists in 1879, Marshall translates the economic problems discussed by Ricardo and Mill into a very elegant and concise mathematical formulation. The need to distinguish from a national and an international theory of values is so explained: the economist, says Marshall,

investigates the equilibrium of trade on the one hand for imaginary places
between which there is perfectly free circulation of capital and labour; and on
the other hand for imaginary places between which capital and labour do not
circulate at all. The first class of problems forms the basis of the pure theory
of the relative values of commodities produced under perfectly free competition 'in the same country' – or, as I shall henceforth call it, 'the pure theory
of domestic values'. The latter class of problems forms the basis of 'the pure
theory of international values' (Whitaker, 1975: vol. II, 119).

The reason for this different treatment of the two cases is that when two
countries exchange their goods there is a complete symmetry in the behaviour of the country acquiring and the country selling a certain commodity.
'The economic causes that govern Germany's willingness to exchange her
linen for English cloth are in every respect homogeneous with those that
govern England's willingness to exchange her cloth for German linen.'
(Marshall, 1930: *Domestic Values*, 1). On the contrary, for the explanation of domestic values the economic causes behind the demand and the
supply are different. For the supply side, the costs of production depend
on the efforts and sacrifices necessary to produce a certain quantity of the
commodity: a discussion of the law of returns of the factors of production employed is the basis for a full explanations of the supply curve. For
international trade this explanation was not required because only two
commodities were exchanged and it was legitimate to take the national
production of the two commodities as given.

Marshall never changed this approach to the theory of value. In his last
book, *Money, Credit and Commerce* (1923), after the experience of the great
international migration of labour and the strong cross-border movements
of capitals before World War I, he maintains that 'problems of "international values" require a different treatment from that which is appropriate
to the relative values of things produced in the same country' (Marshall,
1923: 7). The reason is that 'movements of labour' within a country 'are sufficiently easy and quick to justify the assumption that – as a general rule –
the earnings in occupations of equal difficulties . . . are approximately equal
throughout the country: and further that each Western country's banking
and credit organization secures a prompt flow of capital into any industry
in the country, which yields profits higher than are required to compensate
for the risks and difficulties of that industry; with the result that *net* profits
are kept nearly uniform throughout the country.' (Marshall, 1923: 10–11).
But 'a special study of international values is needed, because a similar
statement cannot be made in regard' (Marshall, 1923: 11) to the dominant
facts regulating international trade and values.

The distinction between the theories of national and international
values is the basis for the existence of that branch of economics called

international economics. A textbook of international economics usually deals with the theory of international trade – based on the assumption that two or more countries, initially closed to external exchanges, open their frontiers to trade with other countries – and the theory of international money – based on the assumption that two or more countries, endowed by a national money and a national central bank, exchange their money against the money of other countries: therefore, the theory of international money boils down to the theory of exchange rates and the balance of payments. Of course, the practical content of the theory depends on the historical circumstances in which the economists live. For instance, in the nineteenth century, the neoclassical school did not inherit the classical model without a lot of reworking and disagreements: 'on the contrary, disagreements sprung precisely from the use of an interpretation of a single model: the international adjustment mechanism described by Cantillon, Vanderlint and Gervaise and finally formalized by Hume in 1752 as the price-specie flow mechanism.' (Gomes, 1990: 144).

In the present study we leave the narrow and conservative point of view of international economics and we try to explore the new land of international integration. Of course, this field of study is not well established and theorized. As a starting point we can take the definition given by Balassa, mainly inspired from European experience.

> In the Western economic literatures, discussions of the types of economic integration of nations states have customarily focused on the various stages of integration. From its lowest to its highest forms, integration has been said to progress through the freeing of barriers to trade ('trade integration'), the liberalization of factor movements ('factor integration'), the harmonization of national economic policies ('policy integration') and the complete unification of these policies ('total integration') (Balassa, 1976: 17).

Concerning the first stage, freedom of trade, we can say that in the global economy trade barriers are no longer high custom duties, which are about on average of 5 per cent, but non-tariff barriers, as the discussions inside the WTO show. The recent financial crisis did not provoke a tariff war, as happened in the years of the Great Depression. National governments have learned the lesson: international cooperation avoided a deterioration of the crisis. Of course, the world economy is not an 'internal market' like the European market, because the development gap of the countries is much wider than in Europe. But, as we try to show in Chapter 2, the main problems concerning the functioning, or malfunctioning, of the global market come mainly from the monetary side, the dollar standard, and not from the so-called global imbalances. Concerning Balassa's second stage, factor integration, in Chapter 3 we try to show that the movements of labour and capital in the world economy are so extensive that it is no longer possible to study income distribution as a national problem, as was customary in the last two centuries. Today, domestic distribution of income has international roots. Balassa's third stage, policy integration, is already a wide and firm practice among national governments, supported by international institutions, such as the UN, the IMF, the World Bank, the WTO, and the various G5s, G7s and G20s which were created with the definite goal of coordinating national policies after the breakdown of the Bretton Woods system and, more recently, the 2007–9 financial crisis. In Chapter 4 we will show how, thanks to this worldwide framework of political and economic cooperation, many groups of countries try to establish regional institutions to capture more advantages from cooperation at a quicker pace than in the global market.

If we want to sum up the previous observations on the first three stages of economic integration, we can affirm that globalization brings about the transformation of the international market in the home market of the Cosmopolitan Commonwealth. But this worldwide process cannot be properly managed if Balassa's fourth stage, complete unification or total integration is not accomplished. However, Balassa's terminology is rather inaccurate because it suggests that total integration is 'national integration', the best-known model of economic integration. But Cosmopolitan Commonwealth is not a nation. On the contrary, the goal of our study is to show that total integration of the world economy is not necessary: world institutions should manage only some specific powers. In order to single out these powers and institutions we prefer to adopt the current distinction between microeconomic and macroeconomic theory. Roughly, this distinction is reminiscent of the private-public dichotomy, which we have already discussed. Our task is to understand what kind of economic power and supranational institutions are required to manage the world economy.

1.7   A SUPRANATIONAL MACROECONOMIC THEORY

Today a supranational trend can be singled out by examining some aspects of international policies. If the four areas of externalities to nation-state sovereignty – as discussed earlier – are real contemporary issues, it is legitimate to look for institutions and policies necessary to govern them. Formally, scholars of global public goods have already studied these problems (Kaul et al, 1999; 2003). However, their point of view is limited by the intellectual boundaries of the traditional international political economy approach. For instance, Scott Barrett (2003: 308) says: 'The difference between national and transnational public goods lies in the institutional response. There is no world government with the authority to coerce states into supplying transnational public goods. Sovereignty safeguards the independence of individual states in this sphere as others. A state can be pressured but not forced to contribute to the supply of a transnational public good. Provision of transnational public goods must be voluntary.' We agree, of course, that 'there is no world government with the authority to coerce states into supplying transnational public goods,' but our aim is precisely that of exploring the need of supranational institutions with the power to provide supranational public goods and not only transnational public goods voluntarily agreed upon by national governments.[2]

The supranational approach is not at all a new idea: it is based on the previous experience of European supranational integration. The process of European integration can be understood as an institutional evolution from an original supranational embryo, the European Coal and Steel Community, which was conceived by Jean Monnet and Robert Schuman, as a first concrete step towards a European Federation (for an explanation of European integration based on this approach see Montani, 2008). Even if the ECSC was limited to the coal and steel sectors, the idea of supranational institutions is clearly visible in its structure: the High Authority (now the Commission) – the executive – was accountable to a European Parliamentary Assembly (now the European Parliament) and the Council of Ministers; it had the power to regulate the two sectors, to levy taxes on coal and steel firms and to issue European bonds; the Court of Justice had the power to settle controversies among European and national institutions and to put European laws into force. Later on the Single European Market and the Economic and Monetary Union were built. These last two achievements can be considered supranational institutions necessary to deliver supranational public goods. The coercive power of the EU is necessary in order to deliver a social market economy and a common European currency to European citizens. The Single European Market can only work properly if the European Commission has the power to forbid national aid to the firms and to detect when competition law is breached; moreover the European Court of Justice ensures the respect of European law by national authorities and people; the ECB provides a stable common currency thanks to the transfer of national monetary sovereignty from nation-states to the EU. Therefore we can affirm that the EU does not have the power to coerce its member states to provide European public goods, but it does have the power to provide European public goods to European citizens. In Europe, the old idea of the nation-state as the unique sovereign political body is over: sovereign powers are shared among nation-states and the EU.[3.]

Here, our purpose is not to develop a new theory of public goods, but only to clarify this notion when it is applied to international problems. A supranational public good is typified by a double failure: a supranational authority providing it becomes necessary not only when the market fails, but also when international cooperation fails. In order to clear this concept, let's first observe that some public goods require a specific institution to be delivered (such as military defence) while some other public goods are delivered freely, or spontaneously, simply because civil society exists: the relativity theory is clearly a global common good for humankind, but it was discovered by the young Einstein when he worked outside academic institutions: no public expenditure sponsored the discovery of this crucial theory of physics. In some other instances, simple cooperation among individuals provides public goods, such as the common law in Anglo-Saxon countries and some trade customs in the local, national and international markets. In a similar way, some global public goods can be provided for in the international community by the voluntary cooperation among national governments, when the will to solve a certain problem exists. Therefore, in the theory of international relations we must distinguish between global public goods provided by voluntary cooperation and global public goods provided by supranational cooperation.

The Montreal Protocol (1987) on substances that deplete the ozone layer was originally conceived as a voluntary agreement among certain states. Its aim was to eliminate chlorofluorocarbons' (CFCs') emissions in the atmosphere. The industrial countries favoured the participation of developing countries in the agreement, which at the time were not very interested in cooperating to reach that goal. But the protection from ultraviolet rays was a global public good attainable only if all countries of the planet cooperated: in such a case the free-rider problems – the lack of compliance of developing countries – should have caused the failure of the agreement. The group of countries limiting the production of CFCs could not reach the objective of saving the ozone layer if other countries continued to produce CFCs. Eventually, the Montreal Protocol was a success because it was possible to find industrial substitutes of CFCs at a low cost. Therefore, the reason for the positive outcome was due more to technical factors than to the will of international cooperation.

The story of the Kyoto Protocol (1997) is different. It was sponsored mainly by the European Union but was not accepted by the US, Japan and several emerging countries, like China and India. The aim of the Kyoto Protocol was to decrease CO_2 and other greenhouse gas (GHG) emissions in the atmosphere in order to avoid dramatic climate change, by means of a cap and trade system. But the Kyoto Protocol had at least two main flaws. The first was the lack of a compliance mechanism: each country had the duty to comply, but the punishment could always have been deferred. The second flaw was that the group of countries willing to go ahead had to face the internal opposition of the industries forced to raise their costs in a global market in which their competitors – placed in countries outside the Kyoto Protocol – were not obliged to comply. An easy solution, similar to the Montreal Protocol, was not possible because at present alternative friendly technologies are not available (like carbon capture and seques-tration) or are not powerful and cheap enough (like photovoltaic power and other renewable energies). Therefore a serious revision of the Kyoto Protocol should take into consideration supranational cooperation: even if the cap and trade system is confirmed a carbon tax should be agreed upon.

Supranational cooperation does not mean that a country is punished with retaliations by other countries if it does not comply. This issue will have the same flaws of private vengeance in uncivilized societies. The expe-rience of the European Union shows that this problem can have a different solution. The countries concerned should accept a treaty limiting their sovereign power – the power to pollute the atmosphere – and to entrust to a supranational institution the power to provide the required global public good. Of course, this supranational institution should also have the power to punish the countries breaching the treaty, according to some common rules already established. This solution cannot be considered a dramatic change of the international order or a utopian plan. Let's consider the problem of climate change again. Jeffrey Sachs (2008) suggests that the yearly cost to save the planet from the danger of climate change is less than 1 per cent of global GNP. If Sachs' proposals are accepted, the UN should manage a budget much smaller than that size (because some of the costs should be shared between the UN and the nation-states) to sponsor scientific research for renewable energies, to finance plans to avoid defor-estations and to protect endangered species, to help poor people to adopt friendly technologies, and so on. A UN budget is a necessary institution to provide the previously mentioned global public goods. Finally, let's observe that when supranational institutions are set up to provide some common public goods, it is easier for member states to agree on some other voluntary public goods.

The example of the Single European Market could bring to mind that complex supranational institutions are required to provide supranational public goods. The international reality is different. WTO is a multilateral institution, which includes agreements among the member countries to settle disputes concerning international trade. Rajan (2010: 210) rightly observes:

The WTO bases its actions on a set of agreements that limit barriers to trade. These agreements have been signed and ratified by member governments after long and arduous negotiations. The WTO has a dispute-resolution process aimed at enforcing participants' adherence to the agreements, and because the rules are relatively clear, adherence can be judged in a quasi-legal setting. Penalties against violators, usually in the form of sanctions on their trade, are easily imposed.

Therefore, in such a case of a 'quasi-legal setting' multilateral institution, it is correct to say that the WTO is a supranational institution, even if its supranational power is limited to a small area of international politics. The case of the WTO shows that the creation of supranational institutions can be flexible and that even a modest achievement can strengthen the peaceful relationships among countries and open the way to further achievements, perhaps in other fields.

The discussion on the relationship between supranational public goods and supranational institutions shows the need to reconsider macroeconomic theory. A supranational macroeconomic theory should take into consideration not only which supranational goods to provide, but also how to finance them and which are the priorities, given the international degree of integration and the political will of the countries to accept more cooperation agreements. Our task is to explore a very complex problem. In order to clear it we can quote a statement by Alfred Marshall, who explains why a 'national spirit' is the required assumption of the economics of the nation-state: 'Hopes and fears, ambitions and anxieties, ideals and disappointments which are common to the whole call for a large common purse; out of which to defray the expenses not only of defence against external foes, but also the costs of national movements connected with religion, education, and provision against infirmity. They call for, and they help to sustain, a common money market, with a unified currency, and an almost perfectly free movement of capital from one part of the country to another' (Marshall, 1923: 108–9). In short, in the nation-state, monetary policy and fiscal policy depend on the same political authority: the national government. In order to understand international integration we should examine the case of a kind of divorce between monetary and fiscal policy. A world monetary union is possible in a community of nation-states maintaining some power over fiscal policy (Montani, 2011b). Therefore, the final two chapters of this study are devoted to problems of the international monetary order and the control of public finance in a multi-tier system: local, national and supranational.

Monetary policy and fiscal policy are the crucial institutional means for public policies; but in today's international framework the distinction between public and private is blurred. Supranational institutions are required in order to maintain a fair balance between the public good and the private interest. National borders cannot limit the public interest of people. Therefore, there is a relationship between the provision and financing of supranational public goods and international democracy: public finance and democratic accountability go hand in hand. We hint at the problem of a cosmopolitan political economy in Appendix A.1.

NOTES

1. In the introduction to his study on the international order, Robbins (1937: 5–6) remarked that liberalism, as well as socialism and nationalism, is a kind of plan, not an anarchical or spontaneous order. 'The question to plan or not to plan, so frequently posed nowadays is essentially a red herring. It has not been seriously suggested that there should be no plan, no order in society. The issue is not between a plan and no plan, it is between different kinds of plan' (Robbins, 1937: 5–6).
2. In his useful and interesting book *Why Cooperate?* (2007), Scott Barrett holds fast to these assumptions. He explores a wide range of global public goods, which can be supplied by voluntary cooperation among sovereign governments, because: 'The institutions every society relies on to supply essential national public goods do not exist at the global level. Global public goods must be supplied by alternative means. Sovereignty essentially implies that they must be supplied voluntarily' (2007, 16–17). This kind of global public good does not require supranational institutions, which do not exist today: 'Lacking a supranational authority capable of compelling states to behave differently, the only alternative available is international cooperation – a kind of organized volunteerism' (19). Of course, these statements are correct. We do not deny that some global public goods, such as smallpox eradication, can be provided by spontaneous international cooperation. But our task is to show that a set of crucial global public goods can be provided only by supranational institutions.
3. The debate on the nature of the EU is wide and uninterrupted (for a survey see Eilstrup-Sangiovanni, 2006; and McCormick, 2008). Here, we do not want to establish whether the EU is a sovereign state, a union of nation-states or a federation. For our discussion it is enough to observe that there is a general agreement on the fact that some 'sovereign powers', such as the currency and the national central banks, were surrendered by nation-states to the Union.

APPENDIX A.1 COSMOPOLITAN POLITICAL ECONOMY AND COSMOPOLITAN DEMOCRACY

The aim of this appendix is to show how the implicit assumption of classical economists about the existence of a cosmopolitan harmonious order among the nations was taken for granted by the neoclassical school and the following economists of our age.[1] This assumption must be abandoned if we wish to frame the supranational institutions of the new multipolar world. There is a link between the supranational macroeconomic theory here discussed and the debate on cosmopolitan democracy.

If we take a glance at the contents of Adam Smith's *The Wealth of Nations* (1776), Jean-Baptiste Say's *Traité d'Economie Politique* (1803), David Ricardo's *Principles of Political Economy* (1817), and Thomas Malthus' *Principles of Political Economy* (1820), which can be considered the most important references of what is called classical political economy, we do not find a chapter nor even a paragraph devoted to international relations as a governance problem. Of course, we can find discussions on the advantages of international trade and the problems of international payments, but the common point of view is that the world market can work properly without a world regulation: the main foreign policy suggested is the doctrine of free trade. Adam Smith, at the beginning of Book IV, says: 'political economy, considered as a branch of the science of a statesman or legislator, proposes . . . to enrich both the people and the sovereign'. Production and distribution of wealth were considered the main goal of political economy. The nation-state was the natural framework of political economy and, as it is clear when the three functions of the state (defence, justice and public works) are discussed by Adam Smith, the relationships among nation-states were also considered a natural framework, a spontaneous order. There is an explanation. Classical political economy was developed as a reaction against the physiocratic and the mercantile systems: labour, and not the natural power of land, was considered the real source of wealth; moreover, the market, an institution in which individual and firms compete to provide 'all the necessaries and conveniences of life', was theorized as a complementary system to the political system. Free trade in the international market was no less necessary than free trade in the home market in order to produce the greatest value for society. Therefore, the first duty of the sovereign was to not restrict trade, and without distinction between internal trade and external trade. In short, the main rule of policy followed by classical economists was: what is good for my country is good for the world. Cosmopolitan wellbeing can be built bit by bit, country by country.

This harmonious vision of the world order was challenged by Friedrich List's *Das Nationale System der politischen Ökonomie* (1841). According to List, the classical school of economists teaches that all the national people should adopt a free trade policy, but they do not recognize that not all national people are undergoing the same stage of development. There are some people still living in the agricultural stage, others living in the agricultural-manufacturing stage, and others experimenting with the agricultural-manufacturing-commercial stage. If we compare England with Germany it is easy to see that England has already reached the most advanced stage of industrialization, with its industries capable of competing successfully all over the world. On the contrary, Germany is living a more backward stage, where most of the population is still devoted to agricultural production and with very few manufacturers. Therefore, so List concludes against the Cosmopolitan approach, for Germany protective custom duties are necessary to promote the development of the national industry. But List does not oppose a free trade policy as the best world economic order: when all the nations reach the same stage of development, the best international policy is free trade.

In the middle of the nineteenth century, despite the vociferous protest of English manufacturers, John Stuart Mill defended the German protection policy for the development of infant industries. Alfred Marshall took the same position, at the beginning of the twentieth century, when a strong internal protest against the protectionist policies of Germany and the United States obliged English producers to share the international market with their new competitors. But the new argument, put forward by Marshall, was not the naïve interest of humankind in free trade, but the national interest of a commercial power, such as Great Britain, with its Commonwealth, to preserve its primacy among the new big commercial powers. Now, a free trade policy was considered a means for foreign policy. When, in the 1930s, Great Britain decided to abandon the traditional policy and to raise custom duties, the same utilitarian argument justified the protectionist policy.

Meanwhile, the theory of value and distribution was taking a new direction, different from the cost of production theory elaborated by classical political economy. In 1871, Stanley Jevons published *The Theory of Political Economy*, Carl Menger the *Grundsätze der Volkwirthschaftlerhe* and, in 1874, Leon Walras the *Eléments D'économie Politique Pure*. The common theoretical ground of this new approach to the theory of value was the explicit reference to the principle of utility and the use of differential calculus as the technical means for the determination of prices, production and income distribution. After the publication, in 1890, of Alfred Marshall's *Principles of Economics*, all economists basically adopted the new neoclassical paradigm. Here we are not interested in discussing the differences and the common aspects of the classical and neoclassical approaches to political economy, but only to take note that the contents of these founding treatises of the new paradigm do not devote a single chapter to the international problem. The international economic order, based on the gold standard and free trade, was a dogma or, from another point of view, a natural gift: a spontaneous order working without a world governance.

At the beginning of the twentieth century, some economists began to notice some contradictions threatening the solidity of the international order. In an essay written in 1909, *The Incompatibility of Socialism and Nationalism*, Edwin Cannan observed the changing nature of nationalism from an ideology aiming merely for internal autonomy, to a political ideology aiming to 'hold that the duty of the good citizen is to promote the welfare of the nation even if the means or the end involve greater ills to the people of other nations' (Cannan, 1912: 283). Socialism, says Cannan, can be realized only on a worldwide scale. A national project of socialism clashes with a reasonable plan of world resources. 'If the capital may not move, the people will move to the capital', observes Cannan, but if, on the other hand, each national area restricts immigration 'each of the richer areas will become closed to immigrants, and. . . the population of the globe will tend to be shut up in a number of watertight compartments' (Cannan, 1912: 289) and finally the world will be divided between rich and poor people. To avoid this segregation of the poor people the reasonable solution is a world socialist government: 'No reasonable person can doubt that a worldwide organization is necessary for the proper working of a socialist system. If territorial units are to exist at all, they must be kept in very strict subordination to the world power.' (Cannan, 1912: 289–290).

After this warning, the nineteenth century balance of power was drawing to an end. The First World War and the 1929 economic crisis obliged the economists to take an explicit position on the international economic and political order. The two extreme points of view are represented by John Maynard Keynes and Lionel Robbins. Since 1923, in his *Tract on Monetary Reform*, Keynes was well aware that the gold standard is dead, it is a barbarous relict, no more adequate to a society with trade unions fighting for a stable or increasing standard of living. If prices and wages are inflexible downward, a flexible monetary policy is required in order to prevent unemployment. But, if every country experiences a different rate of inflation, then a rigid exchange rate, in gold or in some other currency, is impossible: a national government should therefore choose among the internal goal of full employment and the external goal of monetary stability. A system of flexible rates of exchange is the best solution. In the middle of the Great Depression, Keynes faced the same dilemma, but this time he explicitly chose the national goal, abandoning any hope for a reform of the international order. *The General Theory of Employment, Interest and Money* (Keynes, 1936) is an ambiguous work. While the analysis of the capitalist system is carried out for a worldwide economy, in the final two chapters Keynes supports a neo-mercantilist policy and self-sufficiency; achieving national full employment can be considered a contribution to a peaceful international order. A century later, therefore, Keynes restates the classical point of view: 'what is good for my country is good for the world'. There is something correct in this statement, but in the twentieth century international politics was completely different from the century of free trade and the gold standard: one cannot do without observing that Hitler's Germany was in those years reaching full employment, mainly thanks to the armament industry, but it did not contribute to world peace. Keynes changed this extreme position when he was obliged by the American government to think of the reform of the international monetary order. He changed his mind quickly and presented a clever plan for international cooperation at Bretton Woods. But his followers inherited the fundamental ambiguity of his analysis, wavering between national self-sufficiency and international cooperation.

During the 1930s a peaceful international order was only thinkable as a plan for the future of Europe and the world. This task was carried out by Lionel Robbins, whose writings on the international order are virtually forgotten in today's economic thought. In 1934, Robbins published *The Great Depression*, in which he proposed, as a way out of the crisis, the return to the gold standard, free trade and a flexible labour market. But very soon, Robbins realized that the traditional liberal international policy was not feasible in the new international context, dominated by economic nationalism and power politics. If a single country wished to stick to traditional liberal policies it would be smothered by the aggressive policies of the other nation-states. Therefore, says Robbins, the solution to the international crisis is not national, but international or, better, supranational or a federal order. In his *Economic Planning and International Order* (1937), Robbins states clearly that he wants to analyse the problem of the international order from a new point of view. 'The various plans examined are judged according to their effects on the welfare of humanity as a whole. It is assumed that the citizens of different states may be regarded as members of one general world community' (Robbins, 1937: 10). The three plans examined by Robbins are the national plan, the communist plan and the liberal plan. The first two are discarded. The national plan hinders, with trade barriers and national monetary policies, the international division of labour; it is a policy for increasing inefficiency and poverty. The communist plan tries to solve economic problems by means of bureaucratic machinery; of course, with coercive methods it is possible to achieve important productive goals, as the Soviet Union were doing, but even the Pharaohs were able to have pyramids built by slave workers. Communism does not solve the economic problem with democratic means. The third plan is international liberalism, the aim of which is to satisfy the needs of the people by means of the market. But why did the international market collapse in the years of the Great Depression? Robbins' answer is that an international economic order cannot work without a supranational political authority regulating the international market, in the same way in which a national government regulates the internal market. To think that 'a super-national authority' was not necessary was 'a grave error' of classical economists. 'The harmony of interests, which they perceived to be established by the institutions of property and the market necessitated, as they demonstrated, an apparatus for maintaining law and order. But whereas within nation areas such an apparatus, however imperfect, existed, between national areas there was no apparatus at all' (Robbins, 1937: 240–41). We cannot follow Robbins in his analysis of the international economic institutions, especially the penetrating pages devoted to the international monetary problem, which can be solved only with a central supranational bank. His main conclusion is that there is only one solution to the international problem: 'it is necessary that the nations states should surrender certain rights to an international authority . . . they need not give up all their rights of independent government; and the rights of the international authority must also be limited: there must be neither alliance nor complete unification, but Federation.' (Robbins, 1937: 245).

After World War II, the international order was shaped neither according to Keynes' self-sufficiency principle, nor according to Robbins' federalism. The United States conceived the institutions for a global hegemonic international order, with the UN, the Bretton Woods system and the GATT. This global project was realized only partially, because the Soviet Union and its satellites caused the division of the world into two hegemonic spheres. But on the Western side the US hegemonic system worked fairly well. Monetary stability and free trade were the two pillars of the world economic miracle of the post-war decades and, after the fall of the Berlin Wall, even of the full integration of the emerging economies in the world market. In this political framework, based on the principle of hegemonic cooperation, the political and economic theory did not found an incentive to abandon the old Westphalian paradigm or the classical distinction between the theory of internal values and international values.

Only at the dawn of the twenty-first century and especially after the

2007–8 financial crisis it became clear that the international system of states was changing radically: the old hegemonic system, based on the US superpower, was going to be replaced by a new multipolar system. Even if it is not clear which will be the new subjects of the new multipolar system a debate is open on the new world balance of power, the international monetary system alternative to the dollar standard, the danger of a global market insufficiently regulated and the reform of the international institutions, especially the Security Council of the UN. This new political perspective inevitably raises the problem of the future of democracy. The development of democracy and of the nation-state are two parallel and inseparable histories. Now we are approaching a crossroads. Some people rightly fear that in a global market national democracy is at risk: people controlling powerful institutions, such as multinational and global financial corporations, can also have the power to influence, blackmail, hold up or take over national governments. Others, more optimistically, think that national democracy can survive thanks to its capacity to develop international agreements, without developing supranational institutions (see for instance Ladeuer, 2004). Finally, there is an approach to this boundless field of research based on the idea of Cosmopolitan democracy, i.e. that global interdependence among national peoples should be regulated by supranational democratic institutions (Held, 1995; Archibugi, 2008; Brown and Held, 2010; Archibugi and Montani, 2011). In the twenty-first century, the policy point of view of cosmopolitan political economy is: what is good for the world is good for my country.

NOTE

1. In this appendix we draw some ideas from Montani (1996), where the concept of international order in classical political economy, Hamilton, List, Marshall, Robbins and Keynes is discussed.

PART II

Global imbalances, income inequalities and regional integration

2. Global imbalances and the dollar standard

2.1 INTRODUCTION

When trading in the world market, countries usually export part of their domestic production in exchange for imported goods. Because of the monetary nature of the modern economy, importing gives rise to a demand for foreign currency that countries meet by selling goods or services abroad. However, international trade is not necessarily continuously balanced year by year since deficits and surpluses may be temporarily financed through the accumulation or disposal of foreign assets. Historical data show that periods in which countries run a trade deficit (or surplus) are quite normal, often followed by years in which a trade surplus (or deficit) takes over. Developing countries, for example, need investments in an amount that very often exceeds domestic savings so that inflows of foreign funds, associated with the import of capital goods and a trade deficit, occur. When economic growth is consolidated, the external deficit eventually turns into a surplus so that the country's trade is balanced in the medium term. In the language of modern international trade theory, what really matters is that a country satisfies an intertemporal budget constraint in which a current external deficit (or surplus) is matched by the present value of the sum of (expected) future trade surpluses (or deficits). However, if the sequence of deficits is too long and trade surpluses fail to appear, the market would interpret such a situation as a signal of increasing the likelihood of the country going bankrupt, and the subsequent loss of international credibility would rapidly produce both a currency and balance of payments crisis[1].

At a more general level, when persistent economic and geographic disequilibria spread to several countries, in the world economy global imbalances arise and this is a serious issue. We define global imbalances as a situation in which one country, or a group of countries, systematically imports more goods and services than it exports while others persistently do the reverse. Trade deficits must be financed so that a chronic external deficit involves continuous financial flows from surplus (creditor) to deficit (debtor) countries whose foreign debt becomes larger and larger. Sooner

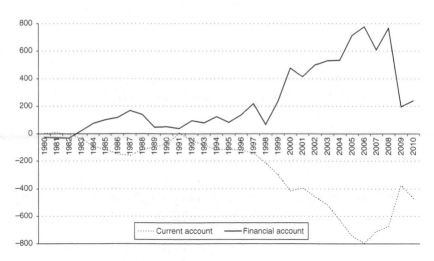

Source: OECD Main Economic Indicators

*Figure 2.1   US current account and financial account (1980 – 2010, USD
            billions)*

or later, in the absence of current account rebalancing, indebted countries
reach a critical point in which they violate their intertemporal budget
constraints and become insolvent. Lasting global imbalances are therefore
likely to result in a balance of payments and currency crisis with costly
adjustment that may spread to the world economy when the originating
country (or group of countries) is sufficiently large and important.

In recent years, in 2007 the burst of the sub-prime bubble was the
US domestic event that in a few months led to the collapse of the US
banking system in 2008 and gave rise to the most severe international
economic crisis since the Great Depression in 1929. However, global
imbalances preceded and accompanied the crisis, dating back years and
characterized by a growing American current account deficit financed by
the huge inflow of foreign capital, mainly from Asian and oil producing
countries[2]. Global imbalances not only contributed to the development of
the US credit bubble but also favoured its subsequent worldwide spread
(Dettman, 2011). Figure 2.1 shows the annual current account, trade
balance and financial account data for the US in the period 1960–2010.
The most striking fact is that, after 1982, the US trade balance has been
constantly negative with a rapid and dramatic deterioration after 1992,
reaching an unprecedented level in 2006. The current account balance
closely follows the trade balance pattern, while the financial account

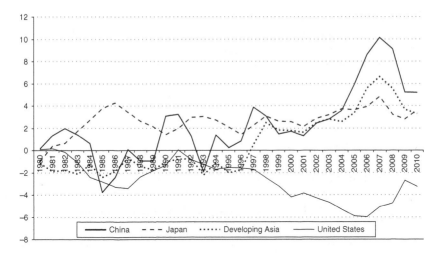

Source: IMF World Economic Outlook Database

Figure 2.2 *Trade balance as a percentage of GDP in the US and Asian countries (1980 – 2010)*

shows the increasing inflows of foreign capital allowing the US economy to finance the trade deficit. Only after the crisis of 2007 did a partial rebalancing occur. The counterpart to the long running US trade deficit was mainly a surplus in Asian countries, including Japan and more recently China (see Figure 2.2).

Parallel to the deterioration of the external trade position of the US was the worsening US foreign asset position. An inevitable consequence of the persistent inflows of foreign capital to finance the trade deficit is the continuous accumulation of foreign debt. US Treasury data shows that, at the end of 2010, foreign debt was $14,457 million and its ratio to GDP was 97 per cent. In early 2012, in absolute terms the US was thus the biggest debtor in the world economy.

Another aspect of the huge trade deficits is that for many years the US acted as the 'buyer of last resort' in the international trade arena, allowing emerging exporting countries such as China to grow at a very high rate. As a result, the slowdown of US domestic demand determined by the crisis caused a sharp negative shock spreading the American recession worldwide.

This picture raises several questions: how could the US sustain such a long period of continuous external deficits? What are the causes of long lasting global imbalances? Why were foreign investors so willing to finance the American economy, notwithstanding clear signs of rapid current account deterioration and foreign debt accumulation? Are global imbalances related to the worldwide financial crisis?

It is not simple to answer these questions because there are many possible causes for the rise and persistence of a trade deficit. Both micro and macroeconomic factors are relevant. On the microeconomic level, elements such as investments, commercial policies or technology transfer by firms[3] may be important because they interfere with the international competitiveness of countries through product and process innovation and the international re-allocation of production. Rapid industrial growth and the large trade surplus of China, for example, are not simply the result of an aggressive exchange rate policy toward the dollar as many US analysts and congressmen believe[4], but largely depend on foreign direct investments (FDI) over the last 15 years by many international companies which moved some or all of their production plants to Asian countries in order to exploit cheap Chinese labour[5].

At the macro level, the status of domestic and foreign trade, fiscal and monetary policy, the degree of protectionism and patterns of international demand affect import and export flows. An excess of domestic demand (absorption) over domestic output creates trade deficits, but real exchange rate appreciation may depress exports and foster imports through changes in the conditions of international trade. Financial and money market equilibria affect nominal exchange rates that in turn are the main drivers of short-term real exchange rate movements. Agents' expectations and the actions taken by the central bank may also have a significant impact on foreign exchange markets.

The shape and functioning of the international monetary system play a very significant role too. One source of global imbalances is the asymmetric nature of the international monetary system in which one national currency, the dollar, is the leading player. It was due to this asymmetry that, in the first decade of the new millennium, emerging countries accumulated dollar reserves that were reinvested in the US financial market allowing the country to ignore external balance of payments constraints, enabling it to finance the sub-prime bubble.

Trade deficits and imbalances in the world economy are complex phenomena that may be analysed from different points of view. Here, we focus on the macro and monetary aspects of global imbalances and their close link with asymmetries of the current dollar-based international monetary system. Our thesis is that profound international monetary reform, including the creation of supranational monetary institution, is necessary to create a more stable world economic environment if we want to prevent the recent pattern of global imbalances from appearing again in the future.

2.2 TRADE ACCOUNT, CURRENT ACCOUNT AND NET FOREIGN DEBT: ACCOUNTING IDENTITIES AND USEFUL ANALYTICAL TOOLS

Before we develop a detailed analysis of global imbalances, we must outline some accounting definitions and analytical tools used in the following discussion.

According to national accounting rules, current account CA is equal to the difference between national savings S and investments I.

$$CA = S - I = S_p + S_g - I \qquad (2.1)$$

In the above equation, national savings S is also written as the sum of two components, private savings S_p and government or public sector savings S_g. The latter is also equal to the government budget, so that a budget deficit represents negative public savings and vice versa. According to the equation 2.1, a trade deficit is always the result of domestic investments exceeding domestic savings. This approach outlines the possibility of twin deficits, namely the co-existence of both trade and government budget deficits, but it says nothing about the sources of differences between savings and investments. A trade deficit that arises because of a change in household consumption and savings behaviour and/or a fiscal expansion that worsens government budget is obviously more problematic in the long run than an external deficit caused by an endogenous increase in investments associated with capital accumulation and higher long-term rates of growth. In the first case the trade deficit may prove unsustainable, which is not necessarily so in the latter case. One should therefore carefully investigate the economic forces behind the dynamics of savings and investments to draw the right conclusions about trade imbalances. As to global imbalances, the savings-investment approach was the starting point of a famous explanation, put forward by Fed Chairman Bernanke (2005), known as the 'global savings glut hypothesis' (GSG), discussed in section 2.3.

A different, probably more direct approach to considering trade deficits and surpluses is the absorption approach (Alexander, 1952) that views the external imbalances of a country as a mismatch between aggregate demand, including both domestic and foreign goods, and domestic output (or the supply of goods and services). Characterizing domestic aggregate demand or absorption as A and output as Y, the trade balance TB is given by $TB = A - Y$. When the domestic supply of goods and services falls short of private and public demand, a deficit emerges while an excess supply over absorption generates a surplus. From standard macroeconomics we know that absorption depends on consumer income, company investments, the real exchange rate and monetary and fiscal policies, so that we may write the following compact trade balance equation:

$$TB = TB(Y, I, R, \gamma, \mu) \tag{2.2}$$

In equation 2.2, I represents investment, R the real exchange rate, while γ and μ are fiscal and monetary policy variables controlled by governments and central banks. Current account CA is closely related to the trade balance and is equal to the latter plus interest income accruing from net foreign assets iB, i being the interest rate earned on the net stock of foreign assets B that domestic residents hold:

$$CA = TB + iB \tag{2.3}$$

The net stock of foreign assets B changes whenever trade is not balanced. At the end of any period, a surplus increases the claims on foreign assets by domestic residents, while a deficit is financed selling liabilities to foreign investors:

$$TB = \Delta B \tag{2.4}$$

$$B_t = B_{t-1} + \Delta B \tag{2.5}$$

According to equations 2.4 and 2.5, a trade deficit or surplus affects the net stock of financial assets and determines the dynamics of foreign debt of a country. Combining equations 2.3, 2.4 and 2.5 we may derive the well known intertemporal solvency condition referred to in the introduction (Osbtfeld and Rogoff, 1996: 66).

$$-B_t = \sum_{s=t}^{\infty} \left(\frac{1}{1+i}\right)^{s-t} TB_{s-t+1} \tag{2.6}$$

Equation 2.6 is an intertemporal constraint that relates the current stock of foreign liabilities to the discounted flow of future trade surpluses and is derived under the assumption that a country cannot accumulate boundless foreign debt. In other words a 'no Ponzi scheme' terminal condition, excluding the possibility that a country can infinitely finance continuous current account deficit borrowing from abroad, is imposed. Equation 2.6 implies that a net current negative foreign asset position ($B < 0$) from the accumulation of past trade deficits, must sooner or later be matched by a sequence of trade surpluses. This is the only way to obtain the resources a country needs to refund foreign investor loans. A balance of payments crisis and economic disruption are the final outcome of violating (or the expected violation) of the intertemporal constraint. When foreign investors think a country is heading into insolvency, they stop financing the indebted country so that the rebalancing of the current account must be achieved through the reduction of domestic absorption through government spending cuts and monetary restrictions that ultimately result in a fall in income, lower consumption and a rise in unemployment[6].

It is important to observe that when national currencies have the same weight in the international monetary system, equation 2.5 symmetrically holds for every country. In this case, each currency plays the same role in international transactions and the conclusion that excessive prolonged trade and current account deficits are not sustainable holds everywhere. The ultimate reason is that the purchase of foreign goods and services requires the holding of foreign exchange balances, so that every country faces the same liquidity constraint and is bound by an intertemporal budget constraint of the same type (Obstfeld and Rogoff, 1996: 595–97).

However, as shown in Appendix A.2, when the international monetary system is asymmetric, based on one national 'key currency', as in the case of the current dollar standard, the issuer faces a less binding constraint and is therefore able to sustain longer sequences of trade deficits than other countries. Asymmetry occurs when the world monetary system is organized around a national currency serving as a worldwide unit of account, medium of exchange and store of value. The consequence of this asymmetry is that the country whose money is the 'key currency' can exert 'seignorage' on real resources traded in the international market, attracting foreign capital, and its intertemporal solvency condition is different from the rest of the world.

We can indicate the long-term implications of an asymmetric international monetary system using a simplified two-country world economy model in which Home and Foreign country face liquidity constraints 'a la Clower' (Clower, 1967; Fiorentini, 2002; Obstfeld and Rogoff, 1998: 595). Full technical details are available in Appendix A.2.

The benchmark case is the symmetric one in which no 'key currency' exists, so that each country is subject to the following liquidity constraints (foreign variables are indicated by asterisks):

$$M_{t-1} \geq P_t C_t \tag{2.7}$$

$$M^*_{t-1} \geq P^*_t C^*_t \tag{2.8}$$

In each period t, the value of consumption of domestic goods cannot exceed the stock of domestic money carried over from the previous period. At the same time, the domestic consumption of imported foreign goods is bound by the stock of foreign money held by domestic residents who obtain it through selling (exporting) goods and services to the other country.

Let us now assume that just one of the two currencies is used as a world-wide means of payment in international transactions. If Home country issues the international 'key currency', then it does not need to accumulate foreign currency reserves because it can purchase both domestic and foreign goods with its own money. On the contrary, Foreign Country, whose money has no role in international markets, has to export goods and services to obtain the 'key currency' it needs to pay for imports from Home country. As a consequence, the liquidity constraints are different. In fact, while Foreign country is still restrained by equations 2.7 and 2.8, Home country has to satisfy the following inequality:

$$M^H_{t-1} \geq P^H_t C^H_t + S_t P^F_t C^F_t \tag{2.9}$$

The meaning of 2.9 is that Home country has the privilege of purchasing both domestic and foreign goods using its own currency. It does not need to accumulate foreign currency by exporting domestic goods in order to import products from abroad. In Appendix A.2 we show that the exist-ence of a 'key currency' has two main implications that are relevant to our discussion. The first is that global imbalances are a natural result of the asymmetric world monetary system because Home country inevitably develops a trade deficit counterbalanced by a stable surplus in Foreign country. The second is that Home and Foreign countries' intertemporal budget constraints are different. In Home country the constraint is:

$$-B^H_{t-1} = \sum_{s=t}^{\infty} P^H_s TB^H_s + \alpha \tag{2.10}$$

while in Foreign country it is:

$$-B^F_{t-1} = \sum_{s=t}^{\infty} \frac{P^H_s}{S_s} TB^F_s - \alpha \tag{2.11}$$

In the equations, α is the terminal value of Foreign consumption of Home goods, S is the exchange rate and P^H is the price of Home country goods. According to equations 2.10 and 2.11, the same initial net foreign debt $B^H_{t-1} = B^F_{t-1}$ requires that the discounted value of the sum of future trade surpluses of Home country is smaller than the sum of Foreign country. In other words, given the same initial condition, Home country may have a longer period of trade deficit than Foreign country before violating the intertemporal constraint. In conclusion, the country whose currency is used as the medium of exchange in world trade benefits from seignorage that in the long run takes the form of a less binding intertemporal constraint. Global imbalances are an endogenous product of international asymmetric monetary systems.

2.3 EXPLANATIONS OF GLOBAL IMBALANCES: THE 'GLOBAL SAVINGS GLUT' HYPOTHESIS

We can now use the definitions and tools of the previous section to analyse global imbalances and their relationship with the dollar standard monetary system. It is known that current account deficits occur whenever domestic investments exceed domestic savings. The data on current account and trade balance shown in Figure 2.1 therefore directly point to the existence of a stable negative gap between savings and investments in the US economy.

The immediate question prompted by this data is: why have savings been systematically below investments in the US since 1982? Does it depend on internal factors or is it the result of international disequilibria to which the US economy has passively adapted? Bernanke (2005) believes the latter explanation. This view, known as the 'global savings glut' (GSG) hypothesis, states that the US current account deficit is the end result of an excess of world savings invested in the efficient American financial market, keeping long-term interest rates very low. Low interest rates in turn caused an expansion of both domestic credit demand and household consumption that depressed savings and gave rise to the current account deficit of recent years.

What can be said about the GSG hypothesis? Obviously, from an accounting point of view, at a worldwide level savings and investments must be balanced, and a savings glut cannot arise. However, a continuous upward trend in world savings after 1997 would be consistent with the GSG hypothesis. IMF data on world saving and investments are shown in Figure 2.3. They indicate that the global savings/GDP rate has been quite stable over the last 30 years, moving in a narrow 20.4–24.1 per cent range.

If we restrict the analysis to the 1997–2005 period in which, according to Bernanke, the GSG was operational, it can be seen that world savings actually decreased until 2002 and increased only after 2003. Yet, the US trade deficit was already declining quickly in 1997, so the GSG hypothesis is not entirely consistent with real global savings data. A disaggregated

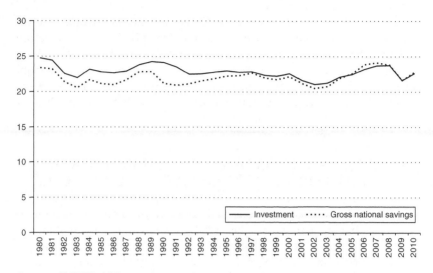

Source: IMF World Economic Outlook Database

Figure 2.3   World saving and investment rates (1980 – 2010)

view of world savings is useful in assessing the GSG explanation of
global imbalances because, by looking at the distribution of savings and
investments in different countries, surplus and deficit areas can be readily
identified. As Figure 2.4 shows, in the 1992–2009 period Asian and oil
producing countries had an excess of savings over domestic investment
while in industrialized countries only the US was in deficit, Japan having a
surplus and the EU area being roughly in equilibrium.

Looking at the US situation, a negative gap between savings and investments already existed in the 1980s but was quite stable up to the end of
the 1990s, oscillating slightly between −2 per cent and −3 per cent. This
trend is the result of different savings and investments dynamics during
the period. In Figure 2.5 three distinct phases are evident. In the 1980s,
there was a general decrease of both investments and savings, so the latter
drove the initial deterioration in the US trade balance. Both the private
and public components contributed (see Figure 2.6). The 1990s show quite
a different picture. The rebalancing of the federal budget by the Clinton
administration improved the gross savings rate, despite a continuous
decrease in private savings. In relation to investments, a popular explanation of the jump from 17.59 per cent in 1983 to 20.86 per cent in 2000 is
that huge investments in ITC were made, raising the GDP growth rate and
making the US an attractive place for foreign investors seeking high real
returns (Blanchard and Milesi-Ferretti, 2009: 8). In this view, it was a rise

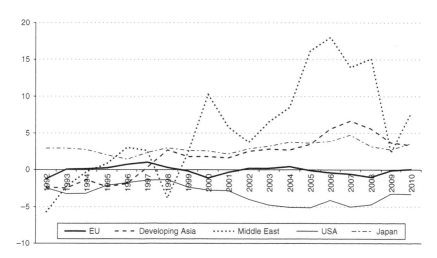

Source: IMF World Economic Outlook Database

Figure 2.4 Saving – investment gap as a percentage of GDP (1992 – 2010)

Source: IMF World Economic Outlook Database

Figure 2.5 US saving and investment rates (1980 – 2010)

Table 2.1   Top ten trading partners of US (1998)

US export	US import	Total trade
Netherlands	Japan	Canada
Brazil	China	Japan
Saudi Arabia	Germany	Mexico
Australia	Canada	Germany
Belgium	Mexico	China
Hong Kong	Taiwan	UK
Korea	Italy	Korea
Egypt	Malaysia	Taiwan
Argentina	Sweden	France
South Africa	Philippine	Singapore

Source: US Census Bureau

in investments and not a fall in savings that drove the savings gap, after accounting for the positive federal budget contribution to national savings (Blanchard and Milesi-Ferretti, 2009: 8). At the beginning of the new millennium, however, the gap grew steadily both due to the deterioration of the Federal Budget under the Bush administration and a steady increase in American household consumption.

The fact that in the last decade the lack of savings has been essentially an American problem seems to be consistent with Bernanke's explanation of the US current account deficit as a passive response to external dynamics. However, if he is right, we should see a strict time sequence between the trade surpluses of other countries and the decrease in the American savings rate after 1998. Since in the last ten years China has become the largest exporter country engaged in bilateral US trade, moving up from fifth to second position in total bilateral American trade (Tables 2.1 and 2.2), we should observe a close relationship between the high Chinese net savings rate and the low American rate.

However, in the US the savings rate actually started to decline *before* the surge in the Chinese current account surplus (Zhou Xiaochuan, 2009b). In fact, in the 1990s, the US savings rate as a percentage of GDP increased, peaking at 18.81 per cent in 1998; subsequently it steadily declined, mainly because of a reduction in the rate of household savings. On the other hand, it was only after 2001 that the Chinese current account surplus soared, from a mere 1 per cent to about 10 per cent of GDP in 2008. Domestic factors seem therefore to be as important as international phenomena in explaining the recent external imbalances of the US economy.

The composition of gross US savings comprising public and personal

Table 2.2   Top ten trading partners of US (2010)

US export	US import	Total trade
Canada	China	Canada
Mexico	Canada	China
China	Mexico	Mexico
Japan	Japan	Japan
UK	Germany	Germany
Germany	UK	UK
Korea	Korea	Korea
Brazil	France	France
Netherlands	Taiwan	Taiwan
Singapore	Ireland	Brazil

Source: US Census Bureau

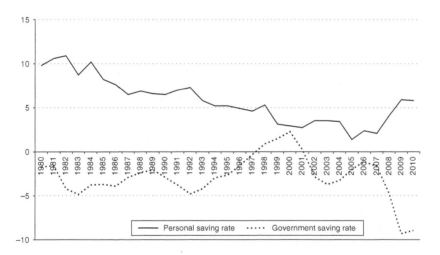

Source: Bureau of Economic Activity NIPA tables

Figure 2.6   US public and personal saving rates (1952 – 2010)

components shown in Figure 2.6 again provides a useful hint of what forces lie behind the deterioration of the US savings rate.

The graph shows that in the last three decades, from 1980 to 2010, the public sector negatively contributed to national savings in the 1980s and 2000s. On the other hand, private savings decreased well before the recent surge of the global imbalance debate focused on the GSG hypothesis.

Annual data on the US personal savings rate show a clear downward trend from 1982 to 2005. In 2006 the trend was reversed, but personal savings rates remained below their 1982 value at a very low level seen in historical perspective.

At the end of the 1980s, several years before Bernanke's speech, in their paper *Why is US National Saving so Low*? Lawrence and Carrol (1987) expressed concern about the low level of savings and growing dependence of the US economy on foreign loans. After careful review of the possible explanations for the declining American savings rate, they concluded that it was the result of a combination of the federal deficit and a long-term downward trend in private and personal savings. Their explanation for the personal savings trend was based on the increasing access of households to credit and the improved economic condition of the elderly, reducing the incentive of younger generations to save.

In the 1990s, although the Clinton administration improved the federal budget so much it went into surplus in 2000, the savings rate of the private sector continued to decline and the issue did not disappear from the economic debate (Gale and Sabelhaus, 1999; Parker, 1999; Maki and Polumbo, 2001; Marquis, 2002; Guidolin and La Jeunesse, 2007). According to Marquis (2002), the persisting decline in private savings in the 1990s was ultimately a consequence of two events: financial innovation relaxing individual financial constraints and fostering a rise in consumption; and the increase in permanent income generated by an upward trend in productivity associated with investments in the ICT sector. Guidolin and La Jeunesse (2007) added wealth effects, demographics, Social Security programmes and macroeconomic stability ('great moderation') to the list of possible explanations.

More recently, rising income inequality in the US has attracted attention as a possible cause of the long-term decrease in the private savings rate. The argument put forward by Rajan (2010) and Reich (2010) goes as follows: since the 1980s, the income of average educated American workers lagged behind productivity growth so their share of national income declined. In order to maintain their level of consumption, they increasingly turned to credit-financed consumption, producing a continuous decline in savings rates. Actually, the increase in the inequality of income distribution is not just an American problem; it is a global one that deserves specific attention (ILO, 2008; OECD, 2008, 2011). For its relevance to the current crisis, we discuss it in Chapter 4. For the moment, this brief review of the economic literature on the causes of the low US household savings rate can be summarized by saying that most explanations put forward are based on domestic factors, and therefore the GSG hypothesis of simple passive adaptation by the US economy to external trends in world savings does not appear to be very convincing. While the negative impact of financial innovation and cheap credit on household savings rates fits the GSG story, these factors were already functioning in the 1980s when Asian and other developing and emerging countries were running trade deficits and accumulating foreign debt rather than running trade surpluses and exporting capital to the US financial market.

Focusing now on the savings surplus outside the US, in the high-saving group of countries China plays a special role as the largest trade partner of the US. This explains why the Chinese savings rate has recently attracted so much attention. Doubtless, what is striking about China is its rapid recent surge in savings which, already high in 2000, peaked at 53 per cent of GDP in 2007 (Yang et al, 2011: 7). Many explanations have been put forward for the very high Chinese savings rate (Leightner, 2010; Chamon and Prasad, 2010; Kraay, 2000; Yang et al, 2011; Xinghua and Yongfu, 2007; Zhou Xiaochuan, 2009b). Overall, the rising trend in Chinese savings is the result of simultaneous positive contributions by companies, the government and households. At the company level, the privatization of many state-owned enterprises increased their efficiency so improved profitability associated with low labour costs and a widespread policy of low dividends resulted in a steady rise in corporate savings. As to the public sector, tax revenues increased more rapidly than expenditure, widening the government surplus. Finally, one of the most accredited explanations for rising household savings is the growing inequality in income distribution associated with a higher propensity to save by richer households; demographic dynamics with a rise in the dependency ratio due to the aging of the population and gender imbalance; the lack of a welfare system that increases private expenditure for health and child care. However, although the savings rate in China was very high, in the second part of the 1990s, when the US trade balance was already deteriorating, Chinese national savings slightly declined so that we do not see a strict correlation between US and Chinese savings, the one declining and the other increasing.

It is worth noting that savings surpluses outside the US would not have been able to cause such a huge trade deficit had it not been for a policy decision by the Fed to accommodate the rapid growth in the supply of credit which ultimately led to the sub-prime bubble. In other words, domestic monetary policy and household attitudes toward debt-financed consumption both played an important role in the dynamics of US internal and external imbalances.

The Fed pursued expansionary policies throughout most of the 1990s and 2000s. Such a stance in monetary policy shows up in Figure 2.7, which shows annual consumer price inflation rates for the US and the EMU area from 1992 to 2010.

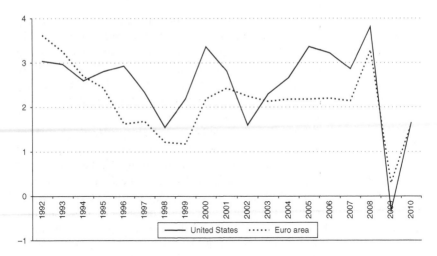

Source: IMF World Economic Outlook Database

Figure 2.7   US and EMU inflation rates (1992 – 2010)

In the sub-period 1995–2008, with the exception of 2002, US inflation rates were above EMU rates. A look at the 2000s shows that between 2002 and 2007 the US inflation rate almost doubled, while in Europe inflation was stable, slightly above the ECB target of 2 per cent. The sharp decline of inflation in 2009 is obviously a consequence of the recession caused by the international economic crisis starting in 2007.

As far as interest rates are concerned, there was a decrease in US short-term rates in the first half of the 2000s (see Figure 2.8), a period of rising US inflation.

As Taylor (2009: 3) has showed, such a trend in US interest rates represents a sharp downward deviation from the path followed in previous years, signalling loose monetary policy. The temporary decline in inflation in the period 2006–2007 is, interestingly, associated with the US overtaking European interest rates (see Figures 2.7 and 2.8), evidence of the tightening of the Fed's monetary policy over previous years. This increase in domestic interest rates contributed to the development of the sub-prime financial crisis. It should be noted, in fact, how the rise in interest rates in the US after 2005 was a shock that caused widespread household defaults in the sub-prime mortgage market. Since real estate was the main collateral in that market, household defaults forced banks to sell a growing number of newly purchased houses, leading to the decline in house prices and to the ultimate burst of the sub-prime bubble.

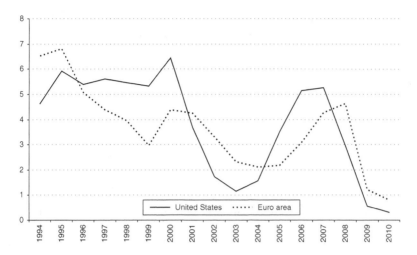

Source: OECD Main Economic Indicators

Figure 2.8 US and EU short term nominal interest rates (1994 – 2010)

To sum up, the GSG hypothesis cannot alone explain the sharp decline in the US savings rate. Other US domestic and external factors must be taken into account. In particular, useful insights come from the analysis of US domestic savings and monetary policy along with an investigation of the causes that led to a situation in which surplus countries accumulate surpluses and simultaneously opt to invest them in the US financial market. The latter is related to the key role of the dollar in the world economy, a topic we shall deal with in the following section.

In relation to why emerging economies willingly financed the US economy in the 2000s, it should be remembered that emerging Asian countries were importers of savings until the severe economic and financial crisis that hit the region in 1997. Subsequently, these countries increasingly became positive net savers. It was the Asian crisis at the end of the 1990s that induced countries to switch their development strategies from a model based on domestic investments financed through foreign debt to an export oriented model in which trade surpluses and foreign asset accumulation were key ingredients (Wolf, 2008). However, we would like also to stress that the specific international role of the dollar helped the US to attract foreign capital flows on a scale no other country could achieve. The bottom line is that, thanks to the asymmetric nature of the dollar standard monetary system, the US has so far been able to ignore balance of payments constraints that in the rest of the world are usually binding (Fiorentini, 2002; McKinnon, 2005).

2.4 EXPLANATIONS OF GLOBAL IMBALANCES: THE 'BRETTON WOODS II' HYPOTHESIS

The explanation of US external imbalances known as the Bretton Woods II (BWII) hypothesis was forcefully expounded in a series of papers by Dooley et al. (2003, 2007 and 2009) and is based on the existence of an implicit bargain among emerging Asian countries and the US. The basic idea of the proponents of the BWII hypothesis is that emerging Asian countries have very high savings rates yet their financial sector is not efficient enough to transform national savings into an adequate flow of domestic investments, so they mainly rely on FDI. In order to attract FDI after the Asian crisis of 1997, these countries started accumulating foreign exchange reserves in dollars, running current account surpluses mainly with the US. The rationale for this strategy is that if a country has enough reserves to service foreign debt, for say 12 months, then its solvency is well established. In other words, foreign reserve accumulation through trade surpluses is both a way to offer collateral to foreign investors and to buy assurance against sudden capital flights and financial crises. This strategy implies a constant flow of financial investment from emerging countries to the US and an exchange rate policy against the dollar that produces a de facto fixed exchange rate regime in the Pacific area. China, for example, after the 40 per cent devaluation of the renminbi in 1995, kept a 2.27 constant RMB/dollar exchange rate up to 2005 when the Chinese Government allowed it to appreciate by 10 per cent in three years, a rather modest revaluation.

In this framework, the role of the US financial sector was to transform incoming Asian savings into an outflow of efficient FDI returning to the originating countries and enhancing the economic development of the area. Since the BWII regime is based on unilateral pegging to the dollar by countries that have bilateral trade surpluses with the US, the consequences for the American economy are that a current account deficit necessarily arises and domestic long run interest rates are kept low. According to this hypothesis, the implicit bargain is therefore the following: the US offers FDI, international liquidity and collateral in the form of growing dollar reserves held by Asian countries. The latter finance the US current account deficit by buying American assets, providing a supply of low cost credit to US households and firms. The bargain between the US and Asian countries (mainly China) is summarized in Figure 2.9.

Available official data do in fact show a huge accumulation of foreign exchange reserves by developing countries. In absolute values, Figure 2.10 shows that Asian countries including China are the most active players in

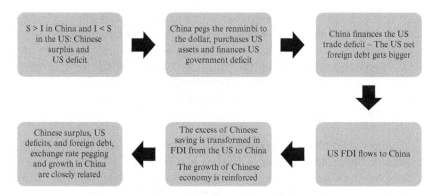

Source: Author's own rendition

Figure 2.9   The Bretton Wood II circuit

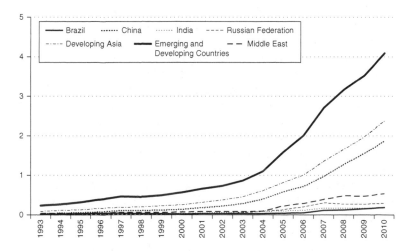

Source: IMF International Financial Statistics

Figure 2.10   Holdings of foreign exchange reserves (1993 – 2010, millions of SDR)

this field. Similarly impressive is the dramatic growth of the reserve/import ratio (IMF). In developing countries as a whole, the ratio started from a value of 46.3 per cent in 1998 and in ten years almost doubled, peaking at 86.7 per cent in 2008. Even more striking is the ratio for Asian countries, increasing from 58.6 per cent in 1999 to 114.8 per cent in 2008. This means that today Asian countries are able to finance one year of imports out of their foreign exchange reserves without exporting any commodities.

Complete data on the foreign currency reserves of central banks are sadly unavailable: many central banks, including the Chinese, disclose no information on these reserves. However, data from the IMF COFER database reported in Chapter 4, Figure 4.5, show that in 2010 about 60 per cent of international reserves were held in dollars, with a euro share of around 26 per cent.

The above evidence supports some aspects of the BWII hypothesis, although the rapid decrease of FDI as a source of funding for Chinese fixed investments contradicts it. In fact, according to data from the China Statistical Yearbook 2009, FDI contributed 11.19 per cent to funding in 1995 and a mere 2.90 per cent in 2008 (Branstetter and Foley, 2010: 513–43; Yang et al, 2011). Furthermore, the hypothesis is less generally relevant than its proponents assert. The so-called BWII appears to be quite specific to the US-China link rather than global (Wolf, 2008: 145). Besides, the phenomenon of the huge accumulation of dollar foreign exchange reserves in emerging countries shows once again that the pattern of global financial imbalances is closely related to the asymmetric nature of the current international monetary system, allowing one country to avoid external constraints thanks to its currency being used and held abroad for trade and precautionary purposes. This kind of imbalance, in which the core of the world economy (the US) acted as buyer and borrower of last resort by absorbing production and excess savings from less developed countries, doubtless contributed to the stabilisation of the world economy after the long wave of international financial crises in the 1990s. However, such a pattern is no longer sustainable now the reserve currency country faces a binding external constraint. The US simply cannot delay the rebalancing of the external position both in real and financial terms. The credit crunch produced by the explosion of the domestic financial crisis associated with the fall in US production and real household incomes has reduced GDP and demand for imports with a negative impact on international trade flows and financial surpluses abroad. Foreign investor confidence in US dollar assets is still intact but it may be eroded if the dollar starts devaluating. In fact, a declining dollar exchange rate is one of the factors that may help to eliminate the US current account deficit (Feldstein, 2008 and 2011) but, at the same time, it reduces the value of US assets owned by foreign investors so that their willingness to purchase dollar bonds, securities and equities may weaken. We do not expect US consumers and companies to be able to purchase large amounts of foreign goods in exchange for cheap credit as in the recent past.

2.5   GLOBAL IMBALANCES, CRISES AND ASYMMETRY

There are several reasons that explain the ability of the US to run long current account deficits, but the core explanation is the asymmetric nature of the dollar standard shaping the international monetary system. Both the GSG and BWII hypotheses have as a key ingredient the willingness of emerging countries to invest their trade surpluses in the US. In the GSG view, such willingness is due to the higher investment opportunities and returns offered by the US financial market; according to the BWII hypothesis, foreign countries need collateral that is well accepted by international lenders. Whatever the reason, the US has recently been able to attract foreign funds well beyond what would be normal for any other country.

A look at US assets held abroad shows that a large share of foreign portfolio investments consists of assets whose returns are not particularly high in comparison to those earned by US owners of foreign assets. At the same time, countries accumulating huge dollar reserves are foregoing better domestic and foreign investment opportunities since returns on foreign currency reserves are lower than returns on FDI or other securities. This fact is well documented by Gourinchas and Rey (2005) and Forbes (2008) among others. The latter, for example, shows that in the period 2002–2006, total average returns (including exchange rate movements) on US assets abroad was 11.2 per cent, while returns on US foreign liabilities was just 4.3 per cent. Looking at returns on private sector investments, Forbes finds that when all securities (equities and bonds) are included, American investors earned on their foreign portfolio an average return of 14.3 per cent, compared to a much lower 5.9 per cent earned by foreign owners of US debt. Even worse is the differential in the case of FDI: the figures are 16.3 per cent for American investors in contrast with a meagre 5.6 per cent on foreign investments in the US. In general, the GSG assumption that foreigners prefer US assets because of their superior performance seems unsupported by real data (Wolf, 2008: 136). We are back to our starting point: why do international financial flows go from less developed countries to the US? Our answer is the role of the dollar in the current international monetary system.

Since the end of World War II, the dollar has been the world's main reserve currency; due to hysteresis, it maintained such a role even after the end of the Bretton Woods era in 1971. In the international economy, there were simply no real alternatives to the dollar as a medium of exchange and a reserve currency. Even today, after the birth of the euro, the dollar is the currency most often used for international trade and finance (see Chapter 4). As issuer of the de facto international reserve currency, the US is able to borrow from abroad by issuing assets in its own currency. A consequence of the capability of borrowing in domestic money is that the debt burden does not depend on exchange rates. This contrasts with the well-known balance of payments and currency crisis in the 1980s and 1990s, which hit several developing countries with large external debt denominated in foreign currency (dollars): Mexico, Brazil, Argentina and Indonesia. The Asian crisis of 1997 is a clear example of the difficulties that countries unable to sell domestic bonds abroad may incur. When for any reason investors stop funding a foreign country and start withdrawing their investments, a sudden devaluation and a dramatic rise in the foreign debt burden creates panic and economic turmoil. Insofar as the dollar is accepted worldwide, the US therefore has the privilege of becoming indebted by issuing dollar-denominated international bonds.

As for net foreign debt, we should recall that, while the US sells dollar foreign debt, at the same time US international assets consist in securities, bonds and equity denominated in foreign currency (yen, euro, sterling), so that any devaluation of the dollar *improves* the US net foreign asset position. This asymmetry in US international portfolio helps to explain why America has so far been able to finance its increasing trade deficit with a cumulative real depreciation of the dollar by 40 per cent in the period 2001–2007. This phenomenon is known in literature as the 'valuation effect' (Gourinchas and Rey, 2005) and has had a substantial positive effect on the US net foreign debt position. Alessandrini and Fratianni (2009a) have used official Bureau of Economic Analysis (BEA) data to show that, in the period 2001–2007, the dollar depreciation increased the dollar value of US foreign assets by $950 billion. That figure helps to explain why, in the same period, the increase in US net foreign debt position was just one quarter of the cumulative current account deficit.

Another asymmetry of the international monetary system is that the most important commodities, raw materials and oil are invoiced in dollars. Almost half of world trade is carried out with the dollar and the US invoices in domestic currency about 95 per cent of its exports and 85 per cent of its imports (Golberg and Tille, 2005; Salvatore, 2000; BCE, 2008). The privilege of being the issuer of the international medium of exchange enables the US to exploit *seignorage* along the lines described in general terms in section 2.2: insofar as the rest of the world is willing to accept the key role of the dollar, the US may obtain foreign resources simply in exchange for domestic money. All other countries have to export something in order to obtain the foreign currency they need to pay for their imports. Leightner (2010: 50) clearly made this point:

Much of the USA's trade deficit is financed by countries, like China, who are willing to take our cash and hoard it. Indeed China's one trillion dollars of USA assets represents the USA receiving one trillion dollars of goods and services from China in exchange for US dollar, US treasury bonds and other US assets. If China would be willing to never spend those dollars, then the USA will have received one trillion dollars of goods and services free.

The limit is that the excessive creation of dollars would fuel world inflation by eroding trust in the dollar as a valuable reserve currency. An increase in world inflation would help to ease the US foreign debt burden but at the cost of a loss of status for the US currency. Countries like China, which hold most of the world's dollar reserves, are well aware of this problem but are in a difficult position. Their rapid accumulation of dollar reserves was the consequence of a policy strategy to exploit the opportunity of rising domestic expenditure in the US. The recent crisis of the US economy would seem to recommend diversification in the currency composition of international reserves. However, a relevant switch away from the dollar, say toward the euro, would result in rapid depreciation of the dollar, reducing the net foreign asset position of dollar-holding countries. It is clear that if the need for foreign currency holdings were removed, the dilemma would be resolved and the stability of the international economy greatly enhanced.

Summing up, until now the US has been able to run large trade deficits financed with foreign debt because of the asymmetry in the international monetary system allowing the country whose money acts as the reserve currency to avoid normal balance of payments constraints. It is therefore unsurprising that in the last decade several emerging countries have found the accumulation of low return dollar reserves useful. The origins of the global imbalances lie in the mutual interests of the US, eager to finance its excess of domestic consumption over production at a low cost, and emerging countries, keen to avoid a repetition of the 1990s financial crisis through export-led growth and the accumulation of dollars, the reserve currency. The cost of such a strategy, one that assured ten years of rapid worldwide growth, is now evident: excessive external and domestic debt in the American economy fuelled by massive inflows of financial capital, and the excessive reliance on the US market by developing countries. This mutual relationship is the main reason for the rapid worldwide spread of the US recession. Global imbalances were not the immediate cause of the US financial crisis of 2007 but they created the conditions for its development. We know that the US financial crisis was the consequence of a credit boom in the housing sector due to a lack of regulation and widespread use of derivative assets traded over the counter. However, the credit boom was global rather than specific to the US, as Astley et al. (2009: 180) and Duncan (2005: 120) have documented. The rapid accumulation of dollar reserves that surplus countries reinvested in the US was tantamount to a global monetary expansion creating a favourable environment for the development of credit and the housing bubble. If it is true, as Reinhart and Rogoff (2009) have recently claimed in their history of financial turmoil, that a rapid credit expansion is the best predictor of financial crisis, the sequence of negative events that hit the world economy in 2007–2008 cannot be considered a surprise, after all.

At the time of writing it is not clear how long the crisis will last, but in our opinion stable recovery requires the profound reform of the international monetary system to avoid a return to the pattern of recent global imbalances. The solution we propose is to create a symmetric monetary system in which none of the national currencies takes on the role the dollar played so far. This amounts to the creation of a supranational world currency with supranational institutions.

NOTES

1. Historical data and an empirical analysis of current account deficits and the crisis can be found in Adalet and Eichengreen (2005), Edwards (2007), Milesi-Ferretti and Razin (1996, 1997), and Reinhart and Rogoff (2009).
2. There is a great deal of literature on global imbalances, which includes: Astley (2009), Bernanke (2005), Blanchard et al. (2005), Blanchard and Milesi-Ferretti (2009), Bracke et al. (2010), Caballero and Krishnamurthly (2009), Clarida (2005, 2007), Edwards (2005a, 2005b), Engel and Rogers (2006), Feldstein (2008), Fiorentini and Montani (2010), Hong (2001), Kouparitsas (2005), Laibson and Mollerstrom (2011), Lee and Chinn (2002), Leightner (2010), Obstfeld (2005), and Obstfeld and Rogoff (2007).
3. The behaviour of foreign companies may affect the time lag with which an exchange rate depreciation contributes to the rebalancing of current account disequilibria. If foreign companies seek to defend their international market share, they do not immediately upwardly adjust the foreign currency price of their products. They prefer to accept a temporary loss of profits. In this case, the pass-through of exchange rate depreciation on prices is slow and related international prices do not change very much. In this event therefore, depreciation does not improve the trade balance. According to Krugman and Baldwin (1987), differences in price policies of American and foreign companies explain the persistence of the US trade deficit after the dollar depreciation in the 1985–1986 period.
4. Among academics, for example, Krugman forcefully maintains that the Chinese trade surplus depends on the policy of pegging an undervalued renmimbi to the dollar.
5. Yang and Liao (2007) showed the existence of a causal link between FDI in China and the development of the trade imbalance between China and the US. It is also worth noting that Hong Kong and Taiwan were particularly active in the field of DFI in mainland China (Branstetter and Foley, 2010: 5).
6. The events that occurred in the Asian crisis of 1997–1998 are a good example of the dramatic economic and social costs of a sudden stop in foreign financing in countries that accumulated a large stock of foreign debt.

APPENDIX A.2   KEY CURRENCY, SEIGNORAGE AND ASYMMETRIC INTERTEMPORAL CONSTRAINTS

In this appendix we develop a simple pure endowment monetary model to show that the existence of an international key currency gives the issuer country both short- and long-term advantages in the form of seignorage and less binding intertemporal solvability conditions.

Consider a simplified world economy with two countries, H and F. In each period t, the two countries are endowed with a given amount of consumption goods Y_t^h and Y_t^f. The only financial assets in this simplified model are the currencies circulating in H and F, namely M_t^h and M_t^f. Trade between the two countries occurs because consumers in H and F want to consume both goods. Consumers are also bound by Clower type liquidity constraints (Clower, 1967) that force individuals to carry money from one period to another because no market transaction can occur without money. In each country, the national currency is necessary to purchase domestic goods but only the M_t^h currency is used in international transactions. In other words, the assumption is that H is the issuer of the 'key currency'. Because of this asymmetry, the consumers in country H can purchase Y_t^h and Y_t^f goods simply using their own domestic currency, while country F consumers with their domestic money can purchase only Y_t^f goods. Therefore, in order to consume the desired amount of Y_t^h goods, country F needs to accumulate reserves of the H currency M_t^h exporting part of their endowment.

Following the discussion in section 2.2, the period t of the current account balance is defined as:

$$CA^i = A_t^i - A_{t-1}^i = Y_t^i - D_t^i \quad (i = h, f) \qquad (A.2.1)$$

where A_{t-1} is the stock of foreign net financial assets held in a country at the beginning of period t, Y_t is the endowment and D_t is the domestic absorption. Since we assumed that the only financial assets are the two currencies, it follows that the stock of net foreign financial assets entirely consists in the foreign currency held at home. As for the money creation process, we assume that in each country money is injected into the economy by the public sector in order to finance any public budget deficit.

The F Country Period t Budget Constraint

In country F, at each date, consumption is bound by the stock of money carried from the previous period according to the following liquidity constraints:

$$M^f_{t-1} \geq P^f_t C^f_t \tag{A.2.2}$$

$$M^{h,f}_{t-1} \geq P^h_t C^{h,f}_t \tag{A.2.3}$$

In inequality A.2.3 $M^{h,f}_{t-1}$ represents the country H money balances held by country F residents and $C^{h,f}_t$ is the consumption of country H goods by country F consumers. P^f_t and P^h_t are the domestic prices of F and H goods. In country F, the consumers' period t aggregate budget constraint is:

$$P^f_t Y^f_t + M^f_{t-1} + E_t M^{h,f}_{t-1} = P^f_t C^f_t + E_t P^h_t C^{h,f}_t + T^f_t + E_t M^{h,f}_t + M^f_t \tag{A.2.4}$$

where E_t is the exchange rate between country H and F currencies. According to A.2.4, the domestic nominal value of income (or endowment $P^f_t Y^f_t$) plus the initial stock of domestic (M^f_{t-1}) and foreign money ($E_t M^{h,f}_{t-1}$) must be equal to the sum of the value of consumption of domestic ($P^f_t C^f_t$) and foreign goods ($E_t P^h_t C^{h,f}_t$) plus taxes (T^f_t) collected by the government and the monetary balances (M^f_t and $E_t M^{h,f}_t$) set aside for use in the next period. The government budget constraint is given by:

$$G^f_t = T^f_t + (MS^f_t - MS^f_{t-1}) \tag{A.2.5}$$

According to A.2.5, a government budget deficit implies a change in the domestic money supply MS^f and since only F inhabitants demand F currency, the money market equilibrium is given by the condition that F money supply be equal to the F resident money demand.

$$MS^f_t = M^f_t \tag{A.2.6}$$

Now, with the help of equation A.2.5, we may eliminate T^f_t and write the consumers' budget constraints A.2.4 as:

$$P^f_t Y^f_t + M^f_{t-1} + E_t M^{h,f}_{t-1} =$$

$$P^f_t C^f_t + E_t P^h_t C^{h,f}_t + G^f_t - MS^f_t + MS^f_{t-1} + E_t M^{h,f}_t + M^f_t \tag{A.2.7}$$

which, thanks to A.2.6 and some simple algebraic simplifications, finally becomes:

$$\frac{E_t(M^{h,f}_t - M^{h,f}_{t-1})}{P^f_t} = Y^f_t - C^f_t - \frac{E_t P^h_t}{P^f_t} C^{h,f}_t - \frac{G^f_t}{P^f_t} \tag{A.2.8}$$

Equation A.2.8 is the country F current account balance. Comparing it with A.2.1 we can see that the right hand side of A.2.8 is nothing but the difference between the endowment and the absorption, which in this case is equal to the sum of private and public consumption $(D_t^f = C_t^f + E_t P_t^h/P_t^f C_t^{h,f} + G_t^f/P_t^f)$. The left hand side represents the accumulation by country F residents of foreign financial assets (country H currency) valued in real terms and converted in domestic currency. When $Y_t^f > D_t^f$ F incurs a current account surplus and accumulates country H currency.

Equation A.2.8 is useful because it reveals the seignorage country H exerts in the international economy. Following Obstfeld and Rogoff (1996: 523), we may formally define seignorage as the increase of key currency stock outside the issuing country H. According to A.2.8 it is equal to the amount of real resources H obtains in the international market (country F exports). A country F current account surplus implies that only a fraction of the endowment is domestically consumed. The remaining is exported in exchange for country H money balances that in the next period allow consumers in country F to purchase country H goods. This is clearer if we assume that the liquidity constraints A.2.2 and A.2.3 hold as strict equalities

$$M_{t-1}^f = P_t^f C_t^f$$

$$M_{t-1}^{h,f} = P_t^h C_t^{h,f}$$

In such a case, equation A.2.8 reduces to:

$$\frac{E_t M_t^{h,f}}{P_t^f} = Y_t^f - C_t^f - \frac{G_t^f}{P_t^f} \tag{A.2.9}$$

or, since $M_t^{h,f} = P_{t+1}^h C_{t+1}^{h,f}$,

$$\frac{E_t P_{t+1}^{h,f}}{P_t^f} = Y_t^f - C_t^f - \frac{G_t^f}{P_t^f} \tag{A.2.10}$$

The latter equation says that, in the case of country F consumers, the future consumption of foreign goods is equal to today's export of domestic goods.

The Country H Period t Budget Constraint

Country H is the issuer of the international key currency so consumers in that country face a completely different liquidity constraint:

$$M_t^h \geq \frac{P_t^f}{E_t} C_t^{f,h} + P_t^h C_t^h \qquad (A.2.11)$$

The economic meaning of A.2.11 is that in country H the value of total consumption of domestic and foreign goods is limited by the stock of domestic money held by residents. They do not need to set aside country F money balances. In mathematical terms, while consumers in country F have simultaneously to satisfy two different constraints, people living in country H have to meet just one.

In the two countries, liquidity constraints differ but the budget constraints of consumers and the government are comparable. In the case of country H they may be written as:

$$P_t^h Y_t^h + M_t^h = \frac{P_t^f}{E_t} C_t^{f,h} + P_t^h C_t^h + T_t^h + M_y^h \qquad (A.2.12)$$

$$G_t^h = T_t^h + (MS_t^h - MS_{t-1}^h) \qquad (A.2.13)$$

The main difference between A.2.4 and A.2.12 is that in the latter, foreign currency holdings (F currency in this case) do not appear since they are useless for H consumers. Another difference with the country F case lies in the condition for money market equilibrium, since demand for H money comes not only from H residents (M_t^h), but also from F consumers ($M_t^{h,f}$). Therefore we have:

$$MS_t^h = M_t^h + M_t^{h,f} \qquad (A.2.14)$$

This equation states that H money supply MS_t^h has to match the world money demand from countries H and F. Using the same mathematical steps as the previous section we obtain the final aggregate H consumers budget constraint or the country H current account balance:

$$\frac{E_t(M_t^{h,f} - M_{t-1}^{h,f})}{P_t^f} = \left[\left(\frac{E_t P_t^h}{P_t^f} C_t^h + C_t^{f,h} + \frac{E_t P_t^h}{P_t^f} G_t^h \right) - \frac{E_t P_t^h}{P_t^f} Y_t^h \right] \qquad (A.2.15)$$

A comparison between A.2.15 and A.2.8 shows us that the left hand side of the two current accounts are the same but, in the case of country H, the right hand side represents a deficit rather than a surplus. In fact, in A.2.15 the right hand side gives us the excess of domestic consumption over domestic endowment or income that is financed through money held by the foreign country F. Put another way, A.2.15 represents the acquisition of real foreign resources through the transfer of 'key currency' in the other country. The left hand side of A.2.15 is therefore country H's net foreign liabilities but, at the same time, in equation A.2.8 it is country F's net foreign assets.

Finally, and importantly, because of the asymmetric liquidity constraints generated by the existence of an international key currency, the country that issues the dominant money inevitably needs to run a current account deficit matched by a current account surplus in the other 'peripheral' country. Global imbalances are therefore a 'natural' consequence of an asymmetric international monetary system.

Intertemporal Budget Constraints and the Sustainability of Current Account Deficits

An important issue in international macroeconomics is the sustainability of current account deficits. We may use the model developed above to derive sustainability conditions that extend uniperiodal constraints to an intertemporal setting.

Let us start with the Country F equation A.2.8. Since the right hand side of it is the current account balance, we can write it simply as:

$$M_t^{h,f} - M_{t-1}^{h,f} = \frac{P_t^f}{E_t}CA_t^f \tag{A.2.16}$$

or

$$-M_{t-1}^{h,f} = \frac{P_t^f}{E_t}CA_t^f - M_t^{h,f} \tag{A.2.17}$$

Forwarding the latter by one period we get:

$$-M_t^{h,f} = \frac{P_{t+1}^f}{E_{t+1}}CA_{t+1}^f - M_{t+1}^{h,f} \tag{A.2.18}$$

Replacing it in the previous equation we obtain:

$$-M_{t-1}^{h,f} = \frac{P_t^f}{E_t}CA_t^f + \frac{P_{t+1}^f}{E_{t+1}}CA_{t+1}^f - M_{t+1}^{h,f} = \sum_{s=t}^{t+1}\frac{P_s^f}{E_s}CA_s^f - M_{t+1}^{h,f} \tag{A.2.19}$$

Iteration of that procedure for all future time periods yields:

$$-M_{t-1}^{h,f} = \sum_{s=t}^{\infty}\frac{P_s^f}{E_s}CA_s^f - \lim_{T\to\infty} M_T^{h,f} \tag{A.2.20}$$

We know that $M_T^{h,f} = P_T^h C_T^{h,f}$ so that the last term in equation A.2.20 represents the terminal consumption of country H goods by country F consumers. Under quite general assumptions about consumer preferences, consumption is positive at all dates so that we may write the following transversality condition:

$$\lim_{t \to \infty} M_T^{h,f} = \lim_{t \to \infty} P_T^h C_T^{h,f} = \alpha > 0 \qquad (A.2.21)$$

Finally, from A.2.20 and A.2.21 we obtain the intertemporal constraints of country F's consumers:

$$-M_{t-1}^{h,f} = \sum_{s=t}^{\infty} \frac{P_s^f}{E_s} CA_s^f - \alpha \qquad (A.2.22)$$

The meaning of the above constraint is that in country F, any initial foreign debt (negative financial assets) must be equal to the sum of the future current account surplus *minus* the terminal value of F consumers' consumption of the H good.

Let's now compare the country F intertemporal constraint with that of country H. Using the same technique described above it can be shown as:

$$M_{t-1}^{h,f} = \sum_{s=t}^{\infty} \frac{P_s^h}{E_s} CA_s^h + \alpha \qquad (A.2.23)$$

Recall that $M_{t-1}^{h,f}$ are money balances held by country F citizens so they represent country H foreign liabilities. Given this, we observe that in the case of country H, the same initial value of foreign debt has to be matched by a *shorter* sequence of future current account surpluses than is the case for country F. In other words, assuming the same initial foreign debt, the sum of future current account surpluses compatible with the country H solvency is smaller because the term α appears with a positive sign in the right hand side of the equation. Whereas, for country F, α enters the intertemporal constraints with negative sign and the sum term in equation A.2.22 has to be greater than in A.2.23. As a conclusion, because of asymmetric liquidity constraints, due to the existence of a key currency, the long-term burden of current external deficits are lighter for the country that issues the international currency. In the long run, seignorage takes the form of less binding intertemporal constraints.

The General Intertemporal Solvency Condition without Liquidity Constraints

We conclude by showing how the intertemporal constraint (2.6) displayed in the main text of the chapter is derived. For convenience, below we write out the relevant equations:

$$CA_t = TB_t + iB_{t-1} \tag{2.3}$$

$$CA_t = \Delta B \tag{2.4}$$

$$\Delta B = B_t - B_{t-1} \tag{2.5}$$

Recall that (2.3) defines the current account as the sum of trade balance and the interest earned on the stock of foreign assets and that (2.4) and (2.5) are the law of motion of the stock of foreign assets. If we substitute (2.4) and (2.5) in (2.3) we obtain

$$\Delta B = B_t - B_{t-1} = TB_t + iB_{t-1} \tag{A.2.24}$$

Rearranging the terms, this becomes

$$-B_{t-1}(1 + i) = TB_t - B_t \tag{A.2.25}$$

Forwarding one period this equation, we find a value for $-B_t$

$$-B_t = \frac{1}{1 + i}(TB_{t+1} - B_{t+1}) \tag{A.2.26}$$

which, when inserted into (A.2.25), yields

$$-B_{t-1}(1 + i) = TB_t + \frac{1}{1 + i}(TB_{t+1} - B_{t+1}) \tag{A.2.27}$$

or

$$-B_{t-1} = \frac{1}{1 + i}TB_t + \left(\frac{1}{1 + i}\right)^2 TB_{t+1} - \left(\frac{1}{1 + i}\right)B_{t+1} =$$

$$\sum_{s=1}^{2}\left(\frac{1}{1 + i}\right)^s TB_{t+s-1} - \left(\frac{1}{1 + i}\right)B_{t+1} \tag{A.2.28}$$

Repeating the same procedure for all future time periods we get

$$-B_{t-1} = \sum_{s=1}^{\infty}\left(\frac{1}{1+i}\right)^{s} TB_{t+s-1} - \lim_{T\to\infty}\left(\frac{1}{1+i}\right)B_{T+1} \quad (\text{A.2.29})$$

Now, since it makes no sense to keep financial assets at the final period of the economy, the limiting value of the second term of A.2.29 must be zero, so that imposing the transversality condition

$$\lim_{T\to\infty}\left(\frac{1}{1+i}\right)B_{T+1} = 0$$

yields the final intertemporal constraint reported in the main text of the chapter:

$$-B_{t-1} = \sum_{s=1}^{\infty}\left(\frac{1}{1+i}\right)^{s} TB_{t+s-1}$$

3. Globalization and income inequalities

3.1 THE PROBLEM OF THE INCREASE OF INCOME INEQUALITIES IN THE WORLD ECONOMY

Since the Industrial Revolution, the history of the world economy has been characterized by a general rise in global inequality. This lengthy trend is the result of the interaction of two types of inequality: growing differences in GDP levels between countries (horizontal or inter-country inequality) and large differences in the income of individuals within each country (vertical or within-country inequality). During the first wave of globalization (1820–1914), although vertical inequality was high, horizontal inequality grew at a faster rate because industrialization in few core European countries initiated an uneven world development process leaving most of the other regions in the world behind. After the 'first globalization' period, in 1914–1945, inter-country inequality continued to increase while income distribution inside countries was more even (Lindert and Williamson, 2001). After World War II, in the Bretton Woods period (1944–1971), inequality between countries continued to rise, albeit at a slower pace because of post-war reconstruction and growth in Japan and Western Europe, offset by the gradual inclusion in the core of the world economy of a group of new industrialized Asian countries, the so-called 'Asian tigers'. These countries were able to increase their per-capita income and reduce poverty through export-led strategies supported by controls on capital flows and domestic investments in capital goods, infrastructure and education. In the same period, within-country inequality remained stable overall with improvements in several advanced and Asian countries. From 1980, in the so-called 'second globalization' era, world economic and, in particular, financial integration accelerated, surpassing the already high level of the first phase of globalization in the years before World War II. Recently, the rapid growth of high-population countries such as China, India and Brazil as well as of other Latin American and South-East Asian countries, has positively affected inter-country inequality but not within-country income inequality which is now rising everywhere.

This trend in within-country income distribution, common to both developed and emerging countries, poses several questions: does it have a positive or a negative impact on economic efficiency and social welfare? Is it an inevitable consequence of greater openness to trade and financial flows in emerging and developing countries? Does it depend upon continuous technological change spreading all over the world? Is it the consequence of liberalization policies mainly driven by international economic institutions such as the WTO, the IMF and the World Bank? Did it have a role in the genesis of the recent financial crisis? Obviously, no simple answer to the above questions can be found and a set of simultaneous explanatory factors, rather than single factor explanations, must be taken into account to explain the worldwide trend in income distribution. Nonetheless, it is difficult to avoid the idea that some causal link between globalization in trade and finance, global imbalances, the financial crisis and inequality does exist. This chapter explains why current trends in income distribution cannot be ignored in the discussion of the causes of the financial crisis and their implication for the redesign of economic theory and the international order. After a discussion of empirical international evidence on within-country income distribution, we analyse the main factors that seem to be at the root of the income distribution problem, taking into account, among other things, the role that policies fostering financial liberalization may have had in the overall increase in income inequality.

From the point of view of economic theory, it is worth noting that, unlike classical economic thought, standard neoclassical economic theory treats income distribution as a relatively minor issue. Assuming perfect competition, owners of the factors of production (labour, capital and land) are rewarded according to their marginal contribution to output. In this context, no conflicts over income distribution exist and changes in income share are viewed as the result of an efficient adjustment of the economy to technologically induced structural changes or to new market equilibria driven by demand or supply shocks. From this, it follows that changes in income distribution are not a problem *per se*. In the neoclassical paradigm, the Heckscher-Ohlin (H-O) model of international trade is one notable exception, in that it predicts unambiguous and sharp distributional effects in countries that open up to trade. In the H-O model, greater openness to international trade increases the real income of the country's abundant factor of production intensively employed in the production of exported goods. At the same time, the real income of owners of the scarce factor decreases, so that the group damaged by international trade is likely to oppose any move toward free trade, calling for some form of protection from foreign competition. Domestic income remuneration policies may therefore be necessary to convince international trade 'losers' to give up their opposition to free trade, allowing the economy to move toward an international Pareto superior equilibrium. Because of these predictions, the H-O theory is sometimes invoked as a possible explanation for the worldwide trend in rising income inequality. However, as we will show later in this chapter, the actual trends in income distribution are not consistent with the 'naïve' H-O view and other explanations need to be found.

Moving away from the narrow static neoclassical world, studies of economic development pay more attention to income inequality. The reason is that developing countries undergo structural changes in their institutions, the labour market and their economic structure, which affect the incomes of different segments of the population in non-uniform ways. The final goal of economic development should be the achievement of better living conditions for populations that are often locked into a poverty trap. However, a high rate of GDP growth does not necessarily mean greater welfare for everybody: it may lead to an improvement in the living standards of the majority of the population and to lower inequality or, on the contrary, it may lead to a growing share of domestic GDP going to a small elite without any real benefit to the poor. The distributional consequences of different development policies cannot be ignored, as shown by a large body of literature on this topic, effectively summarized by Goldberg and Pavcnik (2007).

In developed countries, a growing interest in the theme of income distribution was evident in the US at the beginning of the 2000s, well before the start of the financial crisis (Bryan and Martinez, 2008; Lawrence, 2008). Subsequently, after 2008 a lively discussion took place on the role of US income inequality in the genesis of the financial crisis (Reich, 2010). At a more general level, official reports published by the International Labour Organisation (ILO, 2008) and OECD (2008, 2011a and 2011b) not only show beyond any doubt that the recent period of globalization has also been a period of rising inequalities, but also indicate that the problem of income inequality has become a concern for important international economic institutions often criticised for the support they have given in the past to the 'Washington Consensus' ideology (Stiglitz, 2002).

Why should we be concerned about income inequalities? After all, a degree of inequality is acceptable and can be explained by the fact that high wages are the consequence of high productivity of labour which has to be properly rewarded, according to the neoclassical view. Since the labour force is a heterogeneous aggregate comprising individuals with different skills and levels of education, it is likely that different individuals will have different rates of productivity and hence obtain different rewards as described by Murnane et al. (1995). Therefore, if the composition of the labour force changes and labour demand switches in favour of more educated and skilled workers, the gap between high and low wages will probably increase. As shown in the next section, the problem is that the gap between low and high income individuals has, in several cases, gone well beyond any reasonable and socially acceptable level. Having said that, the social perception of excessive inequality is not sufficient, on its own, to justify concern about its potential negative economic consequences: other factors are in play. For example, in the case of developing and emerging countries, excessive income inequality often correlates with corruption and poverty problems that may hinder both growth and the modernization of the economy. In fact, there is evidence that '. . . longer growth spells are robustly associated with more equality in the income distribution' (Berg and Ostry, 2011) and that equality is beneficial to the long-term sustainability of growth. At a more general level, one concern about income inequalities is that wherever income and wealth are unequally distributed and concentrated, democracy is emptied of any real content, because the growing costs of election campaigns mean that only the wealthy can afford to run for political office. As in the past, personal income, rather than citizenship, becomes the prerequisite for taking an active part in the political life of a country. In addition, it is well known that the wealthiest people and corporations are very often able to influence policy decisions through the ownership of the media and via lobbying, unfairly promoting their interests.

Another problem which is particularly relevant today, in advanced countries severely hit by the recent global financial crisis, is that an excessive concentration of income and wealth in the hands of the upper echelons of a society may depress aggregate demand, generating economic stagnation and inducing low income households and individuals to become increasingly indebted.

In general, the propensities to save or consume from disposable income are not uniform across households and individuals but vary with the income level. High income households have a greater propensity to save whereas low-income households consume a larger proportion of their incomes (Dyan et al, 2004). In formal terms, if we call the consumption propensity of low income households c_L and the consumption propensity of high income households c_H, assuming that $c_L > c_H$, Appendix A.3 shows that the impact on aggregate consumption C of changes in the national income share a of low income households is positive and equal to

$$\frac{\partial c}{\partial \alpha} = (c_L - c_H)\,Y > 0 \qquad (3.1)$$

where Y stands for GDP. Conversely, according to equation 3.1 a lower α, namely a higher proportion of GDP in the hands of wealthy households, depresses aggregate consumption. If income distribution changes in favour of the upper segment of society (a decrease in α) but in the same time GDP grows at a sufficient rate, consumption may still increase because the higher per-capita income may offset the income distribution changes. However, in the case of weak economic growth or particularly adverse distributional changes, aggregate consumption cannot increase in the same proportion as GDP, unless lower income households finance part of their consumption with debt. If enough credit is available, the outcome can be greater and greater private debt, or, if credit to households is constrained, the eventual reduction of the growth rate and economic stagnation due to declining aggregate demand. In its simplicity, this resembles some features of the US economy prior to and after the financial crisis: growing income inequality characterized by a rising concentration of wealth at the very top, the increasing indebtedness of households, a credit bubble that eventually burst followed by a period of stagnant domestic demand, and an uncertain economic outlook (Wolff, 2010).

3.2   EMPIRICAL EVIDENCE ABOUT TRENDS IN WITHIN-COUNTRY INCOME DISTRIBUTION

Before we present empirical data for recent trends in within-country income distribution, a brief discussion about the methods for measuring income inequality may be useful. Statistical studies usually rely on synthetic concentration indices calculated from national income data and surveys, consumption and the wages of households or individuals, depending on reliability and availability. Of the inequality measures, the Gini index[1] and ratios between quintile or decile of the income distribution, such as the D10/D1 or the Q5/Q1 (often along with intermediate ratio such as D10/D5 and D5/D1) are among the most used. The Gini Index takes values in the range between 0 and 1 (or in percentage terms between 0 and 100), with 1 (100) representing the highest and 0 the lowest inequality. If the index were equal to 0, all individuals in a country would have the same income (a full egalitarian society). On the other hand, if the index were equal to 1, all domestic income would go to just one individual. As a consequence, an upward movement of the coefficient signals rising inequality with fewer and fewer people gaining wider shares of GDP at the expense of larger portions of the population. A plot of the time trend of the index may therefore help scholars to identify inequality trends within a country. The international comparison of the Gini Index and the ranking of countries according to their degree of inequality is possible but problematic due to measurement errors and because the sources, quality and reliability of domestic data may differ from one country to another. To facilitate comparative analysis, efforts have been made to create homogenous international databases on income distribution by the OECD, UN, ILO and other research institutes such as the University of Texas Inequality Project (UTIP) and the Cross National Data Center in Luxembourg (LIS). The empirical evidence discussed below draws on such databases.

In so far as comparison of quintile or decile ratios is concerned, an example of how they are useful is that a high D10/D1 ratio can be understood intuitively to represent large inequality because it means that the distance between the income of the richest tenth (D10) and poorest tenth of the population (D1) is very wide. At the same time, intermediate ratios, such as D10/D5 and D5/D1 are also very useful and informative because they give detailed information on the shape of income distribution. It is good practice to use both Gini coefficients and distribution ratios, because the same Gini Index may be associated with different underlying income distributions more easily identified with the help of intermediate ratios. For example, a higher Gini Index due to a larger D5/D1 ratio is likely to represent a less problematic situation than when the increase is the result of a higher D10/D5 ratio because, in this case, there is a higher concentration of income in the hands of relatively few people at the expense of the middle class which, in today's societies, comprises the majority of the population. Hence, the information given by distribution ratios is generally a useful complement to the Gini Index.

Now we can look at empirical evidence. The economic literature is unanimous in identifying greater inequality in within-country income distribution over the last two decades (Cornia, 2003; Berg and Ostry, 2011; Bergh and Nilsson, 2010; Bollè, 2008; Celik and Basdas, 2010; Dreher and Gaston, 2008; Goldberg and Pavcnik, 2007; Jauomotte et al, 2008; Palma, 2006; Qureshi and Wan, 2008, and Ulubasoglu, 2004) and in attributing this trend to the concentration of income at the top of the distribution curve. Two wide-ranging and authoritative studies by the OECD (2008) and ILO (2008) are illustrative in this regard.

According to the OECD (2008: 17), wide differences in the absolute level of inequality between countries exist, as Table 3.1 shows, but income inequality in the last two decades has risen in two thirds of all OECD countries. This is shown in Table 3.2 with the Gini index for pre-tax market incomes in 15 OECD countries. In the table, the index is normalized to 1 in a base year that may be 1975, 1985 or 1995 depending on available data in each country. The table therefore shows changes compared to the starting year, rather than the absolute values of the index. Inequality has increased the most in Canada, Germany, the US, Italy and Finland. A slight decrease occurred recently in the UK and Australia. On average,

Table 3.1   The Gini index for selected countries

Country	Gini index	Year*
Albania	31.2	2004
Argentina	50.3	2005
Bangladesh	33.2	2004
Bolivia	50.4	2004
Brazil	56.4	2004
China	37.2	2002
Egypt	34.4	2004
Finland	26	2006
France	27	2006
Germany	27	2006
India	36.8	2004
Italy	32	2006
Nigeria	43.7	2003
South Africa	56.5	2000
UK	32	2006
USA	46.4	2004

Source: UNI/WIDER Income Inequality Database WIID2c (2008).
*Year depends on availability and reliability of data.

in this OECD sample, inequality, as measured by the index, increased by 12 per cent in the period 1985–2005. It is worth noting that, according to the OECD, the rise in inequality is mainly due to wealthy households improving their position with respect to middle class and poor families. In fact, taking the sample of 22 OECD nations as a whole, the average annual change in the real income of households at the top quintile of the distribution was 2.1 per cent in the period 1985–1995 and 1.9 per cent in the subsequent decade. In contrast, the real income of households at the bottom quintile grew by 1.2 per cent in the first decade and 1.5 per cent in the decade 1995–2005 (OECD, 2008: 29).

The general trends that emerge from the OECD study are particularly evident in the case of the US and are confirmed by other statistical sources. For example, using data from the UNI/WIDER Income Inequality Database WIID2c (2008), Figure 3.1 shows the absolute values of the Gini index from 1968 to 2004 and Table 3.3 shows the Q5/Q1, Q5/Q3 and Q3/Q1 ratios.

The graph shows a steady increase in overall income inequality in the US from 1980. The index is very high for a developed country (Table 3.1). At the same time, the inter distribution ratios of Table 3.3 show a clear concentration of income in favour of the top quintile representing the top

Table 3.2   Pre-tax Gini index trends in 15 OECD countries

	1975	1985	1990	1995	2000	2005
Australia				1.00	1.02	0.98
Belgium		1.00	1.03	1.05	1.03	
Canada	1.00	1.04	1.08	1.11	1.11	1.16
Denmark		1.00	1.06	1.12	1.11	1.12
Finland	1.00	0.97	1.05	1.14	1.13	1.13
France		1.00	0.97	0.92	0.95	0.92
Germany		1.00	0.95	1.04	1.08	1.15
Italy		1.00	1.04	1.21	1.23	1.33
Japan		1.00	1.08	1.17	1.25	1.28
Netherlands	1.00	1.11	1.11	1.14	1.00	1.00
New Zealand		1.00	1.15	1.20	1.19	1.16
Norway		1.00	1.06	1.13	1.17	1.22
Portugal	1.00	0.98	0.95	1.07	1.05	
Sweden	1.00	1.04	1.05	1.13	1.15	1.11
United Kingdom	1.00	1.24	1.30	1.34	1.35	1.30
United States	1.00	1.08	1.13	1.20	1.20	1.22
OECD-15		1.00	1.05	1.10	1.10	1.12

Source: OECD Statlinks http://dx.doi.org/10.1787/420718178732.

Source: UNI/WIDER Income Inequality Database WIID2c (2008)

Figure 3.1   Gini Index for income inequality in the US (1967 – 2004)

Table 3.3   US inter quintile ratios of income distribution in the period 1968 – 2004

	Q5/Q1	Q5/Q3	Q3/Q1
1968	10.19	1.75	4.17
1972	10.71	1.79	4.17
1976	9.84	1.75	3.89
1980	10.16	1.76	3.93
1984	10.95	1.82	4.00
1988	12.18	1.91	4.21
1992	12.34	1.94	4.16
1996	13.24	2.10	4.08
2000	13.78	2.16	4.14
2004	14.74	2.16	4.32

Source: UNI/WIDER Income Inequality Database WIID2c (2008)

20 per cent of US earners. Interestingly, while the Q3/Q1 ratio did not change much over the period, both the Q5/Q1 and Q5/Q3 ratios continuously rose. The rise in the income share of the top 1 per cent of earners is unsurprising. Table 3.4 shows that the improvement in the position of the wealthiest portion of the population is particularly clear in Anglo-Saxon countries, such as Canada, the UK and the US. In the US, the concentration of income in the hands of the wealthiest portion of the population has recently returned to the very high levels prior to the 1929 crisis (see Figure 3.2). Although caution is required in drawing inferences from this, one question is unavoidable: is it a coincidence that in the years before both the 1929 and 2008 crisis income inequality was very high in the US?

The information on inequalities provided by the OECD is confirmed by a recent update (OECD, 2011a) and by the International Labour Organization (2008) report, *Income Inequalities in the Age of Globalization*. In this report, the ILO analyses income distribution changes in countries at different development stages, based on a sample of 73 countries (more than in the OECD study). The main conclusions are the same: inequality has been growing in two thirds of the countries, whether developed or developing (ILO, 2008: 1). The ILO report also contains important additional information on another worrisome phenomenon, namely the decrease of the share of national income that goes to wages and therefore to labour. According to ILO estimates, in 51 countries in the sample, the wage share of domestic income has decreased since 1990, falling by 13 per cent in Latin America and the Caribbean, 10 per cent in Asia and the Pacific and 9 per cent in the Advanced Economies (ILO, 2088: 6).

Table 3.4   *Share of pre-tax income of the top 1 per cent of the distribution*

	Australia	Canada	France	Germany	Ireland	Japan	Netherlands	New Zealand	Spain	Sweden	Switzerland	United Kingdom	United States
1981	4.70	7.80	7.55	10.33	6.44	7.11	5.85	5.54	7.60	3.81	8.40	7.43	8.03
1986	5.21	8.24	7.44	9.90	6.18	7.21	5.87	5.04	8.36	4.09	9.05	8.49	9.13
1991	6.38	9.37	7.97	10.83	7.14	7.54	5.54	8.02	8.09	5.10	8.60	10.19	12.17
1996	7.24	10.62	7.59	9.83	8.41	7.36	5.39	8.93	7.94	5.59	7.76	11.61	14.11
2004										5.72			16.08

Source: OECD Statlinks http://dx.doi.org/10.1787/420757184562

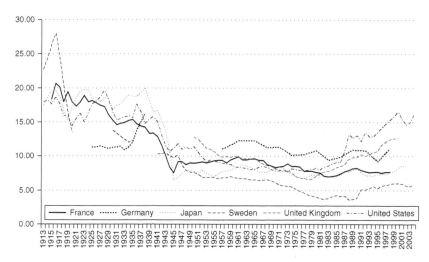

Source: OECD Statlinks http://dx.doi.org/10.1787/420757184562

Figure 3.2 Income share of the top 1 per cent of the population

The decrease in the wage share is closely related to the fact that wage growth generally did not keep pace with productivity improvements. For instance, based on US Bureau of Economic Analysis data, Lawrence (2008) shows that from 1980 to 2006, in the US, labour productivity grew by 70 per cent while real hourly wages rose by a mere 4.4 per cent. ILO (2008: 7) analysed a reduced sample of 32 countries[2] for which data on productivity and wages were available, finding that in 24 countries productivity growth exceeded wage growth in the period 1990–2006. Notable exceptions were China and South Africa where wages performed quite well[3]. It is not difficult to understand that when the output per worker grows faster than wages, the wage share declines in favour of corporate profits and financial rents. Since white and blue collar workers are the majority of the population, the negative consequences for aggregate consumption are obvious, as explained in the previous section.

Another fact, particularly evident in the US and stressed by Lawrence (2008), is that the financial sector was where the profit share grew the most at the expense of wages so a redistribution inside the corporate sector in favour of financial companies also seems to have taken place, in addition to the redistribution between labour and corporations. This observation leads to a related aspect of the inequality issue: not all workers have been hit in the same manner by the fall in income share going to wages because an additional feature of the recent increase in inequality is the widening of the gap between high-wage and low-wage earners. Of course, jobs and pay cannot be equal in view of the technological features of production processes, the composition of the labour force, and the duties of workers and skills required by firms operating in different industries. We expect skilled workers to earn more than unskilled workers so that wage differences are not a surprise. What is surprising is the extent to which the gap has widened in the recent past. A common measure of the wage gap is the ratio between the pay of company executives and average employee wages, which has reached levels that are difficult to justify on the grounds of economic efficiency. In 2007, at the onset of the international financial crisis, for CEOs the ratio ranged from 71 in the Netherlands to 183 in the US, while in the case of average executives it was 43 and 112 respectively (ILO, 2008: 17). The latter estimates are downward biased because they do not include share-based remuneration that actually forms up to 90 per cent of executives' and CEOs' earnings. The practice of share-based remuneration and bonuses is based on the idea that if pay is linked to the economic performance of the company, employees are better motivated to find strategies and take actions that improve the market value of the firms. In many cases, however, that practice has led to distortions resulting in an excessive focus on short-term economic performance rather than long-term strategies capable of producing stable growth. This distortion was evident for banks and financial companies and contributed to the mechanism that led to the sub-prime mortgage bubble in the US. Another distortion is that decisions about the amount of bonuses given to executives and CEOs are often taken by the CEOs themselves, so that the level of share-based remuneration is often unrelated to actual economic performance. The results of empirically analysing the link between company performance and executive pay in different countries are uneven and, on the basis of an extensive analysis of the existing literature, the ILO (2008: 57) concludes that: 'overall, a stable and significant relation between pay and performance has yet to be established'. However, the practice of paying executives with shares and stock options was widespread in the years before the sub-prime mortgage crisis, particularly in financial companies, and apparently persists even after the bursting of the credit bubble in the US, despite very negative public opinion and protests caused by the huge bonuses handed out in the middle of the crisis to AIG and other company executives involved in the financial meltdown of 2007–2008[4]. When the share and stock option components of executive pay are taken into account, the wage gap skyrockets. In the US, the ratio between executive pay and average pay was 370 in 2003 but had almost doubled four years later, reaching 521 in 2007. The case of the US is extreme but not exceptional; similar trends can be observed in other advanced and emerging countries.

So far we have discussed trends in income distribution. However, the wealth of individuals and households also plays an important role in consumption and savings decisions, affecting living standards. Consumption depends not only on income, but also on the ownership of houses and financial assets such as bonds, shares and stock options. We have just seen how, in recent years, stock options have become an increasingly significant part of the remuneration of executives and CEO: inequality in overall wealth distribution cannot be ignored. In this regard, empirical research shows that wealth inequality is correlated to and larger than income inequality. In a groundbreaking article, James B. Davies et al. (2011) computed the level and distribution of world household wealth in 2000 and obtained an estimate of the global Gini Index equal to 0.802. That is very high compared to coefficients for disposable income in individual countries which typically range between 0.3 and 0.5. Looking at the shape of the wealth distribution, they also found that people at the top and very top of the distribution (10, 5 and 1 per cent decile and percentile) respectively hold 70.7, 56.7 and 31.6 per cent of the world's wealth. No clear differences in wealth inequality patterns among developed, low income and medium income emerging countries arose from their study. An international comparison between countries reveals that the US scores first in wealth inequality with a Gini index equal to 0.801, a higher value than that of developing and emerging countries such as Bangladesh (0.660), Indonesia (0.764), Nigeria (0.736), China (0.550) and India (0.669). When we compare wealth distribution in countries at different levels of development, obviously we need to remember that absolute levels of poverty and wealth may differ by a large extent and that medium income or even low income people in advanced countries are often better off than many wealthy people in poor countries. Nonetheless, the fact that wealth inequality in the most advanced country of the world exceeds that of very poor countries where economic inefficiency, unemployment and political corruption are often endemic is something that could be considered scandalous.

In the end, what emerges from a large body of empirical evidence is an ongoing process of income and wealth concentration at the core as well as the periphery of the world economy. There is also evidence that excessive income and wealth inequalities contributed to the financial crisis in the US (Rajan, 2010; Reich, 2010). Finally, inequality is increasingly seen as a problem that may hinder the recovery of the world economy in the aftermath of the financial crisis (OECD, 2011) and reduce the long-term sustainability of growth in developing countries (Berg and Ostry, 2011).

3.3 WHY HAS WITHIN-COUNTRY INCOME INEQUALITY INCREASED?

Why have economic inequalities increased in the 'second globalization' era? It is important to answer this question if we want to design correct economic policies aimed at reducing the negative impact of inequality and, if possible, reverse the trend. In the last 25 years, globalization has grown alongside inequality, making it an automatic suspect. Some tests, examining the hypothesis that globalization is in itself responsible for growing inequalities, regress income distribution data on aggregate indices supposedly capturing the main features of globalization (Bergh and Nilsson, 2010; Dreher and Gaston, 2008). However, globalization is a multifaceted phenomenon with trade, financial and political aspects that often tend to affect income distribution in different directions and have different strengths so that in the literature other studies have tried to isolate and test the impact on inequality of separate components of globalization (Berg and Ostry, 2011; Celik and Basdas, 2010; Cornia, 2003; Goldberg and Pavcnik, 2007; Jauomotte et al, 2008; Palma, 2006; Qureshi and Wan, 2008, and Ulubasoglu, 2004).

In the Bretton Woods era, under the institutional framework of GATT negotiations, world trade expanded greatly, particularly between advanced nations. States became more and more open to international trade and within-country income inequalities were generally constant or decreased. It is worth remembering that, in this period, governments maintained controls on international capital movements in an environment characterized by fixed exchange rates. After 1971, with the breakdown of the Bretton Woods system and the start of the dollar standard era, the liberalization of world trade continued but financial liberalization was the chief innovation in the period. The move toward full economic and financial liberalization was forcefully promoted by advanced countries and endorsed by international institutions, such as the IMF and World Bank, prompting developing countries to introduce domestic reforms aimed at liberalizing their economies and opening their domestic market not only to trade but also to financial flows: so-called 'capital account liberalization'. The implementation of the set of neo-liberalistic monetary and economic policy prescriptions known as the 'Washington Consensus', after Williamson (1990), was supposed to be the key to successful economic development. However, the cluster of financial crises and bursting bubbles in several countries in the 1990s and the 2000s, along with the rise in within-country income inequality, cast serious doubt on the validity of Washington Consensus prescriptions and gave rise to serious criticisms of the IMF and World Bank policies, leading to proposed reforms of leading international economic institutions (Bird, 2001; Florio, 2002; Przesworski and Wreeland, 2002, and Bordo, 2000). The sequence of crises that hit the world economy in the 1990s and the beginning of the 2000s includes: Argentina (1991), Mexico (1994), the Asian crisis (1997, 1998), Brazil (1998, 1999), Russia (1998), Turkey (2000), Argentina (2001). We should also recall the dramatic fall in GDP of Russia and other Eastern Europe countries, which – in the first half of the1990s – attempted to speed up the transition from planned to free market economies by implementing the rapid reforms and liberalization known as 'shock therapy' (Klein and Pomer, 2001).

On the whole, financial liberalization policies have not produced the positive impact on growth that their supporters expected. On the contrary, as Rodrik and Subramanian (2009) clearly show, no correlation between economic growth and financial liberalization in developing countries exists, so that the case in favour of the latter was clearly overstated. At the same time, according to other studies, the idea that capital account liberalization is associated with an increase in income inequality cannot easily be discarded. In any case, the literature confirms the idea that it is useful to separately assess the impacts of the different components of globalization (trade, finance, technology) on income inequality, even where they are interconnected, as in the case of trade and technological change, as discussed below. Table 3.5 summarizes the key results of selected studies of globalization and within-country income inequality.

3.4   TECHNOLOGICAL CHANGES AND INEQUALITY

The hypothesis that technological change widens the wage gap is accredited by many and is generally accepted (Goldberg and Pavcnik, 2007). Certainly, one of the most important events in the last 15 years has been the accelerated pace of technological progress due to the revolution in information and communications technology (ICT). Jorgenson and Vu (2005) estimate that on average, at the world level, the contribution of ICT capital goods to economic growth increased from 10 per cent in 1989–1995 to 15 per cent in 1995–2003. The role of ICT capital goods as a source of growth was particularly important in the case of the advanced G7 countries, where its contribution jumped from 17 to 27 per cent. However, a similar trend is also evident in seven major developing and transition economies (Brazil, China, India, Indonesia, Mexico, Russia and South Korea) where the percentage of economic growth due to the accumulation of ICT capital goods doubled, from 4 to 8 per cent. In this country group, the experience of Brazil (up from 4 to 23 per cent) was particularly

Table 3.5　Results of selected studies on globalization and income inequality

	Effects on within-country income inequality			
	Globalization (aggregate effect)	Trade liberalization	Financial liberalization	Technological progress
Bergh and Nilsson (2010;)	Increased inequality			
Celik and Basdas (2010)		Mixed results		Mixed results: increased inequality in developed countries; Decreased inequality in emerging countries (via FDI)
Cornia (2003)	Increased inequality via domestic reforms	Mixed results	Increased inequality	Increased inequality
Dreher and Gaston (2008)	Increased inequality in OECD countries; mixed results for developing countries			
Galbraith and Jiaqinq (1999)			Increased inequality	
Goldberg and Pavcnik (2007)		May increase inequality in association with unilateral liberalizing trade reforms		May increase inequality interacting with trade openness
ILO (2008)			Increased inequality	Increased inequality
Jauomotte, Lall and Papageorgiou (2008)		Decreased inequality	Increased inequality (minor effect)	Increased inequality (major effect)
OECD (2008)				Increased inequality
OECD (2011)				Increased inequality

striking. Almost everywhere in the world, the share of investments in ICT capital goods increased with important consequences on the organization of production and demand for labour. New technologies made it easier for corporations to split production processes into separate stages that could then be outsourced and moved to other countries. Corporations in advanced countries found it convenient to locate the more labour intensive phases of production processes in less developed countries with a cheap labour force, while keeping at home design, research and development as well as retaining financial and technical control over the entire production process. The consequence on the labour market, in advanced countries, has been a widespread increase in the demand for skilled workers and, at the same time, a reduction in the demand for the unskilled. For this reason, differences in skills may explain differences in earnings (Devroye and Freeman, 2001).

When we talk about skills, it is useful to refer to the classification of working functions proposed by Author et al. (2001). They identify five categories, ranked according to knowledge content and complexity: routine manual, routine cognitive, non-routine manual, non-routine interactive and non-routine analytic. Routine manual functions do not require workers to have a particularly high level of education, while people engaged in non-routine analytic activities need problem-solving capabilities that can be acquired only through years of education and experience. Jobs in factories where workers assemble cars or toys are an example of simple routine manual activities that are increasingly displaced by investment in the automation and informatization of production. Employees in marketing departments devising communication strategies for the sale of new products are an example of workers engaged in non-routine analytic functions. Because of technological progress, the historical trend in the last 30 years has been that of a steady reduction in the demand for routine functions and a continuous increase in the demand for the more knowledge-intensive non-routine functions. The development of a knowledge society necessarily involves these trends in labour demand. An obvious consequence, therefore, is that remuneration for non-routine tasks increases compared to routine functions. Inside firms, many routine manual functions, once assigned to unskilled workers, are carried out by computers or robots, or else outsourced to factories in less developed countries (LDCs) where hourly remuneration is much lower. In developed countries, therefore, the ICT revolution increased the productivity of the labour factor enormously and produced a 'skill biased' change in wage structures, widening the gap not only between low and high pay, but also between blue and white collar workers (Lawrence, 2008). Therefore the rising skills and wage gap depends on two elements:

a technology-propelled surge in the demand for non-routine tasks and skilled workers alongside downward pressure on the pay of individuals employed in routine tasks under the threat of unemployment and job dislocation in foreign countries. Changes in the production organization of corporations through technological progress may, therefore, explain part of the increase in income inequality in developed countries. What still cannot be explained under the heading of the ICT revolution is the excessive concentration of income at the top of the distribution curve and the abnormal increase in the remuneration of the top executives mentioned in the previous section. After all, the gap in wages and salaries due to the skill-biased change in the demand for labour is nothing but a 'premium' for knowledge, while the dramatic increase in the gap between top executive remuneration and average workers' wages seems to be more the result of CEO greed, the decision-making mechanism inside companies and the powers of boards of directors, rather than a direct consequence of above average company performances (ILO, 2008).

What can we say about the impact of technological change on income distribution in emerging or LDCs? Inequalities could be expected to decrease because of an improvement in the salaries of unskilled workers, supposedly the abundant factor of production in these economies. If multinational companies invest in LDCs, buying or building factories in order to exploit abundant cheap labour in these countries, the demand for routine manual and cognitive positions should rise and consequently, so should the remuneration for these tasks. In the end, higher wages of unskilled workers should reduce inequality. On the contrary, as shown in section 3.2, income inequality increased in both LDCs and emerging countries. The prediction of decreasing inequality through stronger demand for unskilled labour is naïve and inaccurate because technological progress also increases the demand for skills and non-routine functions in LDCs, as elsewhere. In this regard, in their review of the literature on the distributional effects of globalization in developing countries, Goldberg and Pavcnik (2007: 52) conclude that 'when we consider the 1980s and the 1990s as a whole, all countries seem to have experienced increases in the skill premium'. They also observe that 'interestingly, the skill premium increases seem to chronologically coincide with the trade reforms in several countries'. This observation raises the important question of the role neoliberal political and institutional reforms may have had in the inequality story. We shall return to it later on in this chapter.

One explanation for the widening wage gap in emerging and developing countries is that domestic investments and FDIs in these countries have led to the adoption of improved technologies. In other words, emerging countries have reduced the distance from the technological frontier and are no more simply dumping grounds for the obsolete technologies of advanced countries. Through FDIs, when new capital goods and equipment are put to work in plants producing intermediate goods, multinational companies actually transfer technology to LDCs. FDIs and outsourcing in LDCs are therefore important parts of the explanation for the skill-bias determined wage gap (Goldberg and Pavcnik, 2007). The technological intensity of new factories in developing countries may be below that of factories in developed economies but it is higher than previous levels, so in emerging economies too a skill bias in the demand for labour arises. Even if the type of skills that corporations demand in developed countries were different from the skills they need in developing economies, the result would be the same: everywhere technological progress would shift demand for labour toward a larger portion of more highly educated and skilled workers. The bottom line is that widespread technological change may negatively affect income distribution in both LDCs and emerging countries (Jauomott et al, 2008; OECD, 2008 and 2011a).

3.5   INTERNATIONAL TRADE AND INEQUALITY

Globalization is a consequence of free trade. The degree of openness to international trade is a common measure of globalization and as such became an explanatory variable in several empirical tests of the causes of income inequality. Why should international trade affect within-country income distribution at all? International trade theory provides one possible answer. According to the standard Heckscher-Ohlin model, greater openness to international trade should improve the marginal productivity of the country's abundant factor of production and therefore its real income. If we believe that skilled labour is abundant in advanced countries, while unskilled (or less skilled) labour is abundant in LCDs and emerging countries, then the straightforward application of this theory leads to one conclusion alone: greater openness to international trade (trade globalization) should increase the wages of skilled workers in developed countries and of unskilled workers in developing countries. The other side of the coin is that unskilled workers in advanced countries and skilled workers in LDCs should suffer from decreasing real wages. In this view, the wage gap increases in advanced economies and decreases elsewhere. However, while there has been a deterioration of the income position of unskilled workers in advanced countries, the same thing is not happening to skilled workers in developing and emerging economies. If trade has anything to do with income distribution, other explanations have to be found.

The previous section discusses how changes in demand for skills due to technological progress explain part of the recent worldwide trend of income inequality. Here we stress how the interaction between trade globalization and technological changes adds another element to the explanation of rising income inequalities. Trade globalization involves the adoption of policies aimed at reducing and eliminating obstacles to trade such as tariffs or import quotas. At the same time, less protection leads to the expansion of the tradeable sector of the economy exposed to international competition, comprising modern export-oriented firms often specializing in the production of intermediate goods. If a dualistic structure emerges, inequalities are very likely to increase.

International trade offers opportunities to developing countries but raises competitive pressure on firms; only the most efficient can survive. In order to do so, companies in the tradeable sector producing finished goods must re-organize and invest in new technologies. Consequently, their demand for skills changes in favour of non-routine functions. As the tradeable sector expands, the wages of employees in that sector rise with respect to wages in the non-tradeable sector and the wage gap widens. In addition, companies in the tradeable sector of emerging countries produce and/or assemble intermediate goods for foreign multinationals. International outsourcing of production creates international trade and contributes to the growth of the tradeable sector in LDCs. Technological progress, trade globalization and outsourcing by multinationals interact and work in the same direction.

However, trade globalization is not always associated with inequality. After all, in the Bretton Woods era and in the 1970s, within-country inequality either increased only slightly or, frequently, decreased as the volume of international trade continued to rise. This is the experience of the European countries that liberalized trade in the 1960s, creating the EEC. According to the OECD WIID2C database, for example in France the Gini Index was 52 in 1962 but 34 in 1970. In the same period it was fairly stable in Germany, at around 38. Another well-known example is that of the Asian countries that globalized trade in the 1960s and 1970s. Singapore, South Korea and Taiwan did not experience increases in income inequality until the 1980s (Cornia, 2003). However, inequality grew in several Latin American countries that liberalized trade in the 1980s and 1990s (Wood, 1999). Different domestic approaches to political reforms and the timing of liberalization may account for this difference. After 1980, trade liberalization was often accompanied by privatization, labour market reforms and financial liberalization. On the other hand, in the 1960s and 1970s, Asian countries did not open their domestic financial markets and when, they did in the 1990s, they were hit by the severe financial crisis of 1997–1998. It is difficult to separate the impact of trade globalization on inequality from the effects of political and institutional reforms accompanying globalization, but the suspicion is that reforms are largely responsible for the recent rise in inequality, as suggested by the different experiences of the 1960s–1970s and 1980s–2000s.

3.6 FINANCIAL GLOBALIZATION, REFORMS AND INEQUALITY

A modern market economy cannot live without a properly functioning financial system. According to economic theory, the role of financial markets is the allocation of otherwise unproductive savings to investment projects, positively contributing to economic growth and welfare. The rapid development of the world economy since the Industrial Revolution owes a great deal to domestic and international finance but financial markets have also been a source of economic instability and crisis, as shown by the fundamental works of Kindleberger and Aliber (2005) and Reinhart and Rogoff (2009). The patterns of global imbalances discussed in Chapter 2 and the recent sequence of regional international financial crises eventually going global in 2007–8, proves that the current functioning of financial markets is far from perfect. The dual nature of finance explains why regulatory and supervisory institutions were set up, although the history of capitalism is one of alternating phases of regulation and deregulation. Prudential regulation and the supervision of banks and stock exchanges by central banks and other institutions such as the Securities and Exchange Commission (SEC) in the US were introduced in order to avoid fraud and minimize the likelihood of financial institutes defaulting and, in the case of default, to prevent contagion, which might threaten the systemic stability of the economy. On occasions, government and monetary authorities over-regulated, imposing interest rate ceilings or credit rationing. These measures interfere with the proper functioning of monetary and financial markets and distort fund allocation, so nowadays the liberalization of domestic monetary and financial markets is generally accepted because it reduces the distortions of over-regulation. Looking back to the events of the last decade, it is clear on the other hand that deregulation went too far. In the US the Glass-Steagall Act separating the activities of commercial and investment banks was partly repealed by the Gramm-Leach-Bliley Act in 1999, allowing US banks to widen the range of their activities, covering new fields and fostering credit default swaps (CDS) and financial derivatives increasingly traded in the non-regulated over-the-counter (OTC) market. The negative role of these changes in the global financial crisis of 2007–8 is now well known. Equally dangerous was the SEC decision in 2004 to allow banks to raise their leverage ratio from 10:1 to 30:1, a move that increased systemic risk enormously and, with it, the likelihood of huge losses, which materialized in 2008.

In relation to the liberalization of international capital flows, as already noted, in the Bretton Woods period the expansion of international trade was accompanied by limited international capital mobility. In a fixed or quasi-fixed exchange rate system, international capital mobility is impeded because central banks are not able to simultaneously target domestic money supply and maintain exchange rate parities in the event of massive capital flight. Because flexible exchange rate systems are compatible with high capital mobility, it is no surprise that after the breakdown of the Bretton Woods exchange rate system in 1971, international capital flows and financial globalization dramatically increased. What is not obvious is that opening domestic markets to international financial flows (financial globalization) is always beneficial to the countries that implement these policies, especially where the domestic market is not suitably reformed.

One of the elements that differentiates the current phase of globalization from the end of the nineteenth century is the preeminent role of economic policies and international institutions (IMF, World Bank and WTO) in shaping domestic reforms in favour of financial openness. Since the end of the 1980s, several developing and emerging medium income countries, pressed by advanced countries, the IMF and the World Bank (Stiglitz, 2002) have abolished controls over external capital flows in the hope of gaining more access to international capital markets and benefits in terms of investments and higher economic growth through financial openness. Financial globalization is thought to exert positive effects partly because of its disciplining effect on domestic monetary and budget policies. In order to attract foreign investments, a government budget has to be 'in order', inflation under control and interest rates free to adapt to international financial market conditions. In turn, lower inflation and the availability of cheaper credit should favour low income households and have a positive effect on inequality. If openness to foreign financial flows actually resulted in higher rates of growth and less poverty nobody would be against it. Empirical evidence, however, shows that financial globalization has had no significant effect on growth rates. Rodrik and Subramanian (2009) estimate that, in the period 1970–2004, the correlation coefficient between levels of financial globalization and annual average growth rate of GDP per capita in a sample of 105 countries is virtually zero at a non-significant −0.0039365 coefficient. The estimate remains the same even if changes, not levels, of globalization are considered. Restricting the analysis to developing countries, Maurice Obstfeld (2009: 63) concludes that 'despite an abundance of cross-sectional, panel and event studies, there is strikingly little convincing documentation of direct positive impact of financial opening on the welfare levels or growth rates of developing countries'. On the contrary, evidence exists that greater financial globalization has had a negative impact on income inequalities (see Table 3.5). One explanation of this is that too rapid financial globalization may have weakened domestic financial systems in LDCs rather than producing modernization and development. This is consistent with the fact that the frequency of banking and financial crises rose dramatically in the 1990s and that, in 1995–2008, they occurred largely in the less developed non-OECD countries (ILO, 2008: 48). The crisis that hit several medium-income countries in the 1990s followed the removal of controls on foreign capital flows in order to attract more international investment. Unfortunately, as the case of the Asian crisis shows, short run foreign speculative investments and mismanagement of foreign loans by domestic banks often increased the vulnerability of domestic markets, rather than improving development prospects. In fact, the resulting financial turmoil had the strongest negative impact on low income households, so that poverty and inequality rose in the countries hit by the 1990s crisis (Galbraith and Jiaqing, 1999; World Bank, 2001). There is also evidence that the presence or absence of strong social institutions and safety nets made the difference as far as the impact of the systemic financial crisis on inequality was concerned (Galbraith and Jiaqing, 1999). The chain of events leading from increased financial openness to the banking and financial crisis and from there to poverty explains why, at the end of the 1990s, several countries in East Asia and the Pacific region reversed their support for unlimited financial openness, reintroducing capital controls and developing trade surpluses in order to accumulate foreign exchange reserves, rather than resorting to international capital flows for development purposes (ILO, 2008; Wolf, 2008). The phenomenon of global imbalances we discussed in Chapter 2, with its paradoxical 'uphill' capital flows from the periphery toward the core US economy, was partly caused by the damage produced in the 1990s by financial liberalization in non-OECD countries.

Another channel through which financial openness has negatively affected within-country income inequality is related to the political dimension of globalization. In general, the decision to open a domestic market to foreign financial flows is part of a broader package of economic and political reforms, which in many cases also negatively affect income equality. Following the prescription of the 'Washington Consensus', in order to attract foreign investors, many governments lowered tax rates on financial investments, reduced progressive taxation, privatized state-owned companies and utilities and reformed the labour market, introducing more 'flexible' contracts along with softening or repealing minimum wage laws. The effect of this set of reforms has generally been a decrease in the bargaining power of trade unions, a compression of wages, a reduction of the wage share of GDP, and a shift of the tax burden from financial companies to industrial companies and from high income households to medium and low income households. One consequence of the reforms is to limit the role of governments in income redistribution policies, a fact that often goes hand in hand with the contraction of welfare systems and social safety nets (Cornia 2003; ILO, 2008; OECD, 2008). One simple way to assess the distributional role of Government is to compare pre-tax with after-tax income inequality. OECD data (2008) show that the latter is lower, confirming the importance of government policies. However, fiscal redistribution in the last two decades has not kept pace with the increase in inequalities. The ILO (2008: 136) estimates that in developed countries, where fiscal redistribution in the late 1990s increased on average by 2.5 per cent, the overall private Gini Index increased by 3.4 per cent, with a net increase in income inequality. The situation in developing countries is even worse, since an adequate direct tax collection system is often lacking and so indirect taxation yields the bulk of government revenues. Reform packages including fiscal reforms that attenuate the progressive nature of direct taxation, along with the already high level of indirect taxes whose regressive nature is well known, increase the tax burden on low income individuals and households, producing a deterioration in income distribution. Social transfers are an additional powerful mechanism for achieving fairer income distribution and reforms that privatize public services and reduce welfare provisions exacerbates income inequality. Trade liberalization and tariff reductions in developing countries also reduce the availability of resources for financing social transfer programmes.

The pressure that financial globalization exerts on domestic policies is not restricted to developing countries. In advanced countries, the reduction of pension benefits and so-called 'structural reform' of the labour market aimed at improving competitiveness were already being called for before the global financial crisis. In the US and EU countries, one unpleasant consequence of the crisis has been the rapid growth of government debts due to the public bail-out of private banks and a fall in tax revenues caused by a fall in GDP. In the EU, in 2007 the average public debt/GDP ratio was below the Maastricht limit of 60 per cent, but three years later in 2010, it rose from 59 to 80 per cent (Eurostat, Table tsieb090). In the same period, federal debt almost doubled in the US, jumping from 35.7 to 61.3 per cent of GDP (OECD, Main Economic Indicators) while the overall gross government debt increased from 61.3 to 94.3 per cent (IMF, World Economic Outlook Database). The private credit bubble which caused the crisis has turned into a sovereign debt crisis because the international financial market, the 'invisible Leviathan' at the origin of the world crisis, saved by government intervention, paradoxically quickly turned its speculative attention to indebted EU countries. So far, the political response of EU governments and institutions has largely been inadequate and mainly based on restrictive domestic budget policies which alone can only deepen the economic and fiscal crisis in the absence of growth. It seems that the survival of the European Monetary Union and the economic and social model which guaranteed decades of peaceful growth and social security in Europe is now seriously threatened. The huge expansion of financial flows in an international environment lacking adequate international regulatory and supervisory mechanisms means the problems of global economic instability and growing inequality cannot be solved at the national level. New supranational rules and cooperative solutions are called for.

NOTES

1. The Gini index was developed by the Italian statistician Corrado Gini in 1912 and is closely related to the Lorentz curve, a graphic representation of income distribution in which individuals are ordered bottom to top on the horizontal axis according to their income, while cumulative income is measured on the vertical axis. In particular, the Gini index represents the ratio of the area between the Lorentz curve and the diagonal of the graph (equidistribution line) and the area of maximum concentration of income, equal to the whole area below the equidistribution line. A practical guide to the use and calculation of the Gini index can be found at www.fao.org/docs/up/easypol/329/gini_index_040EN.pdf.
2. The countries are: Australia, Austria, Belgium, Brazil, Canada, China, Czech Republic, Denmark, Finland, France, Germany, Greece, Hungary, India, Ireland, Italy, Japan, Korea, Luxembourg, Mexico, Netherlands, New Zealand, Norway, Poland, Portugal, Russian Federation, Slovak Republic, South Africa, Spain, Sweden, UK and the US.
3. On the contrary, in other BRICS countries such as Brazil, India and Russia, productivity growth was much higher than wage growth.
4. In 2008, Wall Street executives earned US$18 billion in bonuses (The New York Times, 2011).

APPENDIX A.3   INCOME SHARE AND AGGREGATE CONSUMPTION

This appendix shows that a reduction in the share of domestic GDP by low-income in favour of high-income households may lead to a reduction in aggregate consumption.

Let us consider a simple closed Keynesian economy where two different types of consumers and households live: low income households H_L and high income households H_H. From the macroeconomic point of view the difference between the two household types consists in their consumption (and savings) propensity. The basic assumption is that the consumption propensity of the H_L group c_L is greater than the consumption propensity of the H_H group c_H. As a consequence, the aggregate consumption expenditure is a weighted average of the consumption of the two groups.

The first step is to break down aggregate consumption into two parts, recalling that total consumption is simply the sum of consumption from the two household groups:

$$C = c_L Y_L + c_H Y_H \quad (0 < c_i < 1; i = H, L) \qquad \text{(A.3.1)}$$

$$c_L > c_H \qquad \text{(A.3.2)}$$

The share of domestic income Y that goes to the H_L is α so income can also be broken down as follows:

$$Y = Y_L + Y_H \qquad \text{(A.3.3)}$$

$$Y_L = \alpha Y \qquad \text{(A.3.4)}$$

$$Y_H = (1 - \alpha) Y \qquad \text{(A.3.5)}$$

By replacing A.3.4 and A.3.5 in A.3.1, aggregate consumption can be written as:

$$C = c_L \alpha Y + c_H (1 - \alpha) Y = [c_L \alpha + c_H (1 - \alpha)] Y \qquad \text{(A.3.6)}$$

Equation A.3.6 may now be differentiated to compute the effect of changes in the income distribution parameter α on C:

$$\frac{\partial c}{\partial \alpha} = (c_L - c_H) Y > 0 \qquad \text{(A.3.7)}$$

The partial derivative of aggregate consumption C with respect to the H_L income share α is positive because of assumption A.3.2. The main economic implication of A.3.7 is that a shift of income distribution unfavourable to the H_L group, namely a decrease in α, has a negative impact on consumption.

4. Multipolarity and regional integration

4.1 ARE WE MOVING TOWARD A MULTIPOLAR WORLD ECONOMY?

The economic geography of the world is rapidly changing. The economic contraction and the financial crisis caused by the burst of the sub-prime bubble in the US primarily hit advanced countries where unemployment rose, government budgets deteriorated and prolonged economic stagnation followed the sharp recession of 2008–2009. Outside advanced countries, the consequences of the financial crisis were less severe and emerging economies quickly returned to their previous rapid growth. The different impact of the financial crisis on advanced and emerging countries should not be a surprise because an examination of world development patterns over the last 15 years shows that new economic powers are already eroding centuries-old European and North-American supremacy. We know that, after World War II, the US overtook the UK as the world's leading country and that in the Cold War period the two American and Russian superpowers ruled a bipolar order where alternative social, political and economic models faced off. After the fall of the Berlin Wall in 1989 and the subsequent implosion and disintegration of the USSR, bipolarity ended and Russia, along with many Eastern European countries, started a difficult transition period toward the market economy. Many observers interpreted those dramatic events as the triumph of the 'American century', an era in which the only remaining superpower, the US, would dominate politically and economically for many years. Twenty years later, the reality has proved quite different (Fukuyama, 1992; Kagan, 2008; Kupchan, 2011; Palma, 2009; Zakaria, 2011): the US originated the most severe economic crisis since the Great Depression of the 1920s, sovereign debt besets the EU and in Asia, Japan is unable to come out of a lengthy period of economic stagnation. Meanwhile, India, the largest democracy in the world, is rapidly growing, China has become the world's leading exporter, the second largest economy in absolute GDP terms[1] and the main purchaser of US Treasury Bills; Brazil and South Africa are modernizing and establishing themselves as the main economic and political hubs in their respective continents. The successor of the second superpower of the Cold War era, Russia has completed the transition from a planned to a market economy and has been able to return to the international economic scene as a leading actor due, in part, to its vast endowment of natural energy resources (Aslund, 2007; Hanson, 2004; Malle, 2008). Figures 4.1a, 4.1b and 4.1c give a clear picture of the changing world economy. In the year 2000, the group of advanced countries[2] produced 80 per cent of world GDP, leaving a mere 20 per cent to the others (see Figure 4.1a). Ten years later, the share of emerging and developing economies rose to 34 per cent (Figure 4.1b) but, according to the IMF, the share of this group of countries is bound to further enlarge and in 2016 emerging and developing economies will double their share, totalling 41 per cent of world GDP at the expense of advanced countries whose contribution will fall from 80 to 59 per cent (Figure 4.1c).

Figure 4.2 tells us what is behind such a radical change in the balance of world economic power: in the 2000s, emerging countries have grown twice as fast as advanced countries. Furthermore, in 2008–2009 advanced economies went into recession, while emerging countries merely suffered a slow-down in economic growth. Looking at individual countries in both groups, other trends of interest emerge. Figure 4.3 shows antici-pated changes in GDP in the three major economic areas in the group of advanced countries: the EU, Japan and US. The sharp decrease in the contribution of the US to world GDP is striking. In 2000 the US produced about 31 per cent of world GDP but, according to the IMF, in 2016 that share will fall to around 20 per cent. Figure 4.3 also shows the halving of the Japanese contribution to world GDP, expected to fall from 14.49 to 7.41 per cent. The EU share of world production should be more stable, with a small expected loss of around three percentage points. According to these projections, among advanced countries the US is likely to pay the highest price for the rebalancing of the world economy in terms of relative GDP shares.

Who gains the most from this trend? Emerging and developing coun-tries are rather heterogeneous and comprise a large number of states. However, few of them are acquiring special status both at global and regional levels because of their dimension and/or economic development. In 2000, the BRICS – Brazil, Russia, India, China and South Africa – had a GDP share of just 8.41 per cent which had more than doubled by 2010, reaching 18.18 per cent. The forecast is that in 2016 the joint BRICS GDP will triple on 2000 to 23.8 per cent, above that of the EU. This rebalancing of the world economy is highly significant, but closely related to the performance of the Chinese economy (Figure 4.4). Among BRICS countries, South Africa is still far from reaching true global status as an

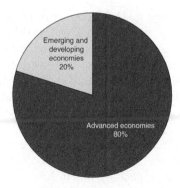

Figure 4.1a   Shares of world GDP (2000)

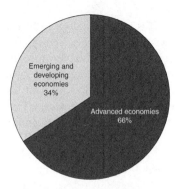

Figure 4.1b   Shares of world GDP (2010)

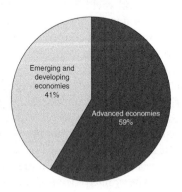

Figure 4.1c   Shares of world GDP (2016*)

Sources: IMF World Economic Outlook Database
* IMF estimates

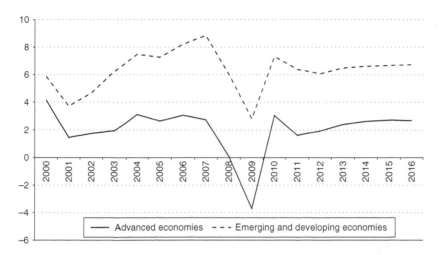

Source: IMF World Economic Outlook Database
* IMF estimates

Figure 4.2 World rate of growth (2000–2016*)

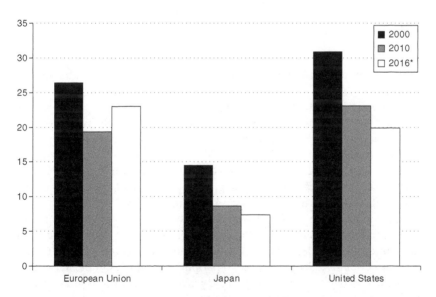

Source: IMF World Economic Outlook Database
* IMF estimates

Figure 4.3 Shares of world GDP: EU, Japan and the US (2000 – 2016*)

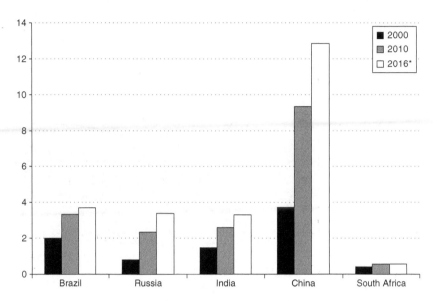

Source: IMF World Economic Outlook Database
* IMF estimates

Figure 4.4   Shares of world GDP: BRICS countries (2000 – 2016*)

economic power, although it is the dominant economy in Sub-Saharan Africa.

Economic projections over a long time horizon are risky and subject to error but the evidence suggests that, under the plausible assumption of unchanged trends in the medium term, the coming decades are likely to be characterized by a multipolar economic order. In the new economic order, countries outside the US and EU will drive world economic growth. In this regard, the theoretical concept of a 'growth pole' recently revamped by the World Bank (2011) may be of use. According to the World Bank definition, a country is a growth pole when domestic growth strengthens growth in other countries as well. This happens when the country is at the hub of a large international network of economic and financial links, so that there is positive spillover from the pole to peripheral countries in the network.

Growth in one country may help the growth of other economies directly and indirectly. The more intense the international trade, the transfer of technology, FDI investment flows and migration, the more likely it is that partner countries benefit from the development of the 'core' country. A straightforward example of a new important growth pole is China, whose emergence as the main industrial pole in Asia is undisputed. According to the World Bank (2011: 20), in the period 2004–2008 along with the EU and the US, China consistently ranked at the top in terms of its ability to activate economic growth in Asia and other parts of the world. Indices of regional polarity show that Saudi Arabia and the other BRICS countries (Brazil, India, Russia, and South Africa) are the main drivers of economic growth in their respective regions (World Bank, 2011: 21). At the same time, other emerging countries such as Mexico, Malaysia and Turkey are strengthening their network of international economic relations and exert a positive influence on world economic growth well beyond their national borders.

A country may be a powerful driver of trade and industrial links but in the absence of truly international financial activities, it cannot hope to become a true world pole. In this regard, a phenomenon that further supports the vision of the coming multipolar world is the rapid growth of international financial flows and FDI originating from emerging countries. Chapter 2 presented and discussed the fact that China and other developing countries are accumulating dollar reserves, purchasing American financial assets and financing the US government deficit. FDI by emerging country-based companies have reached a significant threshold and will further increase in the near future. The geographical dimension of this phenomenon is global, involving both south-south and south-north directions. Major emerging countries are investing in other developing countries but are also purchasing companies in advanced countries. China, for example, is financing infrastructural investments in Africa in order to gain access to strategic raw materials that are abundant in that continent while at the same time acquiring companies in the EU and the US, as can be seen from the acquisition of IBM's personal computer business division by the Chinese company Lenovo in 2005 (Cheng and Ma, 2010)[3]. Another well-known example of expansion is the Indian company Tata, which has made significant investments in the European steel industry and is now a global actor in the world steel and automotive industries (Brautingam, 2010; Evans, 2010; Gu, 2009; Liu, 2007; Mohan and Power, 2008; Strauss and Saavedra, 2009; Taylor, 2011; Wang, 2007). According to the World Bank (2011: 85), in the period 1997–2010, 33 per cent of FDI flows to low-income countries came from the UK, with China scored second at 14 per cent and South Africa, with a share of 5 per cent, performing better than Canada, which sourced 4 per cent of FDI directed toward less developed countries. This evidence clearly shows that emerging countries are not only important international traders and producers of real goods but are also strengthening their strategic position in global financial markets, as the surge in new international bond issues from those countries demonstrates (World Bank, 2011: 98). In the absence of unpredictable catastrophic events, current trends are therefore driving the world economy in the direction of multipolarity.

4.2   THE GLOBAL ECONOMY AND REGIONAL INTEGRATION

In a multi-polar, globalized world, countries large and small find it natural and convenient to cooperate with their neighbours; processes of regional economic integration have become widespread and are today a prominent feature in the spontaneous evolution of the world economy. In Europe, the European Union (EU) is a large integrated area comprising 27 countries; Canada, Mexico and the US created the North American Free Trade Area (NAFTA); in Asia, the Association of Southeast Asian Nations (ASEAN) comprises ten countries (Indonesia, Malaysia, Philippines, Singapore, Thailand, Brunei, Cambodia, Laos, Myanmar and Vietnam); in South America Argentina, Brazil, Uruguay and Paraguay form the MERCOSUR; in Africa the Organization for African Unity (OAU) promoted the establishment of an African Union; in South Africa, the Southern African Development Community includes 15 countries. These are but a few well-known examples of many other experiments in regional economic integration aimed at improving the economic growth and welfare of member countries through the elimination of internal trade barriers and the establishment of common rules.

Why have integrated regional areas become so common in the global world economy? Often, as the gravity model suggests (Anderson, 1979; Anderson and Wincoop, 2003; Bergstrand, 1985; Deardoff, 1998)[4], trade between countries is more intense the closer the countries are geographically. Other factors, such as the sharing of a common history, language, social habits and political institutions seem to positively affect international trade. This simple approach shows why, in the presence of common borders, geographical proximity, cultural and political affinities, the incentive for establishing regional economic agreements is often strong. The advantages of deeper economic integration between countries go beyond the usual arguments about the benefits of free trade based on comparative advantage and international specialization. A coalition of small to medium-sized countries gives individual members a better chance to face up to international competition and political pressure from larger economies. Economic integration resulting in free trade areas (FTAs), customs unions or economic unions creates conditions that, because of access to a larger market and economic synergy, allows member states to improve economic efficiency and achieve faster growth based on a more competitive environment where companies can exploit economies of scale and consumers can choose from a wider range of goods and services. FTAs are agreements in which countries set reciprocal trade tariffs to zero but maintain independent trade policies in relation to countries outside the FTA; hence members may apply different tariffs to the same third country. In customs unions, on the other hand, external tariffs are uniform and members cannot follow independent trade policies. It is clear that customs unions require a higher degree of internal coordination between members than FTAs. Of course, economic agreements of this type may involve distant countries too, if there is a mutual interest in establishing economic relations. For example, the desire to diversify trade flows and reduce excessive dependence on a large neighbour or the opportunity to access promising new emerging markets may result in closer economic cooperation and integration between very distant countries.

Global multilateral trade agreements, as promoted by the WTO (formerly GATT) since 1948 through nine complex negotiation rounds[5], offer economic benefits to participating countries, but it is evident that regional treaties leading to FTAs, customs or economic unions are often simpler to set up, manage and implement since they involve fewer governments than global multilateral discussions between a hundred or so countries which, all too often, have different points of view and conflicting interests. However, the increasing spread of bilateral and regional integration raises the important problem of how this trend relates to WTO multilateral agreements, and the regulations for international trade accepted by 153 countries. The problem is that any bilateral or regional economic agreement determines de facto preferential treatment in favour of member states, a circumstance which may violate the basic non-discriminatory rules of the WTO. The most significant innovation in international trade practice introduced by the WTO was the requirement for any trade agreement to achieve the unanimous approval of countries participating in the multilateral negotiations; in addition, when some members agree on favourable bilateral trade tariff concessions, the agreement must be extended to the other WTO members. For example, if during WTO negotiations a group of countries decides on a mutual tariff reduction in steel products, the same reduction applies to all other WTO partners. Furthermore, the agreement becomes operational only after final approval by all WTO members. This mechanism, known as the 'most favoured nation' clause (MFN), accomplishes the result of generalizing tariff and trade policy concessions where they are agreed upon by small groups of countries.

Since the end of World War II, MFN has been a powerful legal mechanism enabling continuous multilateral reductions in trade barriers in the world economy. Without MFN, a prisoner's dilemma would arise because no country would have the incentive to make the first move to reduce its own trade barriers, such as import tariffs, quotas or export subsidies, in the absence of a credible commitment by all other countries to behave in the same manner. Every country would be better off eliminating the costs and distortions associated with protectionism but none would do so for fear that trade partners would keep the protection of their domestic market intact. In that case, countries abolishing tariffs would incur a net loss because they would find it more difficult to sell their products abroad; at the same time, foreign countries could freely access their markets at the expense of national producers. In the real world, when negotiations involve few countries, a simultaneous reduction or elimination of tariffs can be achieved without too much difficulty. However, on the one hand, although regional processes of economic integration certainly promote free trade among members through reduced internal protection, on the other hand there is also a temptation to protect the internal market of the FTA by means of higher tariffs levied against external third countries. In that event, integrated regional areas would actually segment the world market into separate 'economic fortresses' rather than contribute to the development of global free trade. Therefore, regional treaties, FTAs or customs unions are not the solution to the problem of achieving a more integrated world economy to the benefit of all. Only simultaneous multilateral trade concessions can positively affect global trade and this requires a negotiation mechanism that binds every participating country to the MFN principle. A notable exception to the prohibition of preferential agreement between WTO members is the Generalized System of Preferences (GSP) the WTO established in favour of a group of less developing countries (LDC). The GSP allows developed countries to grant LDCs preferential access to their domestic market on a voluntary base and this exception to the general principle of the most favoured nation is justified by the recognition that in LDCs a full and rapid adoption of the WTO rules would be too costly and reduce welfare sharply so these countries need a longer period of time to adjust their domestic economies to a free trade environment (Stiglitz and Charlton, 2005).

FTAs, customs unions and integrated regional areas existed before the creation of the GATT. This explains Article XXIV of the WTO Charter, which contains provisions for the regulation of these agreements. The basic idea is that FTAs, customs unions or economic unions in regional areas, involving a limited number of countries, are permitted if they follow general WTO rules for free trade. The unavoidable positive discrimination in favour of internal members of regional unions has to be supplemented by the respect of WTO rules with regard to all other WTO members. In other words, countries in an integrated regional area or FTA can internally reduce or eliminate tariffs in order to increase trade between them but they cannot raise tariffs above previous levels against non-member countries in the WTO without explicit negotiation. Notwithstanding the fact that a growing number of countries have decided to join the WTO (154 members including Russia at the end of 2011), in practice many of them also joined local FTAs.

Since the establishment of the WTO, global and regional trade agreements have gone hand in hand with regional agreements, which have become increasingly popular in the last 20 years. Data shows that in 1990 there were 27 FTAs, in 2008 there were 421, up 15-fold (Matsushita, 2008 and 2010). Today, in the world economy FTAs are important and the largest four – the EU, NAFTA, MERCOSUR and ASEAN – represent about 60 per cent of total world trade. In this regard, the stalemate of the multilateral WTO Doha Round reinforced an existing tendency toward the establishment of integrated regional areas. In the absence of a new global agreement on international trade and trade-related issues that are still open or are outside the Doha Round Agenda, bilateral and regional treaties may look like a best rather than a second best option to countries ready to better integrate their economy with that of their closest economic partners or willing to sign agreements on controversial subjects that do not encounter universal support in WTO negotiations. In this sense, local agreements on topics the Doha Round decided not to discuss further, such as investments and competition policies, may be a useful addition to the WTO set of rules. The negative side is that the lack of coordination between FTAs may produce a disorderly accumulation of different rules which could complicate rather than simplify international trade and investments.

To sum up this discussion, regional economic agreements are a very important aspect of the world economy, offering individual countries the way to achieve a stronger position in a rapidly changing international economic environment. At the same time, without a supranational perspective and effective method of cooperative multilateral negotiations, these agreements can segment the world market and ultimately reduce world trade and welfare rather than increase them, as the literature on trade creation and trade diversion shows (Balassa, 1967; Freund and Ornelas, 2010; Fukao et al, 2003; Kreinin, 1959; Matsushita, 2008). The lesson of the 1930s when, in the aftermath of the 1929 crisis, isolationism, nationalism and protectionism spread all over the world, eventually leading to the disruption of international trade, global depression and World War II, must not be forgotten, especially today when recovery after the world financial crisis of 2008 is still uncertain.

4.3   REGIONAL INTEGRATION: EUROPE AND THE OTHERS

A comparison of existing regional experiences shows that the degree of integration between countries varies from simple FTAs to the sharing of complex supranational institutions as in the case of the EU. Chapter 6 discusses the problems and serious risks the EU is facing because of the sovereign debt crisis. Undisputedly, the EU has been the most successful experience of integration among developed modern countries. Based on an intuition of Ernesto Rossi and Altiero Spinelli, the authors of the famous Ventotene Manifesto (1941), the EU is the result of a long process of political and economic integration starting after World War II and involving an initial core of six founding countries (Belgium, France, Germany, Italy, Luxembourg and the Netherlands) led by leaders of the stature of Konrad Adenauer, Alcide de Gasperi, Jean Monet and Robert Schuman. The motivation behind European integration cannot be understood if secular conflicts among European nations causing two world wars and several European conflicts are forgotten. The long-term goal of the founding fathers of modern Europe was to prevent future devastation in Europe via political and economic cooperation and integration, guaranteeing peace and prosperity in the Old Continent. In the intentions of its founders, the final stage of European integration was intended as a federal European state, not merely a customs union or common market. Stable, peaceful economic relations between nations need strong political cooperation and in this perspective, in the light of the conflicts between France and Germany which contributed to two world wars, post-war European leaders have understood that only the permanent linkage of European nations provides the basis for a peaceful future. Former ECB Chairman, Jean-Claude Trichet, made this point clearly, referring to Adenauer, during his speech on 24 October 2011 at Humbold University in Berlin:

> As Konrad Adenauer said in Aachen 57 years ago: "Gerade wird man die Mahnung verstehen, dass Europa uns heute Schicksalsgemeinschaft ist. Dieses Schicksal zu gestalten ist uns übergeben" [Above all, people will understand the call: that Europe, for us today, is a community with a common destiny. It's up to us to shape that destiny].

These are the deep roots of European integration that distinguish it from all other major economic integration projects, none of which have moved much beyond the economic aspects of relations between states, even where they take the EU as an inspiring example, as is the case of ASEAN. ASEAN was set up in 1967 and aims at promoting regional growth through social, political and economic integration. The founder members are Indonesia, Malaysia, the Philippines, Singapore, Thailand and Brunei. Later on, Cambodia, Laos, Myanmar and Vietnam joined the area, which today includes ten countries. The ASEAN focus on the Asia and Pacific region allows the organization to actively collaborate with other major countries, such as China, Japan and South Korea, an aggregation known as 'ASEAN + 3'. In the economic field, ASEAN countries signed a FTA in 1992, whose implementation began in 2002 with the prospect of completion in 15 years. However, the tariff level in the ASEAN FTA may range between 0 and 5 per cent rather than simply being set to zero (Plummer and Clock, 2009: 17). In addition, ASEAN is more open to trade with external partners than the EU. Trade among member countries counts for about one quarter of their total trade, while the figure is two thirds for the EU. ASEAN's most important trade partners are China, Japan, the US and the EU, areas with which ASEAN have very close bilateral trade quotas, varying within a narrow range between 12 and 15 per cent of ASEAN trade. In the Bali Summit of October 2002, ASEAN members agreed on the project for transformation into the ASEAN Economic Community (AEC) by 2020. The major goals of the AEC initiative are to 'establish ASEAN as a single market and production base making ASEAN more dynamic and competitive with new mechanisms and measures to strengthen the implementation of its existing economic initiatives. . .' (ASEAN, 2008).

The EEC and EU experience inspired the AEC project despite the differing starting conditions of the two areas. As stated above, European integration was strongly motivated by the post World War II economic and political environment, including the division of Europe into Eastern and Western zones under the military and political influence of the US and USSR. In Asia and the Pacific area, these problems do not exist. The differences in the economic development and socio-political structures of ASEAN countries are greater than was the case in Europe at the beginning of its integration. Finally, today's international economic environment is very different from that of the 1950s, when the world and European economies were fragmented and countries were relatively closed, whereas today the world economy is largely globalized and ASEAN countries are already open to international trade. Hence it is unlikely that the AEC project will follow the path taken by the EU, particularly with regard to building supranational institutions and relinquishing national sovereignty. The efforts of ASEAN countries to build a new economic community are at the initial stage; much has still to be done to go beyond a simple FTA.

The NAFTA is another major area of economic integration. It was set up by Canada, Mexico and the US in 1992 and became operative in 1994.

NAFTA is a free trade area but, unlike the EU, not a customs union, since members can follow independent trade policies in relation to third countries. NAFTA seems to have reached its economic goal of success-fully strengthening relations and trade flows between the three countries. As shown in Chapter 2 (Tables 2.1 and 2.2), Canada and Mexico have consistently been the first and third trading partners of the US over the last 13 years. According to data from the Office of the United States Trade Representative and the US Bureau of Economic Analysis, total US trade with Canada and Mexico amounted to $1.6 trillion in 2009 – 45 per cent of the American external trade – while US FDI in other NAFTA countries totalled $357.7 billion, an 8.8 per cent increase on 2008. In the same year, NAFTA FDI in the US increased by 16.5 per cent. Despite these excellent results, political and social support for NAFTA in the member states has not been strong, with opposition in the US, Canada and Mexico alike. In Mexico, dislike of NAFTA has even taken the extreme form of armed opposition, as in the Zapatista insurgency in Chapas. Unlike the ASEAN area, NAFTA is not expected to change its nature as an FTA into a more integrated economic union such as that implied by the AEC project.

European integration is an older, dissimilar process. The current struc-ture of the EU emerged through lengthy, gradual integration based on the challenge of post-war economic reconstruction and the founding of the European Community of Steel and Coal (ECSC) in 1952, leading to the creation of the European Economic Community (EEC) in 1957 and to European Economic and Monetary Union in 1992. In this long, stop-and-go journey, the number of European states in the project has continuously grown with membership increasing from the initial six coun-tries in 1952 to 27 in 2007 following five enlargement rounds, the most recent adding Bulgaria and Romania. Now, the EU is a significant albeit incomplete political entity and an economic giant which, with just 7 per cent of the world's population, generates about 20 per cent of world trade flows and rivals or surpasses the US in many economic areas (see Table 4.1). According to data from the EU Commission, about two thirds of EU member trade occurs inside the union with EU partners, showing a high level of economic interdependence.

Economic integration is not the only aspect of the EU; the EU has developed common policies in many social, educational and health fields, and cohesion fund programmes provide member states with financial resources for reducing territorial economic disequilibria. The EU is not (yet) a federal state with a government able to raise taxes and issue bonds. Its financial resources are limited to 1 per cent of EU GDP and depend entirely on transfers by national governments.

The EU is not merely an FTA but a complex economic, monetary and

Table 4.1   US and EU macroeconomic comparison (2010)

	USA	EU
Population (a)	309,997	501,126
GDP (PPS evaluation) (b)	14,526.550	16,242.256
Per-capita GDP (PPS evaluation) (b)	46,860.242	30,455.224
Export of goods(b)	106.52	1712.48
Import of goods (b)	159.43	437.36

Source: Eurostat, IMF World Economic Outlook Database, OECD Main Economic Indicators
(a)   thousands; (b)   billion dollars

political union with supranational institutions such as the democratically elected European Parliament, the European Council and Commission, the European Central Bank (ECB) and the European Court of Justice[6]. The EU is a full customs union which abolished internal trade barriers in 1968. As to political barriers, the Schengen Treaty removed internal frontiers, so that intra-EU borders were not only de facto but also de jure abolished. In a further step forward, in 1992 the Maastricht Treaty established the single European market, a large economic area where the goods, services, citizens and capital of member states can move unrestrictedly. On the basis of the principle 'one market, one currency', the Maastricht and the Lisbon treaties laid down the stages and refined the rules, leading after 1999 to the introduction of the ECB and the euro. On the whole, these achievements are impressive, particularly because they were obtained through cooperation and collective negotiation. However, the push toward the institutional and political unification of the Old Continent came to an abrupt stop when the European Constitution, signed by EU heads of government in 2004, was rejected by French and Dutch citizens in two separate referendums one year later. Since then, no further steps toward deeper political integration have been attempted and the project now appears to be facing the opposition of many European countries. After more than a decade of accelerated integration and enlargement, some respite became necessary. Today, it is not clear whether the process of political integration in Europe will resume or encounter further obstacles. The negative impact of the international financial crisis on the European sovereign bond market, alongside divided and uncertain reactions from European policy makers, have made default by a European state a real possibility for the first time in the history of the EU. Should this happen, the very survival of the euro (and the EU) would be jeopardized because the political, economic, monetary and financial ties between European states would rapidly disseminate the effects of the default throughout the Union. Chapter 6 includes a detailed analysis of the European sovereign debt crisis. Here we limit ourselves to suggesting that the EU will only avoid the high costs of an uncontrolled debt crisis and reduce the likelihood of European collapse by resuming and completing the process of political integration, leading to a federal state where common monetary policy goes hand in hand with common fiscal policy.

This brief review of the main steps in European integration indicates that supranationality and the 'communitaire' method are trademarks of the EU. Supranational institutions mean that the decisions taken at EU level prevail over national policies and that member states must integrate their legislation with EU regulations. Uniquely, member states have gradually surrendered part of their national sovereignty to European institutions as is most evident in the European Economic and Monetary Union established by the Maastricht Treaty, setting up the European Central Bank, a supranational institution issuing the common European currency and managing European monetary policy. What was so new about the introduction of the euro was that independent states in Europe voluntarily gave up one of the major elements of national sovereignty by transferring the control of monetary policy to a common supranational institution.

Much has been written about the theory of optimal currency areas and on the costs, benefits, defects and sustainability of the EMU (De Grauwe, 2007, 2009; Issing, 2008; Eichengreen, 1997; Kenen, 1995; Kenen and Meade, 2008; Masson and Taylor, 1993; McCallum, 1999; McKinnon, 2004; Mulhearn and Vane, 2008). A detailed analysis of the relevant literature is outside the scope of this book. Here we focus on the very different nature of EMU compared to all other, past or existing, monetary unions, whether national or multinational (Bordo and Harold, 2008). National monetary unions have a single monetary authority or central bank, national borders define the dimensions of the monetary area and central national authorities manage both fiscal and monetary policies. In other words, in national monetary unions, fiscal and monetary sovereignty are at the national level. In multinational monetary unions, each country retains its domestic currency and independent central bank; no single monetary authority exists in the currency area. At the same time, the exchange rate between the currencies of the countries in the union is fixed, making national currencies interchangeable. In this type of union, the survival of the area depends on close coordination between national monetary authorities. The Latin and Scandinavian monetary unions are examples of international monetary unions, while the US, Germany and Italy are cases of national monetary unions.

In these three countries, political unity preceded monetary unification. The US became an independent state with a formal constitution in 1789, after the War of Independence. However, a central bank, the Federal Reserve System (FED), was not created until more than a century later, in 1913. Until then, no single central monetary authority existed. Each state regulated the issue of bank notes as it saw fit and many decades passed before US monetary union was achieved.

Italy became an independent state in 1861, under the leadership of the Kingdom of Sardinia, which unified the Italian peninsula politically and militarily, after centuries of division into small independent states under the dominion of foreign powers (for example, north-east Italy was part of the Austrian Empire). Before political unification, a large number of different metallic currencies circulated in the Italian states, making monetary reform urgent after unification. The new Italian government decided to abolish the old currencies and adopted a monetary standard based on the lira (originating in the Kingdom of Sardinia). However, here too, no single central bank was established on unification; in 1884, as many as six different banks were issuing notes. The Italian central bank, the Banca d'Italia, was established in 1893 as a merger between four major Italian banks, including three of the six issuing banknotes. Later, in 1926, the Banca d'Italia became the only authorized money issuer in Italy (Frattianni and Spinelli, 1997). If the creation of a national central bank signals the completion of monetary union, in Italy more than 30 years were needed to achieve it.

German unification was similarly driven by one dominant state, the Kingdom of Prussia. As Italy, before the unification the fragmentation of Germany into free towns, municipalities and small states meant that each independent zone or city had its own coins and banknotes. The first step toward monetary simplification occurred under the Zollverein, a customs union created by 38 German states in 1834, when northern members adopted the thaler as its monetary unit and southern states adopted the gulden. In 1871, after political unification, the German government introduced a new currency, the mark; the central bank was established four years later. Once again monetary unification was neither rapid nor linear.

Quite different is the history of the major international monetary unions of the nineteenth century. Belgium, France, Italy and Switzerland founded the Latin Union in 1865, while Denmark, Norway and Sweden joined in the Scandinavian Union in 1873. Unlike the UK, which adopted the gold standard (and abandoned it in 1931 during the Great Depression), the Latin Union adopted a bimetallic standard, in which both silver and gold coins circulated. It coordinated the creation of token coins with the same silver content in order to prevent the seignorage of one country at the expense of others. Because these Unions did not regulate the issue of paper money, member states retained a great deal of monetary autonomy (Bordo and Harold, 2008: 8). The Scandinavian monetary union was the 'natural' consequence of a situation in which the three countries were using the same unit of account, the risksdaler, and the coins of each country circulated in all. As with the Latin Union, small differences in the silver content between national coins produced money flows from one country to another, and the need for a common coinage emerged. The Scandinavian Monetary Union adopted the gold standard and introduced a new unit of account, the krona. Krona minted in each country had the same gold content. The adherence to a common international monetary standard facilitated the functioning of the two unions, simplifying coordination of the various national monetary policies (Bordo and Harold, 2008; Bordo and Jonung, 1997; Redish, 2000). However, the inconvertibility of currencies and the economic strains produced by World War I brought an end to these experiments in monetary union. In the interwar period, the attempt by the UK, Italy and other countries to return to the gold standard, failed. After World War II, the Bretton Woods exchange rate system was essentially based on the dollar, albeit formally on gold.

Monetary unions are usually created out of the desire to facilitate trade by reducing exchange rate uncertainty, eliminating the costs of multiple currencies and preventing unfair trade policies based on competitive devaluations and seignorage. They are more fragile than national unions because the lack of a single monetary authority renders the implementation of common policies more difficult and the fact that states in the monetary union maintain full political independence makes it less costly to abandon the union in the face of external shocks, diverging domestic economies and/or contrasting economic policy goals than to remain in the union. In contrast, the economic, political and human cost of breaking national monetary unions is very high; usually it is the result of political turmoil such as revolution or civil war ending in the dissolution of the political unity of the country. The peaceful political and monetary division of a state – such as the division of Czechoslovakia into the Czech and Slovakian Republics – is very rare. More common are forms of disintegration such as the former Yugoslavia, with civil war and atrocities on a huge scale.

How do the main features of the EMU compare with these examples of monetary union? The EMU is not an international monetary union because the Maastricht treaty established a common, independent, supranational monetary authority, the ECB, to direct monetary policy for the whole area. Nor is it a national monetary union because the EU is not a national federal state; each member state is independent. Therefore, compared to previous monetary unions, the EMU is unique, as is the introduction of a new single European currency in 17 different states without war or imposition by a single, dominant state. Due to its size and importance, Germany dominated the monetary policy of the EU prior to the creation of the EMU. Although other monetary authorities were formally independent, they followed the Bundesbank policy stance on interest rates and inflation. Paradoxically, after the birth of the euro, the EMU's participating countries lost their formal monetary sovereignty but, at the same time, they gained substantial sovereignty through a mechanism of collective decision-making and via a supranational institution where the German point of view is not necessarily dominant. The reasons why Germany accepted the EMU, giving up its strong mark and dominant position in European monetary policy, are explained in section 6.4. Briefly, European monetary union resulted from the attempt to solve the economic and political problems of German reunification and in order to assure lasting benefits to all the European countries asymmetrically affected by it. Once again, a discussion of the benefits and costs of the EU and the EMU makes no sense without an overview of the historical and political events behind them and the economic and political costs of failure.

4.4   RESERVE CURRENCIES AND MULTIPOLARITY

Chapter 2 analysed global imbalances and asymmetries in the international monetary system, suggesting the need for a supranational world currency and the creation of supranational monetary institutions. Chapter 5 further discusses these topics. The final section of this chapter attempts to answer the following question: without major reforms of the international monetary system, what is the likely evolution of the world in which the dollar remains dominant? If trends in real and financial markets have anticipated changes in foreign exchange markets, then one guess could be that a multipolar international monetary system is likely to emerge in the near future. The international supremacy of the dollar as a reserve and world currency was undisputed until the appearance of the EMU. In the 1950s and 1960s this supremacy was based on the economic dominance of the US; later, after the demise of Bretton Woods, its supremacy remained intact largely due to the lack of viable alternatives. The only implicit competitor of the dollar was the German mark but it was not an international reserve currency and Germany did not have the political will to promote extensive use of the mark in the foreign exchange market. Only after the creation of the EMU and subsequent introduction of the euro did an alternative to the dollar appear (Bergsten, 2002; Chinn and Frankel, 2005; Dutta, 2005; Fiorentini, 2005). Today, the rapid emergence of China, both as the major Asian economy and as a global economic pole, along with the persistent stagnation of Japan, has many observers thinking that, in a few years' time, the Chinese renmimbi will become the third international reserve currency alongside the euro and dollar (Fratzscher and Mehel, 2011; Jayakumar and Weiss, 2011; Kelly, 2009; World Bank, 2011).

The coexistence of multiple reserve currencies is not new, although one currency has always dominated. In the nineteenth century, gold was the basis of the international monetary system and the value of national coins and paper money was defined in terms of their gold content; hence the exchange rate between national currencies was determined automatically. The gold standard was a symmetric system: no single country issued the international key currency. However, because of the predominant position of the City of London financial market, the British pound obtained special status and was largely used as a reserve currency along with gold. In the period between the two world wars, the British economy faded, the US emerged as the new international economic power and the dollar was increasingly used both for trade and reserves. The dollar replaced sterling as the leading international currency after World War II, when the Bretton Woods conference introduced an exchange rate system based on the convertibility of the dollar into gold along with fixed exchange rates between the dollar and other currencies. The Bretton Woods monetary system was a gold exchange standard system, with the dollar functioning as the international key currency. According to Triffin (1960), the dollar overtook sterling very slowly. In the interwar period, both were used as international reserve currencies. Triffin estimates that in 1928, sterling had an 80 per cent share of total foreign exchange reserves, falling to 70 per cent in the following ten years. In 1938, the international role of sterling was still substantial. Other authors such as Aliber (1966) and Chinn and Frankel (2009) confirm Triffin's findings, while Eichengreen and Flandreau (2008) argue that the dollar overtook sterling in the 1920s only to fall behind again after dollar devaluation in 1933. These studies demonstrate that it is possible to have more than one leading international currency. Changes in the economic ranking of a country do not automatically translate into a new ranking for its currency in the foreign exchange market; a currency may continue to dominate after the country has lost its economic supremacy, as explained by network externalities and hysteresis: when a currency has gained international status and is widely used in international transactions as well as being accepted as a reserve currency, it is convenient to continue using the currency despite the decline in the economic and political support of the currency because it is less expensive to use a currency everybody else is using rather than switch to another promising currency traded in a more limited number of transactions. In other words, the persistent dominance of a currency in the foreign exchange market is a product of inertia in international payment technology and represents a case of the advantage of the incumbent. In this regard, other political and institutional elements may affect the international status of a currency. For example, after the fall of the USSR, the fact that the US was the sole military superpower and the hub of a network of international military and strategic alliances, had a positive impact on the international role of the dollar. Partner countries may decide to support the international role of an incumbent currency for political rather than purely economic reasons. The emergence and persistence of key currencies in the world monetary system depend on market forces and on political action and the geopolitical strategies of partner countries (Helleiner and Kirshner, 2009).

What are the economic characteristics of a key reserve currency? As national currencies, any international currency has three main functions: to facilitate trade and investments (medium of exchange function); to denominate prices (unit of account function); and to maintain value through time (store of value function). In a world monetary system based on national currencies, one currency may achieve worldwide importance only if it simultaneously carries out all these three functions in international markets. An international currency is used for trade invoicing and settlements, is a vehicle currency[7] and is used in central bank intervention in foreign exchange markets; it is used for pricing most international commodities and goods, is held for safe private investments and is hoarded in official international reserves. Currently, the dollar meets all these conditions; the euro does so in a more limited manner and the renmimbi still falls short in all areas. However, the trend toward a multipolar world economy is likely to change this static picture.

Not every country can issue a key reserve currency because the international spread and acceptance of a currency requires the economy to be large enough, trade and financial links with other countries to be extensive and domestic financial markets to be liquid, deep and sophisticated (Jayakumar and Weiss, 2011: 97). The frequency with which a currency is used worldwide positively correlates with the intensity of trade and financial flows with foreign partners. Furthermore, it is only when it is widely exchanged in international markets that it can be used to set international prices. Trust in the solidity and solvency of the domestic financial market is essential for the currency to be held as an international reserve abroad. In turn, low inflation, 'sound' economic policies and a market-friendly environment are necessary ingredients for creating and maintaining trust in the currency.

In these terms, how do the dollar, euro and renmimbi compare? Starting from the incumbent, the dollar, notwithstanding the anticipated loss of share in world GDP, the size of the US economy will continue to provide the dollar with a key position in the future. The broad international use of the dollar is shown by the fact that about 65 per cent of all US banknotes circulate outside the US and in 2007, 96 countries followed exchange rate policies that either linked their exchange rate to the dollar through dollarization (seven countries) or pegged exchange rates regimes (Goldberg, 2010). In finance, despite the ongoing crisis, US financial markets remain the deepest and most liquid in the world, and dollar-denominated assets are still in demand and held abroad. IMF data on the composition of global international reserves reveals that the dollar continues to be the major component of allocated reserves,[8] although in the 2000s the share of the US currency declined by roughly 1 per cent each year, falling from 71 to 62 per cent (see Figure 4.5). At the same time, the euro rose from 18 per cent in 2000 to 28 per cent in 2009. In 2010, the euro lost ground, its share falling by two percentage points to 26 per cent. Uncertainty about the prospects of the US recovery, along with the persistent trade deficit and rise in public debt, largely held abroad, suggest that the pattern of imbalances contributing to the crisis persists and the weakness of the US economy is likely to reinforce multipolarity in international finance. As hysteresis and network externalities in the foreign exchange market show, the dollar will continue to have an important role in the international economy unless creditor countries withdraw their support and switch the composition of their financial investments to other currencies. This appears unlikely, because a sudden withdrawal of foreign investments from the US would produce a sharp depreciation of the dollar, which in turn would strongly reduce the value of dollar assets held abroad, causing a dramatic shock in financial markets the world over. More likely is the slow and gradual diversification of the currency composition of international investments and reserves.

For the euro, economic fundamentals such as GDP and trade flows are favourable to the expansion of its international role. The euro is currently the second major currency held in international reserves (Figure 4.5) and is widely used as a medium of exchange in transactions outside the EU. According to the ECB (2011: 10), in 2010, on average, countries belonging to the EMU area invoiced and settled about 68 per cent of their exports and around 53 per cent of imports in euros (EU countries outside the EMU included). Considering only trade with extra-EU countries, these figures fall to 55 and 41 per cent. The ability to use a domestic currency in international transactions is a good index of the international status of the currency. From this point of view, the euro has been a success; its use in international trade has increased constantly since 2000. The areas where

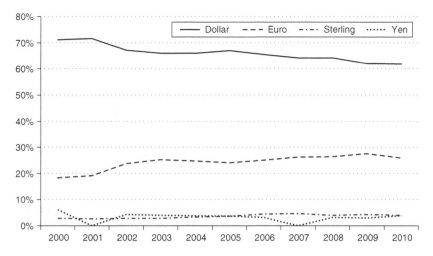

Source: IMF COFER database

Figure 4.5 Currency composition of international reserves (2000 – 2010)

the euro is most commonly used are Africa, Eastern Europe and central Asia, while transactions involving the dollar are predominant in North and South America, the Middle East, and the Asian-Pacific area. As far as international financial markets are concerned, at the end of 2010, euro-denominated securities represented 27.4 per cent of the market, dollar securities had a share of 48.7 per cent and yen securities 6.3 per cent (ECB, 2011: 19). In the same year, in daily foreign exchange market turnover the euro accounted for 19.5 per cent, the dollar 42.4 per cent and the yen 9.5 per cent of global currency transactions (ECB, 2011: 26). Another indication of the degree of internationalization of a currency is how many foreign countries follow exchange rate policies based upon it. In the case of the euro, an array of policies exist, including unilateral euroisation, currency boards, pegs and managed exchange rates based entirely on the euro or including the euro in a basket of major international currencies. The countries that adopt these exchange rate policies are in EU-neighbouring regions. The major obstacles to the expansion of the euro in the world monetary system are related to the institutional structure of the EMU and, in particular, to the fact that fiscal policy coordination in the EU is insufficient because of the absence of a European federal fiscal authority. A single Europe-wide market for government bonds is also lacking; this has contributed to the European sovereign debt crisis allowing speculators to bet against single countries. If the national sovereign debt markets of

Europe were consolidated into a single continental market, as in the Blue Bond proposal (Delpla and von Weizsacker, 2010), its dimension would be comparable to that of the US and profitable speculation would be more difficult.

For the renmimbi, the rapid expansion of Chinese GDP and foreign trade is the major driver behind a broader use of the Chinese currency in international transactions. However, inconvertibility is a major obstacle. The renmimbi exchange rate is currently not market determined and the Chinese government keeps strict controls over capital flows. The export-led growth strategy followed in recent years by the Chinese government has led to the pegging of the renmimbi to the dollar. Furthermore, the desire to avoid a currency crisis, such as occurred in Asia at the end of the 1990s, partly explains the reluctance of the Chinese authorities to liberalize capital flows and ease state control of the exchange rate. However, unless the Chinese authorities take these steps, no further progress in the direction of internationalization is possible. As far as the use of the renmimbi in international trade is concerned, the Chinese government has promoted its use in bilateral swap agreements with Asian and other emerging countries, such as Argentina, Hong Kong, Malaysia, and South Korea. In 2009, China and Brazil also signed an agreement according to which China's import from Brazil are in renmimbi, while Brazil's import from China are paid in real (Kelly, 2009: 2; World Bank, 2011: 141). The aim of these agreements is to reduce these countries' dependence on the dollar in international trade. The renmimbi may also gradually gain ground in the pricing of commodities. Through rapid industrialization, China is the world's largest consumer of metals such as copper, nickel, aluminium and zinc; the need to ensure a stable supply of these materials is the reason for the growing flow of Chinese FDI in Africa. Should this continue, it is reasonable to think that the renmimbi might be used to set the price of such commodities, excluding oil since Chinese demand is unlikely to top that of the US and EU for several years (Kelly, 2009: 9).

China is taking steady steps in the direction of internationalizing the renmimbi; in the long term, the country will have a fundamental role in every aspect of the world economy, including via the renmimbi (Dobson and Masson, 2009). The road is very long, however, and requires sweeping reforms in the still state-controlled Chinese financial sector. Controls over capital flows can only be withdrawn in the presence of a well-regulated, modern, private domestic financial system. In 1997–1998, the weakness of the domestic banking sector contributed to the crisis in Asian countries which had opened their capital accounts to foreign investments (Corsetti et al, 2005). The Chinese authorities have learned this lesson, putting the modernization of the financial side of their economy on the agenda (Barth et al, 2009; Cham et al, 2007; Huang, 2007). Even after this goal is achieved, the use of the renmimbi as a global reserve currency is still not assured, however, because the reputation associated with a reserve currency can only be built up over time, as the history of the dollar and sterling shows. Nonetheless, the renmimbi is likely to replace the yen as the leading currency in the Asian region. In the 1980s, due to its strong economic expansion, technological progress and the efficiency of its production, Japan was set to become the third pole in the international economy, alongside the US and EU, but after 20 years of stagnation, and over ten years of unprecedented Chinese growth, Japan can no longer aspire to this role, nor can the yen remain the only key Asian currency. The growing network of industrial and financial links between China and its Asian neighbour will give the renmimbi a crucial role in economic relations in Asia, as the euro has in Europe and Africa. The spontaneous evolution of the world monetary system will see the continuing central role of the dollar and the formation of two large regional areas dominated by the euro and the renmimbi. The final relative strength among the three currencies in the world monetary system will depend not only on economic variables, but on the ability of the US, the EU and China to face up to political and institutional challenges. In the US the aftermath of the financial crisis led to a huge expansion of public debt, creating new problems and threatening economic recovery, as well as sparking harsh debate between Republicans and Democrats, unable to agree on the solution. In Europe, the survival of the EMU depends on the will of European governments to move toward closer fiscal coordination and true fiscal union. Finally, the Chinese government has the duty to switch the current export-led growth model toward higher domestic demand, simultaneously reforming the financial system along with easing state controls over capital flows and the exchange rate.

Should each currency area be successful, the resulting world economy would nonetheless benefit from a new supranational currency and supranational institutions, because the flaws and asymmetries of an international monetary system based on national currencies would persist in a three-currency world.

NOTES

1. In terms of per-capita GDP, China is still a poor country.
2. The IMF includes the following 34 countries in the Advanced Country group: Australia, Austria, Belgium, Canada, Cyprus, Czech Republic, Denmark, Estonia, Finland, France, Germany, Greece, Hong Kong SAR, Iceland, Ireland, Israel, Italy, Japan,

Korea, Luxembourg, Malta, Netherlands, New Zealand, Norway, Portugal, Singapore, Slovak Republic, Slovenia, Spain, Sweden, Switzerland, Taiwan Province of China, United Kingdom, and the United States.

3. Emerging countries FDI in advanced countries mainly have the form of mergers and acquisitions of existing companies (brownfield investments) rather than investments in newly established companies (greenfield investments).

4. The gravity theory of international trade draws on Newton's well-known gravity equation using trade flows between two countries as the gravity force between two objects. In this view, international trade flows between two countries i and j are positively related to the countries' economic size, typically measured by GDP (Y_i, Y_j), and inversely related to geographical distance D. A typical standard gravity equation is therefore: $T_{ij} = A \cdot Y_i^a \cdot Y_j^b / D^c$ where a, b, c are the weights to be estimated.

5. The GATT promoted the development of international trade adopting a multilateral discussion strategy that was implemented in nine 'discussion rounds' named after the location or the promoter of each round. In sequence, the rounds were: the Geneva Round (1947–1948), the Annecy Round (1949), the Torquay Round (1950–1951), the Geneva Round (1956), the Dillon Round (1960–1962), the Kennedy Round (1963–1967), The Tokyo Round (1973–1979), the Uruguay Round (1986–1993), the Doha Round (2001. . .). The first seven rounds focused on trade in goods and tariff reductions. The Uruguay Round extended discussions to trade-related issues, such as patents and phytosanitary measures, and led to the creation of the WTO. As of today, the Doha Round has not produced any new treaty because of harsh disagreements between advanced and emerging countries on the opening of US and EU agricultural markets.

6. The EU clearly inspired the African Union whose institutions comprise a Commission, an Executive Council and a Pan-African Parliament.

7. A vehicle currency facilitates the exchange between two minor currencies. Currencies with little international supply and demand are more easily exchanged using the vehicle currency in an intermediate step. In the first step 'currency one' is exchanged for the vehicle currency, which is readily available and accepted worldwide. In the second step, the vehicle currency is exchanged for the other minor 'currency two'.

8. The data presented in Figure 4.5 do not offer a complete picture of the currency composition of international reserves due to the lack of information from many countries.

PART III

Money and finance as supranational public goods

5. Money as a supranational public good

5.1 MONEY, FINANCE AND THE NATION-STATE

As we have seen in the previous chapters the global economy is not the simple summation of national economies. Each national economy integrated into the world market accepts common rules – not always explicit – concerning trade, finance and money. As a consequence the power of a national government over its internal economy is greatly affected by external constraints. Even the distribution of income is no longer a simple national matter. The world financial crisis is a clear example of the broad connection between private finance, public finance and the international monetary order.

The aim of this and the following chapter is to discuss international money and international finance – private and public – as interconnected problems, in order to find some guidelines to reform the present international institutions. As far as money is concerned, Davidson (1982: 241) rightly recalls: 'Money can only be studied in an historical and institutional context.' Indeed a historical-institutional approach seems the most appropriate; it gives us the opportunity to study the main features of money and finance as national and international institutions and their evolution since the birth of the modern nation-state. Today the institutional approach in economics is thriving and founded on solid foundations. Thorstein Veblen and John Commons can be considered 'old' institutional economists. The new developments, mainly based on the theory of institutional evolution and the modern methodology of social sciences, are considered 'new' institutional economics (Hodgson, 1998; Williamson, 2000). Moreover, outside the field of economics, scholars of other social sciences and philosophers undertook the study of the place of institutions in society. Among these scholars John Searle (1995, 2010) has achieved important results. According to Searle, institutions are regularized procedures or practices of which we can understand and describe the logical structure. 'The institutional ontology of human civilization, the special ways in which human institutional reality differs from the social structures and behaviour of other animals, is a matter of status functions imposed according to constitutive rules and procedures. Status functions are the glue that holds human societies together' (Searle, 2005: 9). Money, government, property, firms, marriage, football games, churches and so on, are institutions. In the following pages we discuss the evolution of international institutions bearing in mind that institutions do not evolve simply on the basis of Darwinian selection when the environment changes, but that human intentionality can play a role (Hodgson and Knudsen, 2006). To be more precise, we take into consideration the fundamental functions of money, public finance and private finance with the aim of studying their evolution when the economic and political background changes.

Accordingly we need to define some fundamental functions of our institutions. We can say that a certain object (a piece of metal or a piece of paper) can count as money in a certain community if its purchasing power is stable in time, that is that the rate of inflation is zero or near zero. Of course, when paper money becomes a general means of payment the banking system comes into play, because the banking system can create money lending more than its reserves. A certain piece of paper can be considered a public asset (a bond) when the members of the political community expect the capital X they have entrusted to the government to yield an interest R until maturity, when capital X is paid back, as promised by the government. When people loan their money to someone there is always the risk that the promise of repayment will not be fulfilled. The default of a state is possible, but the risk for public loans is often not high. The case of private finance is different. Usually people expect the rate of return of a public bond to be lower than the rate of return on private bonds and on company shares, because of their higher risk. Moreover, private finance is the privileged field of financial innovation since the uncertainty on returns and the value of the investment offer the opportunity to replace some assets with a good return but with a high risk, with other assets with a lower return and a lower risk. The substitution among different financial assets opens the way to speculation and phases of euphoria and panic. The structural problem of private finance is instability, as Minsky (1975) explained.

Minsky's 'financial instability hypothesis' was incorporated in a more general framework by Charles Kindleberger in his book *Manias, Panic and Crashes* (1978 and, with Aliber, 2005, chapter 2). The Minsky-Kindleberger model explains how a financial bubble can start, develop and implode in a relatively independent way from the business cycle. A bubble is a deviation of asset price from its normal value for an extended period of time. Usually the financial bubble starts with a 'displacement,' that is a new sense of optimism about the future of the business cycle and the general economic trend. In this new economic environment, firms and financial institutions are convinced that the increase in the price of financial assets will continue and exceed the interest rate on the money they borrow. Usually, in the upward phase of the bubble the rate of profit of financial investments and institutions increases more rapidly than industrial profit and GDP. But at a certain point the increase in the asset price must slow down and reverse its direction. For the indebted firms and other financial investors it is time to look for more liquidity: the price of assets falls, some investor fails and a phase of panic starts. In the international economy the Minsky-Kindleberger model can be applied easily to the overvaluation (overshooting) and the undervaluation (undershooting) of exchange rates. During the phase of the dollar standard, variation in exchange rates has usually been much bigger than difference in the national level of prices. Crises in exchanges rates go frequently with bank crises, especially in countries obliged to borrow in a foreign currency.

Our reconstruction of the evolution of international economics is to some extent based on a historical trend noticed by Samuel Finer (1993) in his monumental *History of Government from the Earliest Times*. According to Finer, who studied the process of state building from ancient times to the modern age, there is a close connection between the centralization of military force and the centralization of economic resources. The interdependence of the two processes is called the 'coercion-extraction cycle' or, if we consider it the other way round, 'extraction-coercion cycle.' The military force – says Finer – is necessary 'to guarantee the existence of a political community'. But 'military forces call for men, and, once monetization has set in, for money too. . . . The ruler uses a military force to extract taxes, builds up that force, and with it extracts more taxes. There is a fixed connection between absolutism and standing armies' (Finer, 1993: 19–22). This state of affairs advanced dramatically in the nineteenth century, first of all in Europe. 'The reason was the rise of the novel ideology of nationalism. In the name of the nation, individuals were willing to fight and die on a scale quite unknown in the past. Individuals who were prepared to die for their country were equally prepared to pay taxes to sustain it' (Finer, 1993: 20).

In the following pages we try to show that the 'coercion-extraction cycle' reached a turning point after the Second World War. From this time on, a new cycle was visible mainly in Europe. In other continents, such as Asia, Latin America and Africa, the coercion-extraction cycle continues, in the new nation-states created at the end of the colonial phase. But in Europe it is possible to see a 'double-devolution cycle', the devolution of national power downwards, towards local communities and upwards, towards supranational institutions or international organizations. The double-devolution cycle is part and parcel of the evolution of the international economic order. The national rulers have centralized monetary and fiscal power during the last centuries, thus putting an end to the feudal age, but in the post-world wars age they have to face the problem of managing international interdependence and they are obliged, willy-nilly, to share their national power with other national powers: national sovereignty is increasingly becoming an empty shell.

The double-devolution cycle brings about a new relationship between monetary power and fiscal and financial power, which are no longer at the service of a single sovereign or government. In the global economy, where international finance is stronger and stronger, it is necessary to continue the process of centralization of monetary power entrusting monetary policy to a supranational central bank, independent of national governments, as the case of the European Monetary Union shows. Fiscal and financial power should be entrusted to different levels of government: town, region, nation, continent and world institutions. These different centres of expenditure and fiscal power are really autonomous – they are not dependent on some other level of government – if they can manage appropriate own resources and if monetary power is entrusted to an independent institution, which pursues a monetary policy that does not favour one or more governments damaging other governments.

5.2   THE GOLD STANDARD

As mentioned above, the problem of the new world order can be properly studied by means of a historical-institutional approach. This does not mean reconstructing the history of the world economy as the economic historians do. Our main goal is to study some fundamental features and to see how they evolve throughout the centuries. Concerning money, this task is not so difficult since only two main international monetary systems came into existence in modern history: the gold standard and the gold exchange standard (which evolved into the dollar standard). Here we try to analyse these two systems taking into account the following four features: international cooperation; the role of the stabilizer; money as a private or public good; and the coordination of macroeconomic policies.

International Cooperation

The nineteenth century can be considered a century of political revolutions and social turmoil and, at the same time, of international stability because between the end of the Napoleonic wars and the outbreak of World War I no major wars among the European great powers broke out. The historian

David Thomson duly states that there was a crucial difference between the Congress of Vienna (1814–15) and the Congress of Versailles (1919), when President Wilson proposed the League of Nations on the assumption that all states of the international community were democracies, sufficiently like-minded and peace-loving. As a matter of fact, one of the main causes of the League's failure was 'the fact that an increasing number of states ceased to be democratic in structure or peace-loving in purpose.' On the contrary, 'the Congress System of 1815 was more realistic in this respect, that it did not presuppose a greater degree of unity and uniformity in Europe than actually existed. It provided a machinery for peaceful changes by means of periodic consultations between the greatest power-units in Europe' (Thomson, 1972: 98). This system of equilibrium among the European powers functioned fairly well until two important changes occurred: the national unifications of Italy and Germany. Towards the end of the century European politics become uneasy and short-tempered: new forces challenged the old European equilibrium; a reorganization of Europe was in the making. 'The form it took was an attempt to weld together in the heart of Europe the core of a German-dominated empire strong enough to compete on terms of equality with the other great world powers of the time, imperial Russia, the United States, and the British empire. Its outcome was the wars of 1914 and 1939' (Barraclough, 1979: 32).

The balance of power established at the Vienna Congress was stable enough not only to avoid major wars[1] among the European states but also to create the feeling of a lasting truce. This peaceful atmosphere was the breeding ground for free trade and the gold standard, the first international monetary system of post-medieval times. The parallel spread, from England to Europe and to the world, of free trade and the gold standard can be recognized as a symptom of the new disposition of the European powers to cooperate. Indeed, at the beginning of the nineteenth century only England was adopting the gold standard and its Parliament, after the end of Napoleonic wars, took into consideration the abolition of the Corn Laws, which were really repealed only in 1846. England was an island of liberalism surrounded by an ocean of protectionism (Bairoch, 1993: 16). One explanation of this fact is that the industrial revolution started in the eighteenth century in England but the other European states, the US and Japan were the 'second comers,' as the historians call them. After the repeal of the Corn Laws the process towards free trade stepped up. In 1860, France and the UK signed a commercial treaty, which led to tariff disarmament in many other countries thanks to the most-favoured nation clause. After the Franco-German war, exploiting the indemnity paid by France, the German government decided to adopt the gold standard, in order to share the advantages that came from trading in the Commonwealth, the world's greatest market. Thanks to the German decision, bimetallism was abandoned by practically every country. At the beginning of the twentieth century the gold standard was adopted in the US, Russia, Japan, France, Italy, Austria-Hungary, Denmark, Holland, Norway, Sweden, Argentina, Mexico and Peru. India pegged the rupee to the pound in 1898. Only China and some Latin American countries remained on the silver standard (Eichengreen, 1996: 18). England – or some other Great Power – did not plan the birth of the international gold standard: it was really the result of human action but not of human design. 'Such arrangements have arisen spontaneously out of the individual choices of countries constrained by prior decisions of their neighbours and, more generally, by the inheritance of history' (Eichengreen, 1996: 7).

A second piece of evidence of the disposition of European powers to cooperate in the international economy was the behaviour of national central banks and national governments in maintaining the balance of payments in equilibrium in spite of huge international capital movements. The smooth working of the gold standard was based on the convertibility of the national monetary unit of each country with a certain quantity of gold. If the value of each currency is fixed in terms of gold also the 'mint value' or 'par value' of every currency is fixed in the monetary foreign market. According to the classical economists, if a country increases the quantity of paper money in excess of the quantity required by the market – measured as a proportion of production – the commodities' home prices will increase in relation to foreign prices; as a consequence people will bring their paper money to the central bank to change it on a par with gold. Afterwards, people will export gold to buy cheaper commodities on the foreign market. If the national banking system is obliged to maintain a certain balance between the quantity of paper money issued and gold reserves, it has to reduce the issuance of money paper and restrict credit. The export and import of gold from one country to the other is the mechanism – the price-specie-flow mechanism – which brings the balance of trade into equilibrium. However, the classical doctrine of the balance of trade ignored the increasing international circulation of capitals, because it was not so visible at that time; but in the second half of the nineteenth century it was clear that the equilibrium of the balance of payments could not be explained only by the equilibrium of the balance of trade. The behaviour of national central banks and the rate of interest policy could no longer be ignored (Kenwood and Lougheed, 1983: 124–28).

The gold standard can be considered a symmetrical monetary system since no central bank or national government assumed a prominent role even though the Bank of England and the British government were certainly considered the leading authorities: indeed the City of London became in the course of the nineteenth century the financial core of the world economy. Nevertheless the behaviour of central banks did not always follow the model laid down by the economists: in theory, when a country is losing gold reserves the central bank should increase the rate of interest in order to stop the flight and attract foreign capitals. As explained by Eichengreen (1992: chapter 1; 1996: 32–35), on several occasions the Bank of England was in deep waters due to the lack of gold reserves and the impossibility of increasing the rate of interest, so leaving the gold standard was the only option left. In the summer of 1890 some rumours caused a flight of capital from the City; as a consequence the Bank of Russia withdrew its gold deposits. The Bank of England reacted with an increase in the rate of interest but this action was useless, and a further increase in the rate of interest would have been interpreted as a sign that gold reserves were depleted. Luckily the Bank of France offered a loan of two million pounds to the Bank of England and the international market calmed down. In 1907 gold was drained from London towards the United States. The Bank of England reacted by increasing the rate of interest but the measure did not attract much gold because the interest rates were already high in other countries. Once again the Bank of France came to the rescue. Some months later the crisis in the US worsened and there was a new flight of capital from London. This time aid came not only from the Bank of France but also from the German Reichsbank. At the beginning of the twentieth century it was clear that the stability of the gold standard was based on the effective cooperation among national central banks.

The other outcome of international cooperation was the phenomenon of 'stabilizing capital movements.' In normal times when a central bank was in trouble and an interest rate increase was envisaged, to stop a gold flight and to attract foreign capitals, international capitals poured into the country since they expected other central banks not to hinder the manoeuvre and so they could get a capital gain. The central banks were relatively free to maintain the 'external balance' because they were not very worried about the so-called 'internal balance,' that is the maintenance of full employment and price stability. The explanation for this fact is to be found in the social and political environment before the First World War. In those years unemployment was not considered a political and economic problem: there was a problem of poverty, but it was mainly considered an affair of private charities. Trade unions and socialist parties were weak and underrepresented in the national parliaments; social policies were in their infancy. 'The worker susceptible to unemployment when the central bank raised the discount rate had little opportunity to voice his objections,' says Eichengreen (1996: 31), who adds: 'the fact that wages and prices were relatively flexible meant that a shock to the balance of payments that required a reduction in domestic spending could be accommodated by a fall in prices and costs rather than a rise in unemployment . . . For all these reasons the priority that central banks attached to maintaining currency convertibility was rarely challenged.'

The last effect of international cooperation to be considered is the role of the pound sterling as an international reserve currency. As already observed, the Commonwealth was the most important market in the world and the City of London became quite spontaneously, during the nineteenth century, the centre of the world economy, ahead of Antwerp, Amsterdam and Hamburg. The City worked as a clearing board of the world capital market: from the periphery capitals flowed to London where the main markets for commodities and raw materials were set up, and from London they were invested anew in every corner of the world. Thanks to this central position in the world economy the pound sterling was soon considered 'as good as gold' and was utilized in international transactions, substituting gold when necessary and possible. In fact, many scholars of the gold standard observed that the international movements of gold should have been more frequent and greater on the basis of the price-specie-flow doctrine. But the pound sterling, and in a certain measure the French franc and the German mark too, were considered reserve currencies even better than gold because it was possible to invest them instead of keeping them in coffers. At the end of the nineteenth century foreign money reserves were 20 per cent of the total and the pound sterling accounted for 40 per cent of all exchange reserves (Foreman-Peck, 1995: chapter 9; Eichengreen, 1996: 23). Therefore it is possible to say that during the nineteenth century the gold standard began a spontaneous evolution towards a new international monetary system, which was in the following century called the gold-exchange standard. Robert Triffin was the first to observe this slow evolution of the international monetary system; he says: 'the nineteenth century could be far more accurately described as the century of an emerging and growing credit-money standard, and of the euthanasia of gold and silver moneys, rather than as the century of the gold standard' (Triffin, 1968: 21).

The Stabilizer

In his influential study of the great depression, Charles Kindleberger says that for 'the world economy to be stabilized, there has to be a stabilizer – one stabilizer' (Kindleberger, 1987: 304). This statement concludes his analysis of the great depression of the 1930s and the fall, in 1931, of the gold standard, restored after the end of World War I by the UK government in 1925. According to Kindleberger the inter-war period was characterized by the transition from the old political and economic order of the nineteenth century and the emerging new world order of the twentieth century. The explanation is 'that the 1929 depression was so wide, so deep, and so long because the international economic system was rendered unstable by British inability and US unwillingness to assume responsibility for stabilizing it' (Kindleberger, 1987: 289). This analysis, put forward in 1973, was later on the basis for the so-called hegemonic stability theory, widely discussed by scholars of international political economy. Here we are interested in the notion of 'stabilizer' because it mixes the economic and the political function of the leading power. Indeed the UK cannot be considered the hegemonic country of the political system of the nineteenth century. As discussed above the European system of states in the nineteenth century was based on the balance of power and the UK was one of the powers of the system even if, probably, the most important one. But the UK did not have the power – essential to play the role of the leader, like the US or the USSR did after the world war – to prevent war among other powers. When the European balance changed dramatically, after the German reunification, the UK was unable to stop the arms race and the outbreak of war. On the other hand, if we consider the economic role of the UK, until the European balance of power worked, it seems unquestionable that the City was considered the centre of the world economy and that the Bank of England played the role of conductor of the central banks' orchestra. But this leading role of the Bank of England was possible within the general environment of cooperation among central banks: in case of need the other central banks were disposed to aid the Bank of England. One cannot maintain that the Bank of England played the role of an international lender of last resort. During the nineteenth century a central bank was created in every state taking part in the gold standard. The US was the last state to accomplish this step, since the Federal Reserve System was constituted in 1913. Two of the tasks of a central bank were to issue paper money on the basis of a certain quantity of gold reserve established by the law and to regulate the volume of money and credit, in order to avoid banking and financial crisis. The Bank of England was the first central bank to develop these functions skilfully. But when the gold standard collapsed, in 1931, Ralph Hawtrey raised the issue of whether an international lender of last resort should have been able to avoid the crash. In the home money market a central bank can supply liquidity without limit, provided that the bank can issue legal tender. Without this right conferred by the law, the central bank cannot function as a lender of last resort to the home economy. Therefore, Hawtrey says: 'it is by no means taken for granted that an exact parallel can be drawn between an international central bank and a national central bank' (De Boyer des Roches and Solis Rosales, 2011: 198). An international authority which establishes a central bank issuing world money, accepted as legal tender by every state and every central bank, does not exist. In our international monetary system, says Hawtrey, the only way to aid a central bank under stress is through bilateral or multilateral cooperation among central banks, which can provide a supplement of gold reserves for a certain period of time. 'Perhaps some day the Bank of International Settlements will be in a position to meet this need. But as things are, the function can only be undertaken by a foreign central bank or by a group of foreign banks in cooperation' (des Roches and Solis Rosales, 2011). This general statement excludes of course, the possibility that the Bank of England could have played the role of lender of last resort during the gold standard. To conclude, the UK economy, City of London and the Bank of England can together be considered the stabilizers of the world economy during the gold standard, even if they did not wield the power of a hegemonic state.

Money as a Private or Public Good

The basic economic functions of money are three: medium of payments, unit of account and store of value. Money circulates in the market among people who want to buy a commodity and people who are willing to sell it. But in order to perform these tasks money should be produced (issued) and people should trust it. For these reasons, since ancient times, political power – kings, emperors and local authorities – provided the market with a certain piece of metal or paper attesting its value. The history of money shows countless circumstances in which private subjects asked public power to regulate and warrant contracts; in other circumstances public power abused its authority, spoiling the market, for instance clipping coins. Let's recall John Law's disastrous monetary experiment. In 1716 the French monarchy asked the Scottish financier to establish a Banque Royale, in order to reduce the enormous public debt by issuing money in exchange of the debt. In 1717 Law set up the Compagnie de la Lousiane or Compagnie des Indes granting the control of mint and the farming revenue of the colony. People bearing public debt certificates had the chance to change them with shares of the Compagnie. The success was prompt. But the shares were sold at 40 times their value. The crash came in 1720; many people were ruined. The reputation of *banques* collapsed and, in France, for many years, even the name of *banque* was turned down and substituted with *caisse* and *crédit* (Parker, 1974).

The ambiguous status of money, a crucial means for the market but provided by the sovereign, ready to abuse his power, gave rise to the common view that it was necessary to limit the issuing power of the sovereign either with some institutional rule or by entrusting the market directly with the task of producing money. Indeed, money was basically a metal (gold or silver): why not think of money as a commodity produced by the monetary sector and sold to the people who asked for it? This problem was hotly debated during the nineteenth century between the banking school and the currency school until the view of the currency school, which supported the establishment of a central bank, prevailed.

This controversy sparked off in many countries in Europe and in the US, but it is useful to recall a previous debate between Bullionists and Anti-bullionists in England, and especially David Ricardo's position on the role of the central bank, because it shows clearly how paper money and the banking system changed the functioning of the gold standard. During the Napoleonic wars, in 1797, the Bank of England was authorized, with the Restriction Act, to suspend the convertibility of banknotes into gold, until 1819, when convertibility was restored. After the suspension of convertibility, prices of all commodities greatly increased. The Bullionists upheld that the Bank of England was responsible for the high price of bullion, caused by an over issuing of banknotes. The Antibullionists supported the view that the Bank did not issue an excessive quantity of bank notes, but only the quantity required by the market (the real bills doctrine); inflation was caused by other situations, such as a bad harvest. In 1810, Ricardo, in his pamphlet *The High Price of Bullion*, supported the Bullionists' position resolutely. According to Ricardo, gold and silver are distributed in every country according to their need, in other words the total production of commodities and the quantity of money required for their circulation. If the banking system is set up, the banknotes replace gold because paper money is easier to produce, to handle and to transport than specie. But, if convertibility is preserved, commodities prices should be the same inside and outside the nation. Only if convertibility is suspended can the Bank of England issue an excessive quantity of banknotes and provoke inflation. Therefore – this is Ricardo's thesis – the price of bullion is higher than in other countries because people buy gold to export it in order to buy cheaper commodities abroad. The high price of bullion is proof of the inflationary policy of the Bank of England.

During Ricardo's life, the Bank of England was managed by a group of wealthy people, who earned profits from their activity. In many sentences Ricardo defines the Bank of England as a 'company of merchants' and in the *Principles* (Ricardo I, 1951: 356) he writes: 'Experience . . . shews, that neither a state nor a bank ever have had unrestricted power of issuing paper money, without abusing that power.' After the Resumption of Cash, the Act that in 1819 restored convertibility, the Bank of England reduced the bank notes too much and too fast, causing great discontent. Ricardo died in 1823, but after his death, his *Plan for a National Bank* (Ricardo IV, 1951) was published. Here Ricardo proposes to divide the Bank of England into two departments: one working as a commercial bank and the other one as an issuing department, whose gains (seignorage) are transferred entirely to the government. The issuing function is to be entrusted to commissioners paid with a salary and 'not removable from their official situation but by a vote of one or both Houses of Parliament.' Moreover, says Ricardo, 'the commissioners should never, on any pretence, lend money to government . . . If government wanted money, it should be obliged to raise it in the legitimate way; by taxing people, by the issue and sale of exchequer bills, by funded loans, or by borrowing from any of the numerous banks which might exist in the country; but in no case should it be allowed to borrow from those, who have the power of creating money' (Ricardo IV, 1951: 282–83).

This bold position of Ricardo in favour of a public central bank not only anticipates Peel's Act of 1844 and the modern doctrine of the independence of the central bank from political power (Montani, 2012), but it also shows the need for a central bank in a gold standard regime when a banking system exists and paper money circulates. For Ricardo, money is a public good. Nevertheless, during the nineteenth century the debate between the banking school and the currency school was lively and challenging. Vera Smith provided, in 1936, a wide and clear survey of this debate during the gold standard age. Here it is sufficient to recall the position of some economists in the UK, before the central bank reform of 1844. In the 1820s, Sir Henry Parnell upheld that a proper currency should be secured by leaving the business of banking wholly free from all legislative influence. But other economists opposed this point of view. MacCulloch argued that a free system of banking would lead to the over issuing of money, 'the reason being that competition among a number of banks would cause one bank to lower its discount rate in order to increase its business, and all banks would be forced to do the same' (Smith, 1990: 75). The final outcome is that the more daring banks, the banks which lowered their rate of interest more, would spoil the market and transform the banking system into a monopoly. Besides a general over-issue, MacCulloch gave a second reason for the regulation of the banking system by the government: in case of loss or bankruptcy ordinary people, usually poor people unable to distinguish a good banknote from a bad banknote, would bear the cost of inappropriate regulation. This topic was reinforced by Lord Overstone, who said that it is correct to defend competition in a certain sector when 'all the evils arising from errors or miscalculations on the part of the producers will fall on themselves and not on the public,' but in the case of the banking system, in which every bank can issue a paper currency, 'the evil consequence of any error miscalculation upon this point falls in much greater proportion upon the public than upon the issuers' (Smith, 1990: 80). The conclusion of Vera Smith is that the currency school and the movement in favour of central banks prevailed, because 'unless it can be proved that free banking would entirely eliminate the trade cycle and general runs on the banks, the argument for the lender of last resort remains a very powerful argument in defence of central banking' (Smith, 1990: 187).

According to Smith, there is a further argument in favour of a central bank: it is 'an essential instrument for securing international cooperation in monetary policy' (Smith, 1990: 190). As we have already seen, the development of an international financial market and the rate of interest policy adopted by central banks made the task of coordinating central banks easier. Entrance into the 'gold standard club' was an incentive for national governments to create a central bank: it was a means to avoid dramatic credit crises in the national system and a means for stabilizing international monetary and trade cooperation. Towards the end of the gold standard age money became a national public good. At this point, the logic of the development of the international monetary system, based more and more on paper money and free movement of capital, should have warned national governments that the creation of an international lender of last resort was becoming necessary to stabilize the international economy. But the outbreak of World War I stopped any development in this direction. After the war the conditions for a smooth working of the gold standard no longer existed. From a political point of view, the Treaty of Versailles did not allow for peaceful cooperation among European powers. From an economic point of view, it was necessary to take note of the new trade off between the two goals of the external balance (stable rate of exchange and equilibrium of the balance of payments) and internal balance (full employment and price stability): the national interest prevailed over the will of international cooperation. For these reasons the gold standard could be considered an unfinished construction: money was managed by national governments as a national public good and, simultaneously, as an international private good. This discrepancy was fateful for the old system and was only partially overcome after World War II.

Coordination of Macroeconomic Policies

The relationship between monetary and fiscal policies is probably the best lookout post to see how limited the national governments' room for manoeuvre is, in spite of their declared sovereignty. The integration of the national economy into the world market imposes the respect of explicit or tacit rules outside the control of national political institutions.

A comparison of monetary and fiscal rules in France and Great Britain, during the Napoleonic wars, can help us to clarify this point. After John Law's failed experiment, France underwent some other unfortunate experiences during the last decades of the *ancien régime*. In 1759, during the Seven Years' War, the state was obliged to suspend the repayment of capital on its debt and in 1770 there was a new state bankruptcy. After the revolution of 1789, the National Assembly decided to finance its expenses with the issue of *assignats*, a kind of bond, which could be used to buy the nationalized properties of the church. But after the 1792 war, the issue of *assignats* grew to an inflationary level and they were abandoned. The *Directoire* was obliged to raise new taxes. Due to these unhappy financial experiences, Napoleon was forced to finance his war mainly through taxes. In contrast, in Great Britain, also thanks to the Glorious Revolution of 1688 and the Parliament's control of the government, there was a better management of public finance. Taxes, as a percentage of commodity output, did not rise substantially until the Napoleonic wars. After the American War for Independence, William Pitt re-established the sinking fund in 1786 in order to utilize the budget surplus in peacetime to reduce the debt, thereby increasing the credibility of the government. During the war against Napoleon, expenses were financed mainly by issuing a massive debt and, in part, by an inflationary policy which caused the suspension of convertibility in 1797. In 1799 the Pitt government levied an income tax on the propertied class to avoid raising indirect taxes. In conclusion, during this difficult experience, 'given its long record of fiscal probity, coupled with its open budgetary process in Parliament, Great Britain could continue to borrow a substantial fraction of its war expenditures at what were relatively low interest rates.' On the other hand, France 'had squandered her reputation in the last decade of the *ancien régime* and the Revolution. Her dependency on taxation did not reflect any superior fiscal virtues but rather the opposite' (Bordo and White, 1999: 381).

It is useful to study the contrasting experiences of Great Britain and France in order to understand the relationship between fiscal and monetary policies in the nineteenth century. Great Britain's fiscal probity became the model followed by all the countries of the gold standard club, not because of their fiscal virtue, but because they gained many advantages from being members of the world market. They had no serious internal reasons – such as pressure from trade unions and socialist parties for welfare expenses – to breach the rule for a national balanced budget. According to Bordo and Rockoff (1999: 320) the adherence to the gold standard rule 'was evidence of financial rectitude – such as "the Good

Housekeeping seal of approval" – it would signal that a country followed prudent fiscal and monetary policies and would only temporarily run fiscal deficits in well-understood emergencies.' Their empirical research shows that, before 1914, many countries were able to avoid inflation problems and risks of defaulting on external debt thanks to their adherence to the gold standard. Their conclusion is that 'the interest rates charged on long-term bonds in core capital markets during the era of the classical gold standard differed substantially from country to country and these differences were correlated with country's long-term commitment to the gold standard. . . . Indeed, those countries that adhered to the gold standard rule generally had lower fiscal deficits, more stable money growth, and lower inflation rates than those that did not' (Bordo and Rockoff, 1999: 348–9).

In conclusion, the coordination of macroeconomic policies in the gold standard age was the result of historical circumstances that changed dramatically in the twentieth century: the balance of power among the main European states, which created the illusion of a lasting peace, and the possibility for political and monetary national authorities to follow the rule of monetary stability and fiscal probity (a balanced budget). The coordination was not based on the political good will of each single national government but was the spontaneous outcome of the nineteenth century international order. In any case, this model of coordination between monetary and fiscal policies can be considered a legacy for future reforms of the international order, which should achieve the same results avoiding the intrinsic shortcomings of the gold standard.

5.3 THE GOLD-EXCHANGE STANDARD AND THE DOLLAR STANDARD

The gold-exchange standard is the system of fixed, but adjustable, rates of exchange agreed by the two most important subjects – the US and the UK – at the Bretton Woods conference in 1944 and ratified in 1945. It ended on 15 August 1971, when President Nixon declared the inconvertibility of dollar into gold. But the institutions created at Bretton Woods, the International Monetary Fund (IMF) and the World Bank continue to work today, even though their role has changed. However, the dollar went on as the international currency, ushering in the era of the dollar standard. The continuity between the two periods is explained by the hegemonic role of the US in the world economy even if, since World War II, the hegemonic power of the US declined when new political powers became able to act autonomously in the world economy. This section outlines some crucial events showing how the transition from the hegemonic post-war order to the present multipolar world took place.

International Cooperation

The Bretton Woods system was certainly not a spontaneous monetary order, like the previous gold standard. Roosevelt's government put forward the proposal of a new world monetary system as a pillar of the more general framework of the United Nations: the common house to foster a peaceful post-war international order. Forty four representatives of national governments took part in the founding UN Monetary and Financial Conference, but only 29 countries signed the *Articles of Agreement of the International Monetary Fund* in 1945, because the USSR and its allies decided to stay out. Today, the IMF has 187 members, which shows the success of this institution even after the fall of the Berlin Wall and the break-up of the Soviet Union. The Cold War, which brought about a political division in two opposing ideological areas of the world, obliged the US to pursue its project only on the West side where Europe and Japan were the two most important allies. The clear aim of the US was to build, within the UN, an international economic order as a free trade area, thank to the General Agreement on Tariffs and Trade (GATT) and the monetary system of fixed exchange rates. This project was ambitious because it implied, if carried out, the dismantling of the British imperial system of preferences and the European colonial system. If we consider the results achieved before the demise of the Bretton Woods system the judgement cannot be but positive:

'Beginning in the early 1950s, the industrialized countries of the world experienced almost 20 years of sustained economic growth. They recorded an average growth rate of 4.9 per cent per annum from 1950 to 1970, compared with averages of 2.6 per cent for the period 1870–1913 and 1.9 per cent for 1913–1950'.
(Kenwood and Lougheed; 1983: 306)

The Articles of Agreement were a compromise, incorporating proposals of both the White Plan and the Keynes Plan, but the UK was obliged to accept more points supported by the American government. The general objective of the Fund was to promote peaceful cooperation on monetary matters among members. The system of fixed exchange rates was flexible enough – 1 per cent around the agreed par value with a currency (the dollar) convertible into gold – to guarantee a stable system of payments, the growth of the international economy and the maintenance of full employment in every member country. Convertibility of national money was considered a requisite of the system, but capital controls against international speculation were required, in order to avoid the destabilizing movements of the 1930s. Some devices forbade excessive deficits and surpluses of the balance of payments; in case of fundamental disequilibrium, the parity of the currencies could have been changed unilaterally if not above 10 per cent and, if of a greater amount, after consultation with the Fund. The Fund contributed with members' quotas (25 per cent in gold and 75 per cent in currencies) to help countries with deficits to overcome short run imbalances. In such a case the Fund had the power to impose conditions.

In order to highlight the hegemonic role of the US it may be useful to recall the circumstances of the ratification of the Articles of Agreement. During the summer of 1945 the US had already ratified the Agreement but in the UK a strong opposition refused to accept an international treaty incorporating provisions to dismantle the British Empire. The Truman administration decided to push the UK towards a quick solution, declaring that the Lend-Lease agreements, after the end of the war, had to stop. The UK government, since it desperately needed American aid, immediately sent Keynes to Washington to negotiate a delay. But the American government made it clear that the ratification of the *Agreement* was a condition for new financial aid. Before the end of the year the UK government ratified the treaty.

The second interesting episode concerns the demise of the Bretton Woods system and the transition to the dollar standard. The reasons for Nixon's decision of 1971 were several, and included the huge American budget deficit after the Vietnam War and inflationary welfare expenses. Moreover the increasing role of Europe and Japan as new trade powers opened the way to the free cross-border movements of capital. The internal inconsistency of the gold-exchange standard surfaced. This issue was raised and clearly stated by Robert Triffin in his influential *Gold and the Dollar Crisis* (1960), 11 years before the real breakdown of the system. According to Triffin, if the production of gold did not keep pace with the growth of international trade, the US dollar would have been more and more utilized as a reserve currency. Since the Bretton Woods system is founded on the promise of a fixed par value between the dollar and gold (35 dollars per ounce), the accumulation of dollars as a reserve currency must reach an upper limit when central banks and market lose confidence in the convertibility of the dollar into gold. A confidence crisis in the dollar would have been the inevitable ending of the Bretton Woods system. The Triffin dilemma, as it was called, depicted a real trend of the international monetary system at the beginning of the 1960s since the US gold reserves were pouring towards European economies, which grew at rates higher than the American one thanks to the Common Market, created in 1957, causing a deficit in the US balance of payments. In this new changed world, France challenged the US monetary hegemony: in a conference held in 1965 President de Gaulle asked for 'la restauration *de l'étalon-or*' as an alternative to the 'exorbitant privilège' of the issuing country, which had the choice of maintaining an external deficit without reducing its excessive home consumptions.

Many projects of reform of the international monetary system and new proposals for an alternative reserve currency were put on the table during these years. Finally, in 1967, the annual meeting of the IMF approved the First Amendment to the Articles of Agreement, creating the special drawing rights (SDRs), a fiduciary currency, issued by the IMF, based on a basket of national currencies. This decision opened the way for a radical reform of the international monetary system. President Johnson, while signing the US *Special Drawing Rights Act* in 1968, declared: 'For the first time in the world's financial history, nations will be able to create international reserves by deliberate and joint decision, and in amount needed to support sound growth in world trade payments' (Meier, 1982: 91). This statement is astonishing. If taken literally, it means that the IMF had the power to create international reserves, a power it did not receive at Bretton Woods. Indeed, the evolution of the international economy showed very soon that the role of the SDRs, as a reserve currency, was modest, not to say immaterial. After the first SDR allocation in 1970 and the decision in 1971 of the inconvertibility of the dollar into gold, during the 1970s the problem of a 'dollar overhang' substituted the old problem of a dollar scarcity. In 1979 the IMF approved the proposal of a Substitution Account, the aim of which was to allow member states to deposit US dollars and receive an SDR-denominated claim on the Account in return. This claim could be invested in US government bonds. In short, the Substitution Account was conceived as a vehicle for making the substitution of dollar reserves into SDRs easy. But of course the problem was the interest yields on SDRs, whose value changes according to the value of the national currencies in the basket. If the dollar falls, the US government should guarantee the account's soundness 'by paying higher interest rates on US Treasury securities . . . The issue of guarantees backing the account has been the major obstacle to agreement on a substitution account' (Meier, 1982: 250). The experiment of the substitution account came to an end. The reason is that the US government did not want the substitution of the dollar with SDRs because it considered the dollar, as an international reserve currency, not to have any serious competitors and in any case the dollars were coming back into the US. At that time the Europeans had a common market but not a common currency, Japan was economically strong but politically and militarily dependent on aid from the US, and the emerging economies were too weak to be considered, even in the long run, as a challenge to American hegemony. In fact the utilization of the dollar in international trade and finance increased significantly in the following decades, and international cooperation in the world economy was strong enough to guarantee the uninterrupted growth of world output.

The third event to recall is the attempt to coordinate national monetary policies during the phase of floating exchange rates. In the early 1980s Paul Volker, the President of the Federal Reserve System, fostered a restrictive monetary policy, with high interest rates, in order to curb the inflationary process caused by the international monetary and fiscal disorder of the 1970s. The international outcome of this monetary policy was a strong dollar, increasing difficulties for indebted emerging countries and raising inflationary risks for European economies. In 1975, the G6 – very soon enlarged to the G7 with Canada – was created on French initiative. The goal of the informal club (the US, the UK, France, Italy, Germany and Japan) was to coordinate national economic policies, after the fall of the Bretton Woods system. But, without institutions in common, coordination often turns to wishful thinking. The 1985 initiative of European countries to stop the appreciation of the dollar is a good example of the inefficacy of this kind of non-institutional cooperation. After some wavering of the US government, in February 1985 the European central banks of the EMS, coordinated by the Bundesbank and the Bank of Japan, intervened on the foreign exchange market selling dollars against national currencies. The intervention was successful causing a 10 per cent devaluation of the dollar. In September, during a meeting at the Plaza Hotel in New York, the representatives of the G6 came to an agreement to reduce the US public debt, to foster growth in Europe and Japan in order to reduce their balance of payment surplus, and to 'appreciate' the non-dollar currencies against the dollar (and thus to depreciate the dollar). This agreement seemed to work for a certain time, but in 1986 the central banks' monetary policies began to diverge. Therefore, in February 1987, it was necessary to establish 'reference zones' for the exchanges rates in the Louvre Accord. But in the following years, this step raised disagreements, especially in the US, where it was considered an excessive limitation to national sovereignty. Also, in Europe and Japan internal policy issues prevailed over the international agreement. In conclusion 'there was, in essence, a consensual separation from policy coordination. It would be wrong to conclude that the G7 was obliged to drop it due to the hostility of the market' (Saccomanni, 2008: 184–85). International cooperation without supranational institutions only works occasionally.

The failure of the G7 to coordinate the industrial countries' monetary policy, even with the weak 'reference zones' mechanism, is proof that the US embraced, during the phase of the dollar standard, a policy of 'benign neglect' towards the international monetary order. National objectives were the priority while international bonds were considered unbearable obligations. David Calleo, in a survey of American policy, observes: 'During the Nixon and Carter presidencies the floating exchange rate was generally accompanied by an easy monetary policy. In President Reagan's era, by contrast, floating was generally accompanied by tight money . . . Each formula was able to finance deficits and manage the dollar, but each also had its own particular weakness that eventually forced it to be abandoned' (Calleo, 2009: 168–69). After the end of the Cold War the US had the opportunity to cut military spending. 'In many respects, the United States under the Clinton administration seized that chance. Deep cuts in defence spending led toward a fiscal surplus. And despite a still rising external deficit, the dollar stabilized' (Calleo, 2009: 171). But, during the Bush presidency, the internal and external deficits increased out of proportion, until the 2007–9 financial crisis. This was preceded by the Japanese crisis (1990), the Mexican crisis (1994–5), the Asian crisis (1997), the Russian and Brazilian crises (1998–9), the Turkish crisis (2000–1) and the Argentinian crisis (2001). Of course, every crisis had its specific causes and its history, but the general trend seems to point toward a 'leaderless currency system', as Benjamin Cohen defines the present state of the monetary order in which the dollar, the euro, the yen and, in few years maybe the renminbi, compete. 'A weakening dollar is unlikely to be replaced by any other currency', observes Cohen; nevertheless 'a more fragmented currency system, with three or four monies in direct competition in different parts of the world' is the only alternative, and 'sustained cooperation among the major players is unlikely, except in the event of a serious crisis' (Cohen, 2009: 163). Hegemonic power has many aspects: in order to understand the international role of a superpower – as the US was called during the Cold War – we need to consider its political, military, economic and cultural impact on other countries. It is difficult to advance a clear-cut judgement on the demise of the American hegemony. The need for cooperation is strong among all the people of the world and some form of political hegemony can already help to overcome international frictions. But as far as the monetary problem is concerned, we can affirm that the dollar today plays a role similar to that of gold in the spontaneous international order of the nineteenth century: international trade and finance are based on the dollar because that is the legacy of the past. The Fed looks after the problems of the American economy; nobody gets worried about the future of the international monetary order.

The Stabilizer

In order to understand the changed role of the United States as stabilizer of the world economy it is useful to compare the immediate post-war years with the present situation. As a matter of fact, the US were not only the architects of the Bretton Woods system but also one of the main international institutions of the new world order (Gardner, 1969). The Roosevelt government worked hard to shape the post-war order because it was aware that, this time, the US could not repeat the error it committed after World War I, with the failed League of Nations. International peaceful cooperation can work only if the people and the states abide by the rules established by a common government and, since a government does not exist in the international community, the US proposed to build the UN with a Security Council, including the five big powers, in order to settle international disputes. The UN is founded on the principle of national sovereignty, but the five powers of the Security Council have a veto right; in such a way the five governments in the Security Council have more powers than the other members of the UN. All the other international institutions, including the IMF and the World Bank, were planned as agencies of the UN, but when the Cold War broke out they were not included in the UN systems. In any case, if one considers the position of the US in these institutions it is easy to see that the US government preserves a leading position: no decision and no change of statute are possible without the consent of the US government.

It is correct to maintain that the US acted as a stabilizer of the world economy by means of the international institutions built during the war or just after the war and that, when the institutions were not able to cope with certain emergencies, the US administration created new instruments and new policies. The best example is the Marshall Plan. The first aim of the WB was the 'reconstruction and development' of European economies, which collapsed during the effort of the war. But when it was clear that the Western European countries were not able to come out from the depression and destructions of the war and that even democracy was in danger due to social discontent, in June 1947 General Marshall launched a plan, over four years (1948–52), of 13 billion dollars for the recovery of the European economies. The aid was not given to each European government but to common institutions, the Organisation for European Economic Co-operation (OEEC), in order to foster European integration and to solve the German problem, because according to Marshall, the solution to the old conflicts among Europeans was: 'a Europe which includes Germany' (Eichengreen, 2007: 64–70). Moreover, the US government understood that the so-called dollar shortage problem, caused by the inability of the Europeans to export their goods to the US and to import the machineries and commodities needed for their recovery, required new institutions, different from the IMF. The IMF was built and could function only among convertible currencies, but the European currencies were not convertible because the European states did not have gold or any other reserve money as a guarantee of their par value. In 1949 the pound sterling and other 23 moneys were devalued against the dollar to favour exportations. In 1950, Triffin's project for a European Payments Union (EPU) was set up to remove all restrictions to trade transactions among European countries. The model of this regional monetary institution was the Keynes Plan for a Clearing Union, elaborated in view of the Bretton Woods conference. The EPU was a success and, in 1958, convertibility was achieved for all European moneys. By allowing EPU countries to eliminate their restrictions more quickly than other countries of the IMF, (to pursue discriminatory policies), the US 'admitted what had gone unsaid at Bretton Woods: that the post-war international monetary regime was an asymmetric system in which the United States and the dollar played exceptional roles' (Eichengreen, 1996: 107).

The history of this asymmetric or hegemonic role of the US suffered some setbacks, like the Vietnam and the Iraq wars, and some moments of glory, like the break-up of the USSR. Some historians (Kennedy, 1988) had already foreseen the long-term decline of the American superpower, even before the fall of the USSR. Here, our aim is to clarify why, in spite of the declining power of the US, the world today is not moving towards an anarchic society of nation states, and to explain that there are opportunities for peaceful international cooperation. In truth, if we seriously consider Kindleberger's (1987, chapter 14) theory of hegemonic stability, the logical outcome of the historical decline of the hegemonic power – whose main task is to provide some crucial international public goods, such as an international money, free trade and security – is the disruption of the international world order. Indeed, these international public goods are uncertain, frail and even under siege (think of the endless criticism of WTO, of IMF and of the powerless UN). But if we look beneath the surface of the institutions of the old international order, a glimmer of hope for positive change comes into sight. The international institutions built by the US after World War II were designed not only to guarantee the control of a hegemonic power, but first of all to work for the common good of humankind: peace and the development of the international economy. Of course, they were not perfect, but their universal vocation is recognized *ex post* by the present unanimous acceptance of their existence by every country. All the countries of the world are today members of the UN, the IMF or the WTO. What was not possible during the Cold War is a reality today. Therefore, international cooperation continues within these institutions, though not without problems, because the new members – and not only the new ones – ask for new rules of governance, for fairer distribution of powers and responsibilities. The true 'stabilizer' in the present international community is no longer the US alone, but the UN, the IMF and the WTO (and all the other international agencies and organizations). The American citizens and the US government should understand that it is in their interest and in the interest of the world to reform the institutions of the old international system in order to give all people and all states the power to rule the world economy more democratically.

Money as a Private or Public Good

The creation and demise of the Bretton Woods system and the birth of the Economic and Monetary Union (EMU) are the two main monetary events of the twentieth century. From the countless debates concerning these events – the bulk of which revolved around the dilemma of fixed exchange rates versus floating rates – it is interesting for us to recall the question of the 'denationalisation of money,' raised by Friedrich Hayek, even if this question was not at the forefront of the academic and political debate. In 1976 Hayek published a booklet (extended in 1978), in which he proposed: 'to do away altogether with the monopoly of government supplying money and to allow private enterprise to supply the public with other media of exchange it may prefer' (Hayek, 1999: 135). This proposal was elaborated upon just before the creation of the European Monetary System, conceived as the first step toward a European monetary union. Hayek was not opposed to European integration, but he clarified that: 'Though I strongly sympathise with the desire to complete the economic unification of Western Europe by completely freeing the flow of money between them, I have grave doubts about the desirability of doing so by creating a new European currency managed by any sort of supra-national authority' (Hayek, 1999: 133).

Hayek's proposal is different from the free banking of the nineteenth century, which was based on the gold standard. Hayek recognizes that the age of the gold standard is once and for all over and that we are living in the age of fiat money, currently in use as bank notes. Therefore, he proposes that every bank willing to do so can issue bank notes under the condition that: a) each bank note be redeemable in other bank notes already in circulation at a declared rate; b) that the banks announce the purchasing power of their money in terms of a basket of commodities; the commodity standard can be changed at any moment by the bank according to the circumstances and the revealed preferences of the public (Hayek, 1999:

153). Competition among the issuing banks will provide the public with stable money in terms of the declared commodity standard because the public will choose the stable money and discard the weak or bad money. Here, Hayek clarifies that Gresham's Law, (that is: bad money drives out good money), will apply 'only to different kinds of money between which a fixed rate of exchange is enforced by law' (Hayek, 1999: 150), but that is not the case here, where there is a variable rate of exchange between the currencies issued by the private banks. The status of 'legal tender' for private money is not required in Hayek's scheme.

Hayek's practical scheme entails remarkable theoretical consequences: the foundations of the macroeconomic theory fall down. In Hayek's economic system, where different currencies circulate without having a constant relative value, 'the aggregate amount in circulation can only be derived from the relative value of the currencies and has no meaning apart from it'. Moreover, 'in a multi-currency system there is no such a thing as the magnitude of the demand for money' (Hayek, 1999: 180). Therefore, the quantity theory of money has no meaning in this type of economy: no central bank is necessary to regulate the supply of money and, of course, national governments will lose the power to manipulate the value of money and price level. 'Monetary policy as we know it could not exist' (Hayek, 1999: 200). With only one stroke, Hayek scrapped Keynes' macroeconomic theory and Friedman's monetarism. Moreover, in a world in which all nations adopt Hayek's scheme no international economics, in theory and practice, will exist, because private currencies not national currencies would circulate. Hayek says that he remains 'opposed to monetary nationalism or flexible rates of exchange between national currencies as ever. But [he] prefers now abolishing monetary frontiers altogether to merely making national currencies convertible into each other at a fixed rate' (Hayek, 1999: 213).

Since Hayek's scheme is a challenge to the macroeconomic theory, it deserves careful discussion and critique. Otmar Issing, the first chief economist of the ECB, carried out this task with great expertise. Issing acknowledged the cultural influence of Hayek's writings on his education as a young economist, but from his lookout at the ECB he was now able to see the weak points of Hayek's scheme clearly. Here we try to summarize the main objections:

a) Hayek's recommendations neglect 'the "public good" aspect of money, which derives from its function as a unit of account. Money with stable purchasing power serves as the universally acceptable unit of account even for agents who do not use it as a medium of exchange or a store of value' (Issing, 2000: 24).

b) The competition among the issuing banks involves a struggle among inflationary and non-inflationary currencies, therefore the 'discovery process would itself be characterised by inflation'.
c) If a single stable currency did initially emerge from the discovery process, having established a monopoly, the private issuer can start to engage in inflationary over-issue so as to maximize seignorage.
d) Even if a few issuers were to survive, one cannot be sure that the resulting oligopoly situation would not result in collusion or instability.

After these objections to the economic consistency of Hayek's scheme, Issing maintains that the central banks will continue to play an important role as regulators of the financial system. In this regard, the positive experience of the European monetary unification is very important. 'The monetary policy in the euro countries has been denationalized and is being conducted by a supranational central bank, which is politically independent of governments of the member states. Furthermore, any monetary financing of the public sector or privileged access to financial institutions is prohibited. The separation between public finance and monetary policy is thereby ensured' (Issing, 2000: 30–1).

Now let us add a comment to the first objection put forward by Issing, regarding the relationship between money as a unit of account and the public aspect of money. The unit of account function of money is also crucial for the two other essential functions: money as a means of payment and as a store of value. After the gold standard, the problem of the standard of a monetary system can be based only on shared unequivocal conventions between the people and the public power, which issues the money. During the transition age of the gold-exchange standard, an artificial link between gold and national monies was maintained, but with the dollar standard any link with an 'objective' standard was abandoned: national monies are a piece of paper with a value which depends on their purchasing power, that is the quantity of commodities a unit of money can buy. Therefore, it is clear that the value of money depends on two conventions: the first is the basket of commodities taken as a measure of value; the second the capability of the authority (or the market, for Hayek) to maintain the purchasing power stable. Let's consider for example the metre, which is a convention equal to a certain fraction of the earth's meridian and today, more precisely, the distance covered by light in a certain amount of time. We can therefore say that the metre is a physical unit of measurement, because it is based on something outside the behaviour of human beings. The same is not true for the basket of commodities taken as a point of reference for the value of money, which for the euro is the Harmonized Index of Consumer Prices (HICP). The value of this basket is measured on the basis of statistical rules that can be improved and, most of all, of consumer tastes, which cause changes of commodity prices year after year. Therefore, it is almost impossible to guarantee that after 10 or 15 years money will have the same purchasing power as it does today. Hayek's proposal that every issuing bank can change the standard 'at any moment' is simply a fantasy without any basis in the real world. Imagine the poor citizens in Hayek's economy who, before going to work every morning, check whether their money has changed its value in terms of the other moneys and whether their bank has changed the standard. But there is a second problem concerning the money standard: the authority in charge of the monetary policies should avoid excessive inflation or deflation. And here the central banks and national governments come into play. Hayek is right in saying that money should be 'denationalized' because history, and especially modern history, shows that political power has abused the confidence of citizens covering deficits by issuing money: inflation is a hidden tax. But the way out is not to entrust the power to issue money to the market. Hicks, following the teachings of Carl Merger to whom Hayek also refers, says: 'Money, for the greater part of recorded history, has meant coinage; pieces of metal with the "image and super-scription" of some ruler stamped upon them. Money has thus appeared to be the creation of the state,' but money was not created by the state. 'There was money before there was coinage. In its origin, money was a creation of the mercantile economy; though it was the first creation of the mercantile economy which governments . . . learned to take over' (Hicks, 1969: 63). Therefore, it is correct to say that money was created by the market, the mercantile system as Hicks says, and it is also correct to consider mercantile money as a public good, as Menger understood, as language, common law and family are. And it is also correct to say that it was in the interest of the mercantile system to ask for a 'sovereign' to issue money, because it was easier to exchange pieces of metal of the same 'certified' weight. It was only at this stage that it became possible for the sovereign to deceive its subject by clipping the coins and, in modern times, creating an inflationary process. But this is not a good reason to throw the baby out with the bathwater, as Hayek proposes, removing the public aspect of money. Here, the problem that was not explained clearly in economic literature is that if money is a public good there should also be a free rider, – somebody who can get an advantage from the existence of the public good without paying a contribution for its production. Money is an especially intricate case because the 'sovereign' is at the same time the guarantor of the value of money and the free rider: indeed he can get an advantage from his public privilege (if badly regulated, the banking system can also behave as a free-rider). Therefore, the problem is institutional or constitutional: to check the power with a counter power. The solution discovered in Europe is going in the right direction: money has been denationalized because the issuance power was entrusted to the European Central Bank (ECB) and the goal of the monetary policy for the euro area was defined in an European Treaty. National governments maintain the bulk of fiscal power, but they have to respect some European constraints in order to avoid interfering with the monetary policy of the ECB and, since every national government has different and contrasting interests, the ECB can develop a fairly autonomous monetary policy. In Europe, even if this architecture is perfectible, 'the separation between public finance and monetary policy is ensured.'

Finally, we should say something about the dollar, the present international monetary standard. We already saw how the dollar became the international money during the Bretton Woods age. Afterwards the emerging economies, eager to take part in the international trade system, simply adopted the dollar as international money merely because it was there. In this limited sense the dollar standard is a spontaneous order created by the world mercantile system. But we cannot ignore that the 'sovereign' is the US government and that the main goal of American monetary policy is the stability and growth of the American economy, not of the global economy. Therefore, the dollar is a global public good managed by a private, or monopolistic, power (the free rider). This is the main political contradiction of the present international monetary order.

Coordination of Macroeconomic Policies

The relationship between monetary policy and fiscal policy was intensively studied in international economics, especially after World War II. The Mundell-Fleming model is the reference point for macroeconomic analysis in every textbook of international economics. On the basis of this model, important conclusions can be drawn for the efficacy of monetary policy and fiscal policy in fixed and flexible exchange rate regimes. However, this approach is based on purely economic variables and cannot explain specific historical changes, such as the evolution of the international monetary system and the different role of national fiscal policy during the eras of the gold-exchange standard and the dollar standard. Likewise, the most useful concept to explain this historical change is the coercion-extraction cycle put forward by Samuel Finer. For instance, Finer explains how Cromwell, with his New Model Army, strikingly demonstrated 'the basic technique of absolutism: high taxation enforced by standing army which in turn is maintained by the high taxation it enforces – the coercion-extraction cycle'

(Finer, 1999: 1340). The coercion-extraction cycle reached the maximum point of perfection with the creation of the nation state, the banking system and paper money, issued by a central bank. With these means the national government was able not only to collect more and more taxes – including the loyalty and the life of its subjects in case of war – but also to vastly increase its capacity for indebtedness. The money-bank-debt system is explained clearly by John Hicks. The banking system is able to create money: 'The money which it lends is money that it itself creates' (Hicks, 1969: 96). This is a big opportunity for the sovereign. 'There is no longer a danger of the state's defaulting, on debt expressed in its own currency, since it is always possible for it to borrow from the banking system; the banks are not able to refuse to lend, since they can always create money to finance their loans: The power that thus passes into the hands of the state is very great' (ibid.). It was this power that was the basis of the Keynesian revolution. 'The lesson that Keynes taught was of the existence of the power that I have just described. It already existed, and Keynes had only to urge that it should be taken up' (ibid.).

These observations are enough to explain why the gold standard in the nineteenth century worked smoothly: the public promise of the convertibility of paper money into gold put a brake on the inflationary policy and was a guarantee of stable money and stable rates of exchange. Fiscal policy did not interfere with monetary policy. The same basic principles were included in the Bretton Woods agreement. But since the link between monetary and fiscal policy had already been discovered, this agreement was based on the gold standard for the international order and the paper standard for the member nation states. Finally, to maintain the national sovereign's power to tax the citizens, a clause banning international movement of capitals was added. Roughly the states taking part in the Bretton Woods agreement, accepting a fixed rate of exchange with the dollar, surrendered their monetary policy to the hegemonic power, but retained the control of their fiscal policy.

Now, if we consider the control of national public indebtedness as an indication of the fiscal power of the state – taking the public debt as a substitute of taxation – we can see that the Bretton Woods agreement worked fairly well in the post-war years. Reinhart and Sbrancia (2011) studied the policy the industrialized countries utilized to reduce the exorbitant debt they had accumulated during World War II. According to this study the debt was restructured using a kind of taxation that occurred via financial repression. Financial repression means controlled interest rates, controlled credit and persistent inflation rates. Today it is a method utilized by China to reduce its domestic debt. In Europe and the US, savers deposited their money in banks or invested it in government bonds, whose interest rate was below the level of inflation. The real interest rate was negative. At maturity the government returned the same quantity of money deposited, but with lower purchasing power. The savers' loss was equal to the correspondent improvement in the government's public balance. For the UK – with a debt to GDP ratio of 238 per cent in 1947 – and the US, the annual rate of debt liquidation was of 3 to 4 per cent per year and for Australia and Italy 5 per cent. Reinhart and Sbrancia (2011: 6) say: 'The Second World War debt overhang was importantly liquidated via the combination of financial repression and inflation . . . This was possible because debts were predominantly domestic and denominated in domestic currencies.' The link of financial repression with the international monetary system is clear: 'The financial repression route taken at the creation of the Bretton Woods system was facilitated by initial conditions after the war, which left a legacy of pervasive domestic and financial restrictions' (Reinhart and Sbrancia, 2011: 18).

If we take into consideration the post-war recovery of Western countries, and especially the high rate of growth of European countries and Japan, we can understand why the decades foregoing the collapse of the Bretton Woods system can be considered the heyday of Keynesianism. The stability of the world market and the possibility for national governments to manage the internal demand strengthened the confidence of citizens in the effectiveness of economic policy. But the collapse of the Bretton Woods system changed the institutional framework dramatically. The floating rates of exchange and the free movement of capitals narrowed the margin of national economic policies. The Keynesian policy is effective only in closed economies. In Europe the new constraint was perceived clearly with the Mitterrand experiment of 1981–82, just after his victorious election as French President. His government launched a Keynesian expansionary programme based on increased minimum wages, new public investments financed by a deficit spending, a shorter working week and some capital control compatible with the EMS, which had recently been created with the other European partners in order to shelter the European market from the floating dollar. But very soon, increased inflation and capital flight caused two devaluations of the French franc. The effect of the French expansionary policy was modest since, in an open market, the French bought European commodities, not necessarily made in France. At the end, Mitterrand understood that he had to choose between a European policy and a national one, which meant quitting the EMS, the CAP, the Common Market and the leading role of France in Europe. Mitterrand's experiment ended with a cut of public spending and new taxes. 'This was a turning point for France and for Europe. The Socialists had learned that unilateral expansionism was not possible . . . If growth-friendly macroeconomic policies were to be put in place, this would now have to occur at the EU level' (Eichengreen, 2007: 290).

The second effect of the collapse of the Bretton Woods system was the explosion of national debts. The trend is carefully highlighted in an IMF study (Abbas et al, 2010: 13):

> [by 1960] advanced G-20 economy [Australia, Canada, France, Germany, Italy, Japan, Korea, UK and USA] average debt ratio declined to 50% of GDP, due to rapid growth and inflation. Average advanced G-20 economy debt ratios trended down further through the early 1970s; however, debt began to accumulate starting in the mid-1970s, with the end of the Bretton Woods system of exchange rates and two oil price shocks.

The upward trend continued until the current global financial crisis, reaching 90 to 100 per cent of GDP. There is not a simple explanation for this upward indebtedness. The expansion of public spending, especially in Europe, was due to the different causes of previous peaks, as happened during the two world wars. It was mainly due to the consolidation of the welfare state, with more spending in subsidies and transfers, education, health, pensions and unemployment insurance. 'The rapid expansion of public expenditure between 1960 and 1980 is remarkable because it occurred when most countries were not engaged in war effort; there was no depression, and the demographic developments were generally fiscally friendly' (Tanzi and Schuknecht 2000: 16). The Keynesian policies survived not as a means to save the country from depression and mass unemployment, but as a rationale for more and more expenses: for many policy makers more public expenses meant a useful promise of more growth and more employment before the elections (as noticed by Buchanan and Wagner, 1977). As a result, 'public expenditure as a share of GDP increased from around 28 per cent in 1960 to around 43 per cent in 1980. The share almost doubled in Belgium, Ireland, Japan, Spain, Sweden, and Switzerland, and increased rapidly in most of the other industrialized countries. By 1980, public expenditure exceeded 50 per cent of GDP in Belgium, the Netherlands, and Sweden' (ibid). The real problem, behind this trend, is that the increased expenditures were financed mainly by the expansion of the national debt, with grave consequences for the national budget: in Belgium and Italy interest payments exceeded 10 per cent of GDP and were 20 per cent of total government expenditure (Tanzi and Schuknecht, 2000: 46).

In 1903, Amilcare Puviani worked out the theory of fiscal illusion to explain how a national government was able to increase its public spending by deceiving the taxpayers. In our case we should talk of an international fiscal illusion, caused by floating exchange rates and free movement of capital, the main features of the dollar standard. But, in the last resort, the governments themselves are the victims of the illusion. With floating exchange rates the national governments deceived themselves on the feasibility of controlling their internal monetary policy and the rate of interest: in the long run the rate of interest followed an international trend, affected mainly by the monetary policy of the US (as the debt crisis of emerging countries in the 1980s showed). The illusion of controlling the interest rate could have led some governments to cover new expenses with a new debt. In other cases, the governments found it easy to sell their bonds on the international market: in fact, in the 1980s, 'a number of governments took the view that they could borrow on international financial markets at more favourable terms than the private sector' (de Fontenay et al, 1997: 207). In 1984, Belgium reached 24 per cent and Ireland almost 50 per cent in foreign currencies debt. For the same reason, today, many governments of the emerging economies prefer to borrow in dollars, with increasing risks for their economic system in case of a rate of exchange crisis. Anyway, both for a debt denominated in national currency and for a debt in foreign currencies the chance to turn to fiscal repression via inflation is over. In a world market in which capital can go freely from one country to another, if a country tries to get negative interest rates, investors will immediately sell its bonds. 'The development of real interest rates on public debt reflects in the increase in government financial liabilities over the past decades. In the 1980s and early 1990s, all governments have had to pay much higher real rates than in the 1960s or 1970s. Real interest rates also became more similar across countries probably as a consequence of greater capital mobility and less intervention into domestic capital markets. In other words, a world capital market came into existence' (Tanzi and Schuknecht 2000: 107).

There is a more profound explanation for international fiscal illusion. After the Second World War the national governments were able to put into practice fiscal repression via inflation because they were integrated in the Bretton Woods system and the American hegemony was considered to be the essential pillar of international solidarity and cohesion. After the collapse of the Bretton Woods system the European countries, Japan and the other Western states acquired greater degrees of freedom towards the hegemonic power. In Europe the development of the welfare states was the result of several requests and pressures coming from many quarters: trade unions, public sector employees, teachers, universities, taxi drivers, local governments, and so on. The national governments were not able to stop these claims when the national revenue was not enough, nor was it able to raise more taxes: the only way out was to increase the debt. Therefore, the case of 'big government' cannot be compared to that of a powerful

Leviathan: on the contrary, it is the display of a weak state, if the main function of the state is to make the public interest prevail over private and corporative interests. Some keen historians (Reinhard, 1999: chapter 21) have rightly pointed out that the inordinate expansion of the welfare state in Europe is the unambiguous sign of its crisis. It is therefore an illusion to think that the old states, with their own forces, will be able to put into practice a long-term policy for fiscal consolidation, as the supporters of the liberal school think, when they propose to tame the Leviathan. In the global financial market, the nation state is no longer the Leviathan: it has lost some of its fiscal power forever.

5.4   A WORLD MONETARY UNION

Today it is unlikely to find an economist who takes the proposal for a world currency seriously. For instance, Barry Eichengreen says:

> The case for a global currency issued and managed by a global central bank is compelling in the abstract: . . . But as a practical matter, so long as there is no global government to hold it accountable for its actions, there will be no global central bank. No global government, which means no global central bank, means no global currency. Full stop. (Eichengreen, 2011: 141)

This statement has a political implication, as is clear in the last paragraph of Eichengreen's book, when he says of the US, 'it is within our grasp to avoid the worst,' that is a dollar crash. For Eichengreen the future of the dollar and the international economic order depends only on the good will of the US government. That is simply not true: the US cannot stop the rising powers of China, India, Brazil, the EU and so on, and avoid the international disorder which will eventually be brought on by several currencies in competition. A leaderless international monetary system can only be a step towards a new global financial and monetary crash. The social scientist has the duty to explore the institutional way out from the present financial and economic turmoil. The Bretton Woods system was the product of American and British foresight. It may be useful to recall that, in 1941, in view of the Bretton Woods conference, Keynes drafted a proposal for an 'International Currency Union.' The time is ripe, after 70 years, to explore the main features of a World Monetary Union and its significance for the international order.

The creation of a world currency means a step towards a world government, or as some people prefer to say, global governance, requiring an effective cooperation among national governments. Of course, we cannot expect international state building to follow the same pattern of national state building. History is an open process. We are aware that the construction of new world institutions should be based on the smooth evolution of the existing international institutions. The aim of the following discussion is to single out the steps necessary to build a World Monetary Union (WMU). In other words, since an institution is a set of rules of behaviour of individuals, who seek to cooperate to attain a certain aim, we try to investigate the main lines of the rules, which can lead to a world monetary order founded on a world currency and a world central bank (WCB). The limit of our approach is that we focus mainly on economic institutions, even if it is clear that a greater involvement of national people in the government of the global economy should be explored. Of course, there is a connection between cosmopolitan political economy and cosmopolitan democracy, as we have hinted at in Appendix A.1.

International Cooperation

Today no national government is willing and able to point out a global exit strategy from the financial crisis. After the G20 meeting in London in April 2009, when an agreement for joint monetary and fiscal expansion was reached, some decisions were made to reinforce the IMF and to work out new rules for financial supervision. Two years later each national government has concentrated its efforts on internal problems. A creeping neo-mercantilism is under way. Bremmer and Roubini say: 'the G20 has gone from a modestly effective international institution to an effective arena of conflict.' A policy to overcome the present slowdown of the global economy would require 'much greater international coordination on the regulation and supervision of the financial system.' Future global monetary and financial stability 'may even require a global super-regulator, given that capital is mobile while regulatory policies remain national' (Bremmer and Roubini, 2011: 2–4). Indeed, outside the United States, it is difficult to see a global player able to propose a global exit strategy. Japan is again struggling with its internal financial crisis and the tragedy caused by the 2011 tsunami. Russia is a military power and a crucial energy supplier, especially for Europe, but it is certainly not a monetary and financial global power. China is the prominent emerging power: its GDP is likely to surpass the US's by 2030. China's ambition is to challenge the US's position in East Asia, but its present monetary and financial power is not enough to enable China to become the pivot of a new world monetary order. The renminbi will be a global money only if it becomes convertible, but to reach this target the Chinese government must strengthen its domestic banking system, where there is a ceiling on bank deposit rates which allows for a policy of fiscal repression, liberalize the inflow and outflow of capital and move to a flexible exchange rate. This set of reforms will require about a decade (Lardy and Douglass, 2011). The euro is the only global money that can become an alternative to the dollar, even as a reserve currency. But the European Union is today wrestling with the agonizing problem of sovereign debts and it is unlikely that the European Union will be able to act as a world player without root-and-branch institutional reforms: the EU needs a democratic government, not a confused and ineffective governance.

If we turn our eyes towards the US we find a difficult debate on the transition from the American hegemonic era to the reality of a multipolar world. The mistakes of Bush's foreign policy – unilateralism and the pretension to export democracy with force – greatly tarnished the traditional image of the US as the champion of liberal democracy and lowered its capacity to solve international problems. The past lies heavily on present events. A debate is open on the historical decline of American hegemony (see Ikenberry, 2011 among others). But, even when the reforms of the international institutions are taken into consideration, the assumption is always the preservation of the American hegemony (Brooks and Wohlforth, 2011). A more pragmatic approach is required. International power is based on different aspects of power politics: there is military, economic, cultural and social power. It is true that the US will maintain for the next years absolute supremacy of military power even if their capacity to intervene on land has certainly weakened. In some cases, the military power of the US is necessary and suitable (as Robert Kaplan argues) for the preservation of peace in the Indian Ocean, a vast region, which extends from the Eastern coastline of Africa to the South China Sea (Kaplan, 2009). Following this pragmatic approach, Joseph Nye observes that: 'the country's capacity to maintain alliances and create networks will be an important dimension of its hard and soft power' (Nye, 2010: 12). This line of thought is correct. Every reform of the international order must increase the power of the US, but it must also increase the power of the other states, which should share the power and responsibilities of the US. In short, the proposed reform must concern the provision of some global public good by supranational institutions.

The field in which there is an urgent need for reform is monetary and financial stability. Here an American initiative, or an American and European initiative, is certainly welcome. The proposal should go beyond the Bretton Woods system with the creation, among a group of founding countries, of a World Monetary Union open to all countries willing to accept the rules and duties necessary to make the WMU work. The time is ripe for this bold step. The seriousness and length of the financial crisis has triggered a debate on the changing role of central banks in the global economy. For instance, Goodhart (2010: 9) observes that: 'the essence of central banking lies in its power to create liquidity, by manipulating its own balance sheet,' but the crisis has shown that a separate financial stability authority is required too. Goodhart infers from that 'that the financial stability authority has to be given command over liquidity management; but that also implies that the financial stability authority would have command over the central bank balance sheet. Indeed, the financial stability authority would then, de facto, become the true central bank.'[2] Harold James's remarks on the relationship between independence of central banks and centralization are also very interesting. 'Centralized states such as France or Japan exercised a political control over central banks. Independent central banks were fundamentally suited to federal states such as Germany, Switzerland or the United States (and hence also . . . the European Union)' (James, 2010: 15). James also explains the reason for that: 'Central bank autonomy becomes more important as more emphasis is given to policy coordination between different tiers of political authority. This may be in one country, within a federal system; but the same principles apply to regional integration and international cooperation and coordination. Without central bank autonomy, monetary policy can rapidly become a cause of disintegration and political fragmentation' (ibid).

We shall explore these useful remarks made by Goodhart and James to define our proposal of a WMU. Of course, the founding countries will come out from the future international political debate. Here we can only advance an academic but reasonable assumption. Today the US dollar, the euro, the British pound and the yen are the currencies most used to make payments for international transactions. According to the IMF (Moghadam, 2011: 20), those four currencies make up the bulk of global international reserves – 96 per cent in 2010 – and enter the SDR basket. Therefore we can imagine that the US, the EU, the UK and Japan decide to create a WMU entrusting to a world board of central banks, chaired by a president and constituted by representatives of member central banks, the task of managing a common monetary policy: for instance the stability of the price levels of the WMU (an inflation target). The main features of such a decision are the following:

a) A group of four industrialized countries take the lead to build a WMU, but the union is open to all other countries which agree on the rules adopted (for instance South Korea, Brazil, New Zealand and later on, when they are willing, China, India and Brazil).

b) No fixed rate of exchange is established among the members of the WMU but, if the world board pursues a common monetary policy, harmonizing the interest rates, in the long run, there will be a convergence of exchange rates towards a central parity, even without control of capital movements (in compliance with the inconsistent triad theorem).

c)   The WMU is the institutional basis for the creation of a 'global super-regulator', essential to rule the global financial market effectively.

d)   The stability of the exchange rates among the four currencies entering the SDRs allows the emerging economies to issue their national debt denominated in SDRs without adopting either a demeaning dollarization or fearing a twin crisis, a banking and a currency crisis, as happened during the Asian crisis of 1997 (Kaminsky and Reinhart, 1999).

e)   The changeover of the four currencies into a world money is not necessary, so that the main international markets – such as the oil market – can go on with their traditional standard of value.

In the following pages we will further investigate this proposal (for a similar proposal see Mundell, 2005). For the time being it is enough to say that its more general message is that the global economy, up to now based on international cooperation among national governments, is entering a new phase of supranational integration.

The Stabilizer

In Kindleberger's texts the meaning of the terms 'stabilizer' and 'lender of last resort' often overlap, for instance when he says that Great Britain, during the gold standard, acted as a lender of last resort. Here we try to distinguish the function of the lender of last resort, which can be carried out only by an agency (a central bank) issuing a legal tender, as Hawtrey explained, and the more political function of the stabilizer, which should decide to employ the taxpayers' money in order to face emergency circumstances, as happened with the Marshall Plan. In a monetary union the institutions of monetary policy and the institutions of fiscal policy should be relatively independent, even if in extraordinary circumstances (as the experiment of the European Monetary Unions during the sovereign debt crisis shows), monetary policy and fiscal policy interact and collide, putting into danger the very existence of the Union. Let us consider the case of Country A, with a zero per cent debt, and Country B with debts of 100 per cent of its GDP. If the common central bank causes inflation and a negative interest rate, citizens of A and B must bear the burden of fiscal repression, but only the government of Country B benefits from the erosion of its debt. In such a case there is a horizontal transfer of income from Country A to Country B. As Harold James noticed, 'without central bank autonomy, monetary policy can rapidly become a cause of disintegration and political fragmentation.' Therefore, for a monetary union it is necessary to plan institutions that respect a clear dividing line between monetary and fiscal policy.

The WMU – established among the US, the EU (with UK) and Japan – should have as its main goal the monetary and financial stability of the world market. Of course, the countries supporting the project must also endorse an agreement, similar to the SGP, establishing an acceptable reference value of debt to GDP and deficit to GDP. After the financial crisis, these countries are aware of the need to reduce their total indebtedness, and to have a common goal to calm the market and public opinion. But for Japan it is necessary to provide some special clause because of its huge debt (more than 200 per cent of GDP). The stability pact is desirable for the WMU countries because the political aim of this project is to provide monetary and financial stability for the global economy.

The linchpin of the WMU is the World Central Bank (WCB). The WCB should be accountable to the World Council, consisting of the representatives of the governments of the founding countries. This institutional framework can ensure a real economic governance of the global economy. For the first time in the history of international economy, the WCB can act as a real lender of last resort. The WCB can coordinate the four monetary policies effectively, since it has the power to control the liquidity of the four currencies. We can compare the power of the WCB to the power of the ECB from 1999 to 2002, when the national currencies were already circulating but the real power to control the liquidity of the Eurozone was entrusted to the ECB; the only difference is that in the Eurozone the rates of exchange were fixed in view of the changeover of the national currencies into euro on 1 January 2002, while in our proposal the rate of exchange among the four currencies will converge to an average value if the WCB is able to guarantee a common monetary target (for instance an inflation target) in every member country. Of course, the WCB can act as a lender of last resort only within the WMU, but if it is able to manage a common liquidity policy and a common rate of interest policy, the convergence of the rate of exchange among the four currencies (of the SDRs) will facilitate the stability of all other currencies and the financial market of emerging countries, which can issue their debt in SDRs without fearing a sudden flight of capital and a change in the external value of their currency.

We should now consider, among the present international institutions, which one can evolve into a WCB. There are two candidates: the IMF and the Bank for International Settlements (BIS). The IMF was established, at Bretton Woods, as a kind of international treasury (a fund), endowed with a capital consisting of national quotas (gold and national currencies). It acted more as the financial weapon of the political stabilizer (the US, which had veto power in the IMF) than as a lender of last resort. At the beginning it helped distressed countries incapable of maintaining the fixed rate of exchange with the dollar. Loans from the fund had to be repaid and the fund usually linked the loan to strict conditions. In 1969, the proposal for SDRs was approved and during the 1970s many economists debated the functions of the fund and the use of the SDRs as reserve money. There was also the proposal to use the SDRs to finance plans for developing poor countries. Joseph Stiglitz (2006) recently resumed this suggestion. In the 1970s, developed economies opposed this proposal. After the breakdown of the Bretton Woods system the role of the IMF changed and, even though the US maintained considerable power, there was growing pressure from emerging economies to gain more power in the IMF executive board. In any case, without a radical reform, the role of the IMF as a world lender of last resort is either doubtful or impossible (Fischer, 2000; Jeanne and Wyplosz, 2001).

The BIS was established in 1930: it is the oldest international financial organization and it works as the main centre for international bank cooperation. It acts as a 'bank of central banks.' The mission of the BIS is to facilitate the collaboration among central banks, acting as a prime counterparty for central banks in their financial transactions, serving as an agent in international financial transactions and promoting reforms to foster international financial stability. The BIS acted as the agent for the European Payment Union (EPU) and for the European Monetary System (EMS). It can obviously act as an agent for the WCB.

It is not this chapter's task to make a choice between the IMF and the BIS as a candidate to lodge the WCB. Here we are interested only in the WCB's monetary mission, which should be distinguished from the fiscal function. In this perspective, merely as an assumption, it is better to preserve the role of the IMF as an international 'emergency financial fund', ready to give limited and conditional aid to distressed countries, and to place the WCB within the BIS which already carries out the function of 'bank of the central banks'. The reason for this division of functions between the IMF and the BIS will be further investigated in the following pages.

Money as a Private or Public Good

While among economists a fairly common agreement exists on the meaning of monetary stability – the stability of the price level or the inflation rate over a certain period – the notion of financial stability is more disputed. Here we assume that a systemic financial risk entails a loss of confidence in the value of financial assets in a proportion capable of causing momentous damage to the real economy: a substantial fall in output and employment. Therefore, there is a link between a financial crisis and a real economy crisis. Moreover, there is also a link between a monetary crisis and a financial crisis. 'In the midst of a financial crisis there could be a run on liquidity ... So when there is a financial instability, there is likely to be monetary instability. This establishes a link between the natural role of the central bank as the provider of payments finality and its role in financial stability' (Schinasi, 2003: 9). Here we examine how the public institutions for world monetary policy, the WMU, can act to provide the efficient regulation of the international financial market in order to avoid a new systemic financial crisis.

The world financial crisis discredited the efficient market hypothesis, the tenet of global financial milieus, and pushed governments and central banks to strengthen the regulation of the banking and financial system. Experience shows that this task can be made difficult due to the behaviour of the national authorities, which should have been able to oversee and guarantee a smooth functioning of the financial market. For instance, in the US, Levine (2010) remarks that the Fed, in 1996, permitted banks to use CDS to reduce capital reserve and when, in 2004, the FBI warned about committing fraud in subprime lending, 'the Fed maintained its capital regulations.' The other regulating authority, the SEC, authorized investment banks 'to use their own mathematical models of asset and portfolio risk to compute appropriate capital levels.' The result was that the SEC, according to Levine, became 'an accomplice in causing the global financial crisis' (Levine, 2010). These observations show that poor financial regulation in a country as crucial as the US can provoke disasters all over the world. The regulation of the financial market cannot continue to be a national responsibility in the global economy. Moreover, the new case of sovereign wealth funds must be taken into consideration by supranational authorities, which should monitor the behaviour and the transparency of these quasi-public actors in the global market (Quadrio Curzio and Miceli, 2010).

The first reaction came from the central banks. In 2010 the Basel Committee on Banking Supervision approved the so-called Basel III Accord, which is the first response to the deficiencies in the financial regulation revealed by the world financial crisis. Basel III requires banks to increase their common equity capital and to produce additional safeguards against risk-weighted assets. Moreover it introduces a series of measures to increase capital buffers in good times that can be drawn upon in periods of stress, in order to promote countercyclical buffers. Basel III is an example of international cooperation among central banks which can succeed, with the agreement of their government, in improving the stability of the banking and financial system. But it is not certainly enough.

In 2008, after the Lehman Brothers default, national governments in the US and Europe were obliged to intervene to avoid a systemic crisis of the banking and financial system. The liquidity crisis became very soon an insolvency crisis and the only way out was to inject a huge quantity of the taxpayers' money into ailing banks. The result was an impressive increase of public debt. The intervention of public authorities was inevitable and appropriate, because they were able to restore the confidence of the public in the banking system and to stop the rush to the bank deposits. But this policy entails serious negative consequences: there were a certain number of banks considered too big to fail, and for this reason they could behave outside the prudential rules established by public authorities. It is a textbook case of moral hazard: since they do not fear bankruptcy, they can invest their capital in exorbitant, risky activities. The private banking system can thus divert savings towards unproductive goals being certain that, in the last resort, public money will come to the rescue. In order to give a rough idea of the amount of money involved in this tug of war among the private and public sectors let us bear in mind that the assets of Britain's most important banks are 4.5 times bigger than its GDP and that the assets of the two biggest banks of Switzerland are six times its GDP (*The Economist*, 2011: 31). These financial mammoths are not only too big to fail but also too big to be saved by their national governments.

In the US and Europe a reform is underway to reduce the structural risk of the banking system. During the Great Depression, in 1933, the US approved the Glass-Steagall Act, which imposed a separation between commercial banks and investments banks. But the Glass-Steagall Act was repealed in 1999, opening the way for all banks to invest in risky prospects, within their countries and abroad. Today, there is the will to go back to the old division between commercial and investment activities, but in a global market this step is difficult, because commercial banks can become unable to compete with other more lucrative financial institutions.[3] In the EU, as far the Eurozone is concerned, a European Systemic Risk Board (ESRB), responsible for the macro-prudential oversight of the financial system and chaired by the President of the ECB, has already been set up. But it can only advise European and national authorities about possible systemic risks; it has no power to impose measures to avoid the risks. In the meantime, the Commission is studying how to strengthen the mechanism of macro-prudential oversight.

These examples show that the efforts of national governments to control and impose rules on the financial system are likely to be doomed to failure because financial capital can always go 'abroad' in search of higher rates of return. The ideal solution to this problem is therefore a world supervisor authority endowed with the power to enforce the rules required for the macro-prudential oversight of global finance, in whatever country the saving is collected and in whatever country it is invested. The WMU can represent a first step in this direction, since the member countries represent a huge proportion of the global financial market and can set the main rules for the international market.

Global financial rules are not enough to guarantee the stability of the world financial system. Even if the rules are well shaped and enforced it is impossible to avoid some banking failures and the spread of panic. Human rules and human institutions are always imperfect: as the Minsky-Kindleberger model teaches, some bubbles can always grow and implode. Inside the WMU a resolution authority should be set up. The recent financial crisis has taught us that panic spread after the bankruptcy of Lehman Brothers. Public authorities should try to avoid bankruptcy causing systemic risks by intervening *ex-ante* and not *ex-post*. A resolution authority may decide 'to seize the bank when it is still functioning, take control and separate or sell certain parts or assets of the bank, remove its management, freeze the rights of shareholders and creditors and reorganize or wind down the bank . . . All this will reduce the disorder and damage in the financial markets and result in orderly liquidation or merger' (Ruding, 2010: 3). The main difficulty in establishing a resolution authority is that the decision to save or not to save a certain bank should be taken in a very short period of time and that this decision involves a cost, sometimes a considerable one, to the taxpayers. In a study of the IMF for the establishment of a European Resolution Authority (ERA), the authors say: 'The resolution agency would need access to financing. In essence, it would be a true Lender of Last Resort (coming even after the emergency liquidity assistance). This requires established channels of communication and consultation with the fiscal authorities. In essence the ERA would be positioned in between supervisors and Ministries of Finance' (Fonteyne et al, 2010: 58).

In the WMU the Resolution Authority can be allocated within the IMF, where a Financial Stability Board (FSB) has already been set up. The IMF should be relieved of many of its present financial duties, since among the countries of the WMU the stability of exchange rates becomes a task of the WCB and in a financial world in which exchange rates are fairly stable the 'twin crises' in emerging markets should also become infrequent. Therefore the IMF can employ its financial resources to help distressed countries to overcome temporary financial crisis caused by errors in macroeconomic policies or by extraordinary circumstances (drought, famine or tsunamis, for example). The IMF is financed with the taxpayers' money of the member countries. Its role is not that of a lender of last resort (this task belongs to the WCB, which provides liquidity), but that of a financial aid of last resort. It can become a tool for limited – because its financial resources are limited – supranational solidarity among countries which support a policy of global financial stability.

Coordination of Macroeconomic Policies

The WMU is not an end in itself. Certainly it is an institutional framework whose main goals are the monetary and financial stability of the global market. But it must be more than that, because a political project which has the ambition of replacing the Bretton Woods system should also offer some prospects of progress. In short, if we consider the most dramatic problems discussed within the United Nations – such as world famine and poverty, climate change, international terrorism, international migration, pandemics and human health – we can also understand that the WMU can help the member countries reach some of the Millennium goals. Even without a world government, an effective cooperation is possible by exploiting the institutional framework of the WMU (in the next chapter, we try to show how this framework can be improved and how to increase the degree of cooperation).

If we consider the main troubles of the three economic zones – the US, the EU and Japan – it is easy to find remarkable issues in common even if, of course, each zone has its own peculiarities.[4] The exhaustion of monetary policy – the interest rates are very low everywhere – and fiscal policy are problems the three economic zones have in common. The governments of the US, the EU and Japan can exploit the WMU to promote a coordinated plan for sustainable growth and employment. Keynes's policies to spur effective demand are no longer possible in small national economies, but can be effective in the world economy or in very large economic areas. In 2010, the three developed economic areas of the WMU constituted 57 per cent of world GDP. Fiscal consolidation is necessary in the WMU, but to cut deficits and debts (the numerator) is easier if the GDP (the denominator) increases. In this perspective, policymakers should be aware that it is possible to promote two effective policies: a) a simultaneous plan for sustainable growth and employment in the WMU, and b) to spur purchases and aggregate demand supporting low-income groups. Public expenditure in infrastructures, renewable energies, green technologies, research and education can be financed to exploit the fiscal space available, for instance by means of public agencies such as the EIB and the issuance of project bonds. The advantage of launching simultaneous plans for sustainable growth is clear. Consider the car industry: if the

EU initiates a development plan, Europeans will not only buy European cars but also Japanese and American cars. A share of the income spent in the EU will enrich the budget of Japanese and American car producers. On the contrary, if the US and Japanese governments simultaneously start a plan for sustainable growth, more European cars will be sold in the US and Japan. In short, the value of the Keynesian multiplier increases in the case of joint and coordinated expenditure plans.

The second policy suggested – supporting low-income groups by means of a harmonized fiscal policy – encounters fierce opposition especially in the US, but it can be justified on economic and political bases. As we have seen in Chapter 3, the gap between low-income people and high-income people has greatly increased in the last decades. In its *Trade and Development Report 2011*, UNCTAD remarks: 'In Europe, Japan and the United States, the current recovery is characterized not only by jobless growth . . . but also by stagnating wages, which hitherto had been a phenomenon observed mainly in Japan' (UNCTAD, 2011: 1). This trend started with globalization in the last decades of the twentieth century, when 'the share of national income accruing to labour declined in most developed and developing countries' (UNCTAD, 2011: 17). In this social context fiscal policy can play an important role, because there is the possibility of redirecting taxes and spending in a more expansionary way: on the contrary, within a floating exchange rate system this policy is impossible. 'A more equitable distribution of income would make economic recovery more self-sustaining and improve the chances of achieving fiscal consolidation. In this sense, increasing real wages in line with productivity, and . . . government transfers to low-income segments of society, are important complements to fiscal expansion' (UNCTAD, 2011: 82). These recommendations should be considered with the awareness that, in small national economies, a fiscal policy based on financial capital taxation and higher wages is not possible. In a global market a fair and equitable distribution of income can be realized either by a world government or by effective coordination among great important economies: a harmonized fiscal policy can be a transitory way round.

Finally, the WMU can also be useful in helping emerging economies to catch up with developed countries. If the WCB is able to guarantee monetary and financial stability – a stable price level – and stable rates of exchange between the main currencies, emerging economies can borrow in the global financial market on the basis of a stable SDR value and low rates of interest. They can develop their home banking and financial system without fearing a 'sudden flight' of capital and dramatic devaluations of their currency. Moreover they can save international reserves, today hoarded up against exchange rate risks, and employ them for domestic investments. Of course, the member countries of the WMU can do more to help emerging economies to develop and to catch up with developed countries: in the following chapter we shall discuss this issue.

NOTES

1. Paul Kennedy remarks: 'With the important exception of the American Civil War, the period 1815–1885 had not witnessed any lengthy, mutually exhausting military struggles. The lesser campaigns of this age, like the Franco-Austrian clash in 1859 or the Russian attack upon Turkey in 1877, did little to affect the Great Power system.' Later on he adds: 'the half-century which followed the battle of Waterloo had been characterized by the steady growth of an international economy, by large-scale productive increases caused by industrial development and technical change, by the relative stability of the Great Power system and the occurrence of only localized and short-term wars.' (Kennedy, 1988: 191–92).
2. We cannot agree with Goodhart's conclusion that 'the idea of the central bank as an independent institution will be put outside' (Goodhart, 2010: 15), as happened during the years between the two world wars, a period of government domination over subservient central banks. According to Goodhart, only during the age of the gold standard and, more recently, of the inflation targeting monetary policy, a relative independence of central banks from national governments was granted. Maybe, the trend towards subservient central banks is inevitable if central banks remain national state banks, but not – for the reason Harold James explains afterwards – if supranational central banks, as we propose, are set up.
3. As a matter of fact the American Dodd-Frank Act includes the Volker Rule, which involves trading restrictions for financial institutions which are divided into two branches: investment banks, private equity, hedge funds and commercial banks. Banks are not allowed to simultaneously enter an advisory and creditor role with clients, as with private equity firms. Moreover the rule limits the liabilities that the largest banks can hold. The purpose is to reduce banking activities and their size, to avoid the 'too big to fail' problem. But many financial institutions dispute the implementation of the Dodd-Frank Act and especially the Volker Rule. In 2011 in Great Britain, the Independent Commission on Banking, chaired by John Vickers, suggested splitting the banking sector into two parts: the commercial banks and the investment banks. The retail or commercial bank will hold buffer equities higher (10 per cent) than the international standard (7 per cent): the deposit guarantee scheme applies only to commercial banks, which collect money mainly within its country. But some objections have already been raised against a rule that makes British banks less competitive in the global market.
4. The US must face the problem of external and internal deficits, which can cause a sudden stop in lending to the US, pushing the dollar down and the interest rates up. As Fred Bergsten says: 'US policymakers must recognize that large external deficits, the dominance of the dollar, and the large capital inflows that necessarily accompany deficits and currency dominance are no longer in the United States' national interest' (Bergsten, 2009: 21). According to Jeffrey Sachs (2011: 11): 'Americans harbor fundamental doubts about the motivations, ethics, and competency of their federal government.' He proposes long-term reforms based on a more fair fiscal system, on investments and structural changes in the labour market, education, health care, energy security and foreign policy. 'A key to success will be much smarter foreign policy, especially a shift from 'hard' power (military) approaches to 'soft' power (diplomacy and assistance) strategies' (Sachs, 2011: 188).

    After the financial crisis the European Union was besieged by the sovereign debt crisis. We shall discuss the European case in the next chapter. Here, suffice it to say the EMU is at risk if a fiscal union and an economic government are not set up. In order to overcome the EU crisis the European Commission recognizes that 'the first step is to quickly fix the way we respond to sovereign debt crisis . . .We need to complete our monetary union with an economic union.' (Barroso, 2011). Europe does not only need austerity policies but also growth policies.

Japan suffered two decades of stagnation – the Japanese great recession – after the land and financial bubble burst in 1990. Recovery in Japan is very difficult because of the links between the real economy and the financial system. The banking system misallocated funds, subsidizing inefficient firms (Hoshi and Kashyap, 2004). Fiscal consolidation is necessary but within a plan to boost consumer and business confidence (Berkmen, 2011; Singh, 2011).

6. Finance as a supranational public good

6.1 FISCAL POLICY AND INTERNATIONAL SOLIDARITY

Today when people talk about international solidarity two situations usually come to their minds: the first is the policy of international aid from developed to underdeveloped countries; the second is spontaneous solidarity among peoples of different countries on the occasion of natural disasters – famine, tsunamis, epidemic diseases – or tragedies caused by human beings, such as wars and genocides. These instances of international solidarity are often criticized for their occasional nature. Among contemporary philosophers a debate has been enlivened by scholars who support the need to go over the limited notion of international solidarity among closed national societies, which provide solidarity policies for fellow citizens, but are quite indifferent to individuals who live in conditions of extreme poverty in other states and other continents (Singer, 2002; Pogge, 2010). Other philosophers think that international solidarity, or international justice, cannot overcome the limits of international politics, which is founded on relationships among sovereign nation states. For instance, Thomas Nagel says that the way he deals with the problem of international ethics is similar to John Rawls's *The Law of Peoples*, that is 'the moral units of this international morality are not individual human beings but separate societies, or peoples' (Nagel, 2010: 79) and for this reason he refutes the cosmopolitan notion of international justice. For cosmopolitan philosophers all human beings should be entitled to satisfy their basic needs, such as food, clean water, a decent shelter, and so on. For Nagel the members of different societies do not have a direct link, but an indirect contact filtered through the relations of different governments. 'That is because as Rawls puts it, societies have a "moral nature" that deserves equal respect, provided they meet the basic conditions of decency. But individuals per se are not entitled to equal treatment internationally' (Nagel, 2010: 80).

In the following pages we do not take part in this philosophical debate. Our aim is to outline institutional reforms for a fairer international economic order. The institutional reforms we propose should be considered progressive, in the sense that they can be regarded as a first step towards the ideal of international justice championed by the cosmopolitan philosophers. It may be useful to recall that national solidarity among the citizens of the same nation state is not spontaneous behaviour but the result, in modern history, of political struggles among different classes and social ranks. The equality of opportunities was the goal of nineteenth and twentieth century reformers for the creation of what is today called the social state or the welfare state. The international reforms here proposed go in the same direction, though we do acknowledge that, even if basic needs are warranted to all people, wide differences in wealth and per-capita income will endure between different nations.

The WMU risks being a lame duck, if the complementary problem of fiscal solidarity is not solved properly. Concerning this point, the comparison with the European Union is not appropriate. The difficulties the EU faced after the financial crisis are due to the fact that the EMU was built without enough governmental power to coordinate national fiscal policies: the Stability and Growth Pact (SGP) was too stiff and inappropriate a substitute. As we try to clarify later, the EU needs a fiscal union and a democratic government to coordinate national fiscal policies. The WMU, if agreed among the most important developed economies, some of continental size, can work smoothly for many years with an agreement similar to the SGP on fiscal discipline as a financial framework; contrary to the EMU, the WMU rates of exchange converge to a target decided upon by the WCB but are not fixed forever. Nevertheless we think that the states and the people who decide to build a WMU should also take into consideration the construction of a World Eco-Monetary Union (WEMU), where 'eco' means both an economic and an ecological union. In fact, in the twenty-first century, if we set aside security, two great problems are on the forefront of international politics: the eradication of extreme poverty in developing countries and the struggle against an irreversible ecological crisis. These are two global public goods, which can be addressed properly only by supranational institutions, endowed with the power to enforce the decisions taken collectively in order to overcome the free rider problem.

As far as the fight against climate change is concerned, the vicissitudes of the Kyoto protocol are instructive. It was adopted in 1997 in the institutional framework of the UN with the aim to stabilize the climate by means of a cap and trade system. It was supported mainly by the EU, but in the end only 18 industrialized countries agreed to impose limits on their carbon emissions. Many important countries, such as the US, China, India and Australia, did not comply. Since the Kyoto protocol does not have an effective clause to oblige a state to comply, at the end it was necessary to open a new set of deals inside the UN to find a way out. As Scott Barrett rightly says, the problem with the Kyoto approach is that 'Its success depends on effective enforcement, so that all essential countries are assured of participating, and all participating countries of complying' (Barrett, 2007: 93). Let's now consider the problem of global development, whose main objective is to fight extreme poverty. Barrett says: 'Global public goods are neither supplied nor enjoyed in a vacuum. Countries with the wherewithal to supply global public goods have other options. Faced with free riding incentives, they choose to substitute national public goods for global public goods, leaving other countries to help themselves' (Barrett, 2007: 167). In other words, national governments prefer to sponsor policies favouring national social groups – since they get votes and political consensus from their fellow citizens – instead of financing social policies for people who do not vote for them. It is clear that only a radical reform of international institutions can change the rules of the game.

In recent years these two problems, extreme poverty eradication and climate change mitigation, are increasingly becoming a single problem: sustainable development. The link is clearly shown in the World Bank Report *Development and Climate Change* (2010), which states that poverty reduction and sustainable environment are core global priorities because a quarter of the population of developing countries lives on less than 1.25 dollars a day and climate change especially threatens developing countries. Therefore this report recommends that developed countries assist developing countries. High-income countries must:

> . . . assist them with the finance and technology to meet the increased challenges to development, ensure they are not locked into permanently low shares of the global commons, and establish mechanisms that decouple where mitigation happens from those who pay for it. Most emissions growth will occur in developing nations, whose current carbon footprint is disproportionately low and whose economies must grow rapidly to reduce poverty. High-income countries must provide financial and technical assistance for both adaptation and low-carbon growth in developing countries. . . Current financing for adaptation and mitigation is less than 5 per cent of what may be needed annually by 2030, but the shortfalls can be met through innovative financing mechanisms.' (WB, 2010: xxi)

It is only necessary to add to this clear statement that a bold policy for sustainable development has also to take into consideration the dramatic question of security. In its 2011 Report, the World Bank states that: '21st century violence does not fit the 20th century mold. Interstate war and civil war are still threats in some regions, but they have declined over the last 25 years' (WB, 2011: 2). Today, 1.5 billion people live in areas affected by conflict and violence caused by the fragility of state institutions. Since security and economic stress are linked, an effective programme for sustainable development should also provide a set of institutional reforms, for national governments and regional economic and political areas (including the African Union and ASEAN), to eradicate organized criminal violence and strengthen civil society security.

Public finance is the kernel of a world policy for sustainable development. An effective proposal for financing global public goods is crucial. 'The prevailing method of financing global public goods is to determine an overall budget, and then, somehow, to get countries to pay their share of the total' (Barrett, 2007: 105). A collective agreement on how to finance global public goods is itself a global public good because 'compliance is helped when countries can verify which countries have paid their dues and which have not. . . . If countries make their contributions contingent on other states contributing, each state has an incentive to contribute' (Barrett, 2007: 123). These statements deserve a full discussion: the place of national fiscal policies in a global market and within the WEMU must be elucidated. In order to discuss this problem we start from some major historical experiences: the existent federal states in every continent, but especially in the US – the first example of a constitutional federal state – are very useful in studying the behaviour and the relationships of multi-layered fiscal systems. Their specificity is the existence not only of horizontal relationships among fiscal administrations but also vertical relationships among different levels of government (local, regional, national and continental). In the next three sections, after the study of some historical examples of federal states, we consider the special case of the European Union. In the final section we conclude, showing the main features of the WEMU.

6.2   HAMILTON'S PROBLEM

In an innovative study, Jonathan Rodden (2006) examines Hamilton's Paradox, as he christened it. Rodden's study is useful because it clarifies that fiscal institutions must be studied in relation to political institutions. A number of economic essays on fiscal federalism are based on the wrong assumption that it is possible to discuss the problems of a multitier system of government without also considering the historical and political background in which it is rooted. Federal institutions inevitably have specific historical roots. Hamilton's Paradox is the outcome of the foundation of the American federation. According to Rodden, we can talk about Hamilton's 'ambiguous intellectual and political legacies' because he 'did not believe in the wisdom of dividing sovereignty between central and state governments', but at the same time he was one of the authors of *The Federalist*, the most 'eloquent defence of federalism that has stood the test of time and served as the starting point for generations of theory and analysis that celebrate the virtues of divided sovereignty' (Rodden, 2006: xii).

We prefer to deal with Hamilton's Problem rather than Hamilton's Paradox. A paradox is a statement which says two opposing things, but which has some truth in it. A problem is a difficulty, practical or intellectual, for which a solution or an answer can be found. Certainly the problem of fiscal federalism, and that of the related political federal institutions, is very complex, and here we do not claim we are able to give a definitive answer to a problem that is two centuries old, but we hope to elucidate some crucial points. The European experience can shed some light on the relationship between monetary and fiscal policy in a multitier system of governments. We will discuss this issue in the next paragraph. For the moment let's recall how Kenneth Wheare, a well-known scholar of federalism, defines fiscal federalism:

'The peculiar federal problem – says Wheare – is this. The federal principle requires that the general and regional governments of a country shall be independent each of the other within its sphere, shall be not subordinate one to another but co-ordinate with each other. Now if this principle is to operate not merely as a matter of strict law but also in practice, it follows that both general and regional governments must each have under its own independent control financial resources sufficient to perform its exclusive functions'.

(Wheare, 1967: 93)

On the basis of this comprehensive definition of the federal problem we can better understand how the significance and the political background of Hamilton's Problem has changed since the foundation of the American federation. Hamilton, as Secretary of the Treasury of the Washington government, in January 1790 presented his *Report Relative to a Provision for the Support of Public Credit* to Congress. After the victorious revolution, many states were highly indebted with foreign and domestic lenders. Hamilton recommended the federal government to assume all debts of the states for two main reasons: first, 'states, like individuals, who observe their engagements, are respected and trusted' and the new American federal government needed to be trusted especially by European powers and capital market; second, the debts of the states 'was the price of liberty', and therefore the federal government had the duty to assume them entirely (Cooke, 1964: 3–4). Hamilton's aim was to reinforce the federal government, which was, in the first years of the American federation, very weak compared to the power of the member states. Indeed, the only considerable federal revenue was made up of custom duties.

The federal assumption of the states' debts had an unexpected outcome. State governments relied more and more upon federal financial aid. In the first half of the nineteenth century states avoided significant taxation and, in order to build railroads, canals and other public goods, they significantly increased borrowing not only in the US, but also in Europe, especially in the London money market. On the contrary, the federal government was able to pay all its debt and get a budget surplus, which it decided to transfer to the States. In 1837 a financial crisis hit the American economy and in 1840 a banking collapse obliged nine states (Arkansas, Florida, Illinois, Indiana, Louisiana, Maryland, Michigan, Mississippi and Pennsylvania) to default, between 1841 and 1842. Before defaulting, many states asked for a bail out from the federal government reckoning on the fact that foreign lenders expected an implicit guarantee of the federal government. Indeed, 'British investors ultimately argued forcefully that the debts carried an implicit federal guarantee, and placed immense pressure in the US federal government to assume state debts' (Rodden, 2006: 60). At the end of a passionate debate in Congress, the federal government decided not to assume the debts of the nine defaulting states for two main reasons: the bail out was considered by not indebted states as an unfair shifting of debt burdens, and the great majority of creditors were foreigners.

Looking at the first default of nine member states of the American federation we can better understand the concept of divided sovereignty, typical of a federal state. Thanks to the age in which it happened, the age of the gold standard or, better, of the gold and silver standard, the monetary problem was not a concern. Neither the single states nor the federal government could issue money to pay for the debts. The difference with the present European Union crisis is clear: in the age of fiat money the Central Bank cannot avoid being involved in the sovereign debt crisis. But the American federal government, even if it had no debt, was considered, by international financial markets, responsible for the states' solvency. The sovereignty muddle partly depended on the Constitution, partly on the relative power between states and the federal government, and partly on the position of the country in the international order. Since Europeans invested again in the American states in 1850, it seems fair to say that: 'resisting calls for assumption, the federal government established . . . that the states [were] truly sovereigns' (Rodden, 2006: 63). In fact, the American citizens experienced a condition of fiscal illusion, as if public goods were heaven-sent. After the debt crisis, the states started to levy direct taxes and to reform their constitutions, inserting the balanced budget rule, in order to increase their creditworthiness. Nevertheless, the states' sovereignty and federal government sovereignty were entering an uncertain and stormy phase. After the Civil War the balance between the states' power and federal power changed significantly during the industrialization phase and the new status of the US as a new world power in the international order. At the beginning of the twentieth century, the federal government markedly increased its power, thanks to the possibility of levying an income tax, the creation of the Federal Reserve System and its crucial military participation in World War I. In the years of the Great Depression, the Roosevelt administration concentrated many financial resources and expenses, especially welfare programmes, at the federal level. Today, we can affirm that the US is a federal state with a strong federal centre, since the federal government supports almost two thirds of the total expenses. Moreover, federal grants to states and local governments are more than 3 per cent of GDP or 17 per cent of total federal expenditure: according to the US Census Bureau, in 2009 state government revenue was composed of 47.8 per cent taxes and 32.0 per cent federal grants; moreover, while state government taxes fell by 8.5 per cent in 2009, during the financial crisis, federal grants increased by 13.0 per cent.

From these data we can infer that the state governments can hardly be considered sovereign, in the same sense in which we consider the US government sovereign. The role of grants in the US federal system is well explained by Wildasin, who remarks that if federal grants were abolished state governments should increase taxes, cut expenses or issue more debts. The federal government has some comparative advantage in borrowing: it can get lower interest rates on the internal and the international market. Therefore, it is convenient for state governments to rely on a federal government which, 'in effect, bundles together the loans of many lower-level governments into a single debt operation, disbursing the proceeds of its borrowing to the latter in the form of intergovernmental transfers' (Wildasin, 2004: 265). The high amount of federal grants in the US federation also blurs the distinction between soft and hard budget constraints. A government has to face the problem of a hard budget when, as a corporation, it can avoid bankruptcy (or default) only by drawing money from its own resources. If it can avoid default by drawing financial help from higher-level governments, its budget is soft. Therefore, even if in our century we cannot record major cases of state default in the US, it is inaccurate to ascribe this fact to the existence of hard budget constraints.

6.3 SOME INSTANCES OF HARD BUDGET CONSTRAINTS

In the next paragraph we shall discuss the atypical case of the European Union and its attempt to find an answer to Hamilton's Problem. Now it is useful to give a look at the hard budget constraints in some existing federations.

In Brazil, the 1988 constitution included 26 states and a federal district, Brasilia. The states and municipalities were responsible for a third of the revenue collected and 40 per cent of total public debt. The federal grants to the states were an important source of revenue for some states: in the 1990s Sao Paulo received 7 per cent of its revenue and Acre 75 per cent (Rodden, 2006: 193). In effect, according to the constitution state governments must provide some essential services to the population and they continuously bargain with the central government for grants and loans at low interest rates. From a political point of view, the federal government can be considered a coalition of state and local lobbies. In the 1980s the international debt crisis had a dramatic impact on Brazil. Since, during these years, the monetary policy of the central bank was inflationary, state governments were able to sustain their debt keeping the local salaries constant. But when the central bank launched a monetary plan to cut inflation, the states were unable to avoid real increases in salaries, pensions and debt obligations. Sao Paulo, Rio de Janeiro, Minas Gerais and Rio Grande do Sul, unable to pay up their debt, were obliged to default. The federal government accepted to assume state debts, which were in this way 'federalized.'

The German constitution allows the Länder limited powers of taxation, but unlimited powers of indebtedness. Tax revenues are shared by a constitutional formula between the Bund, the federal government and the Länder. Instead of a grant system similar to the American model, the German constitution establishes a fiscal equalization system, which redistributes revenues from wealthy to poor Länder according to parameters negotiated by the Länder and the federal government. In the 1980s the land of Saarland and the city of Bremen were hit by severe economic downturns, with high rates of unemployment. In Germany, every Länder must observe the self-imposed golden rule according to which borrowed money should be used only for investment plans. But Saarland and Bremen disregarded this constraint because of the dramatic economic crisis. In 1985, they asked the other Länder and the Bund for aid. Finally, they submitted their case for a bail out to the Constitutional Court, which in 1986 and again in 1992 decided that the federal government had the duty to aid the two distressed Länder, on the basis of a constitutional solidarity clause. Rodden rightly observes that in Brazil 'bailouts [were] a matter of political bargaining' while in Germany 'debt reduction for Saarland and Bremen was shaped by court decision more than interstate bargaining' and this difference matters, because 'the courts enhance bailout expectations primarily among the poorest and smaller states' (Rodden, 2006: 223–24) and not also for affluent states, as in Brazil.

India and China represent two other interesting models. India's constitution, approved in 1950, regulated the relationship between the central or union government and state governments. Indian states must provide and regulate essential services – such as public health, agriculture, education, water use and roads – and raise less than half of their revenue from their own resources. State revenues are between 5 and 6 per cent of GDP and expenditures are 16 per cent of GDP: the central government finances the difference. There are four kinds of federal grants. First, a Finance Commission establishes every five years how much to devolve to states as a share of taxes collected by the central government, for reasons of efficiency. The Commission does not establish general rules so that, even if population and per capita income are taken into consideration, a political evaluation of state needs is inevitable, especially for debt forgiveness. Second, the Planning Commission has the task of coordinating the development plans between the centre and the states, in order to reduce poverty and income inequalities among the states. Third, the federal government allows conditional grants, covering 50 to 80 per cent of the costs, for programmes concerning education, child nutrition, public works and so on. Fourth, the central government finances a share of the states' deficits. This system of intergovernmental transfers decreases the financial responsibility of the lower levels of government. 'States and municipalities are likely to assume that consequences of a potential default will not be catastrophic because partial bailout will be arranged by either creditors or senior levels of government' (McCarten, 2003: 264). In India, dramatic public default did not occur, but many local authorities experienced serious financial problems, which were resolved by higher levels of government. The hard budget constraint was made effective mainly by administrative machinery and not by the control of a capital market, which is rather underdeveloped in India. In conclusion, 'the Indian case suggests that hierarchical institutions alone are not an optimal mechanism for policing sub-national finances . . . should state fiscal problems appear intractable, a paternalistic central government will step into the shoes of state governments and provide adequate financial resources to resolve the problem' (McCarten, 2003: 282).

China is the last interesting case. China does not have a federal constitution and is not a democratic state, but the decisive reform of the late 1970s, which gave more fiscal power to local governments, contributed positively to its amazing growth (Weingast, 1995). Decentralization was regulated in the 1980s when central and sub-national governments decided to share fiscal revenue on the basis of a fixed quota. The peculiar Chinese system allows local authorities – provincial, municipal, county and township governments – full responsibility for collecting taxes and remitting a portion to higher level of government. This system produced a perverse effect because local authorities found ways to retain revenues, causing a decline in the central revenue as a percentage of the total. Moreover, local authorities collected many extra-budgetary revenues – tax surcharges, agricultural surcharges, funds from local agencies and state-owned enterprises (SOEs) – with the consequence that rich provinces raised more funds than poor provinces. To react to this dangerous trend, in 1994 the central government fostered a tax assignment reform. Some taxes were considered exclusive to the central government, such as tariff duties and income taxes on SOEs under the jurisdiction of the central government; some taxes – sales taxes and income taxes on SOEs under the control of the provincial governments – were considered exclusive to the provincial governments; and some taxes (including VAT and taxes on natural resources) were shared. Moreover, in order to strengthen the control of local spending, all budgets had to be in balance. This reform was quite effective: in 1993 the central share of the total revenue was 22 per cent; in 1994 it was 55.7 per cent. Nevertheless, it was difficult to control local revenues and expenses effectively because the habit of extra-budgetary revenues continued and the credit policy of the banking system was greatly affected by local authorities. These practices undermine central control and eventually lead to corruption. Local governments 'gained substantial control over the credit supply, which has become a source of soft budget constraint of local governments and SOEs, as well as inflation' (Jing Jin and Zou, 2003: 307). The tax system in China certainly needs new reforms, for instance to eliminate discrimination against domestic investors in favour of foreign ones and trade discrimination in favour of special economic zones. But the most important shortcoming is that 'a hard budget constraint on local governments and SOEs cannot be established until local governments and the banking sector are separated' (Jing Jin and Zou, 2003: 320).

The five cases here examined allow us to draw some final observations on fiscal federalism. Of course, Switzerland, Australia and Canada are other interesting cases, which should be studied to better understand how the hard budget constraint works. But our aim is only to compare the model of fiscal federalism set out in Kenneth Wheare's neat sentence and the historical realizations here recalled. According to Wheare, the governments in a federal state should be independent and coordinate: there is not a hierarchy among them and, therefore, each government must rely on its own financial resources to perform its functions. These very general conditions are not met in our five cases: we have seen that the central government has a clear advantage over state and local governments in the

US, Germany, Brazil, India and China. This observation is sufficient to understand why the notion of hard budget constraint is blurred even in the most ancient and structured federation of the world, the US. Some explanations can be found in a paper by Ronal McKinnon, who studies the four conditions for government hard budgets. These are as follow:

1) Borrowing to finance current account spending is not allowed.
2) Revenue from other governments, including grants from the central government, should be strictly delimited.
3) There must be free circulation across jurisdictions of goods, capital and people.
4) Restrictions on tax competition to attract capital and labour from other jurisdictions are not allowed. In this way, every government can levy taxes in its jurisdiction only to finance public goods or to provide general services to its citizens (taxpayers).

These four conditions are more or less adopted in some federations, but as far the central government is concerned, McKinnon remarks, 'Despite the fact that the Federal Reserve system may be quite independent in formulating monetary policy . . . the federal budget constraint is inherently soft relative to the budget constraints of the states' (McKinnon, 1997: 77).

The reason for this fundamental asymmetry of economic power among different levels of government in a federation is the concentration of the monetary policy and the fiscal policy in the hands of the central government. The existing federations share some of the main features of the nation state, which is the historical outcome of the coercion-extraction cycle. Therefore they, whatever their constitution, are obliged to compete in a world system of states with other nation states, equipped with the power to use monetary policy and fiscal policy as tools of foreign policy: for instance, they can exploit the rate of exchange to spur domestic exportations. Moreover, when a central government wishes to reduce its debt, it asks its central bank to print money so that the citizens are obliged to bear an inflation tax. The tacit acknowledgment of this reality is mirrored in the terminology defining the theory of fiscal federalism today: fiscal decentralization (for a survey see Oates, 2008). But, according to Wheare, a system of federal governments is neither decentralized nor centralized: the governments have to be independent and coordinate. The present practical and theoretical problem is therefore to look for the conditions to realize a true federal government. McKinnon clearly sees the essence of the problem when he says: 'The greater the separation between monetary and fiscal policies, the less likely governments will encroach on markets and the more likely that mercantile competition among them will enhance economic welfare' (McKinnon, 1997: 73). In the next paragraph we shall explore the European search for a new model of fiscal union to overcome the asymmetry among different levels of government.

6.4 HAMILTON'S PROBLEM AND EUROPE'S ANSWER

Before examining the measures adopted in Europe, we must point out some events leading to the Maastricht Treaty because the present difficulty of the EU in facing the financial crisis goes back to the political compromise between France and Germany of December 1991. After the demise of the Bretton Woods system and the economic crisis of the 1970s, the European Monetary System (EMS) established a zone of monetary stability in Europe in a world of floating currencies. But, even if the final goal was a fully-fledged monetary and economic union, the European governments continuously delayed the final step. The decisive event was the fall of the Berlin Wall in 1989 and German unification in 1990. In those years the unavoidable choice was: either a European Germany or a German Europe. Many European governments, but especially France, were extremely anxious about this perspective. The French President asked for a European Monetary Union. The German Chancellor Kohl proposed a project for 'A united Germany in a united Europe.' The German proposal included a political union too, not only a monetary union. But on the French side something went wrong. According to a keen witness of French politics: 'The entire art of French diplomacy during the negotiation leading to the Maastricht Treaty, signed in February 1992, consisted in achieving the monetary union without the political union Kohl wished.' (Toulemon, 2007: 28). It is likely that, even though the details of the Franco-German compromise have not been entirely disclosed, the French unwillingness to accept a political union was at the basis of the 'minimum government' of the EU decided at Maastricht. Tommaso Padoa-Schioppa, at that time Secretary of the Delors Committee for the establishment of the EMU, wrote: 'the market-oriented political philosophy of a hard adversary of the Community, such as Margaret Thatcher, contributed to point out the possible way to establish the single market and, with the same minimum government logic, it helped to hinder the proposals for integrating budget policies' (Padoa-Schioppa, 1992: xv).

The Maastricht Treaty can be considered an important step forward for European integration, but not big enough. Concerning public finance, in 1997, the European governments of the Eurozone agreed the Stability and Growth Pact (SGP), which sets only the upper limit of 3 per cent of GDP for the budget deficit and 60 per cent of GDP for the national debt. In other words, in the European Union money became a federal institution, but public finance remained a national responsibility. Moreover the SGP, in spite of its name, does not provide anything for the growth of the European economy. The budget of the EU, the tool to finance European public goods, was little more than 1 per cent of GDP before Maastricht and was not increased afterwards (on the contrary, many national governments tried to lower it to less than 1 per cent). From a political point of view it is inevitable to consider the Maastricht Treaty a missed opportunity. The fall of the Berlin Wall, the end of communist regimes and the urgent demand of Eastern European countries to enter the European Union fostered an atmosphere of reconciliation after decades of division. 'A political union founded on the ruins of the Berlin Wall, on the enthusiasm of liberation and close reunification of the entire Continent should have raised the support of young people' (Toulemon, 2007: 28). The *contradiction française*, says Toulemon, was the real cause of the missed opportunity. We can therefore understand why in the following years, after the enlargement of the union to 27 member states and the Union's inability to act in foreign policy and on the global market, a wave of euroscepticism spread through political parties and public opinion.

Although this book will go to press before the crisis of the European Union is over – and the danger of the breakdown of the EMU[1] under the attack of financial markets is concrete – here we try to outline the main guidelines of the reforms undertaken, to show that a new model of federal state is on the way. Of course, this model can be considered viable only if the EU survives. Our exercise however is not useless, because the problems here discussed are crucial for the creation of a world economic order founded on peaceful cooperation among national peoples and states. The European reactions to the financial crisis, which started seriously in Europe in October 2008, were imposed by the urgency to stop a leak and not by a comprehensive political design. The goal of a Fiscal Union was certainly not in the mind of the European leaders at the very beginning of the crisis. But, in the Council of December 2010, the heads of State and Government were obliged to declare: 'they stand ready to do whatever is required to ensure the stability of the euro area as a whole.' Since then, the Hegelian cunning of reason helped the disunited European governments to find a way out. If they continue along the way undertaken, a Fiscal Union and a Political Union will take shape alongside the EMU. Here, we first discuss the political backdrop beneath the reforms proposed and what they mean for the austerity policies, the EU budget and growth policies and, finally, the sovereign debt management.

The Political Backdrop

The European project is a work in progress because national governments did not surrender to the Union the powers required for its complete implementation. The integration among the peoples and states of Europe was gradual, slow and full of contradictions. Nonetheless, after every crisis European integration went ahead. Today, the EMU can be saved with a new step forward, the new surrendering of national sovereignty to the Union: the power to tax and to issue debt. This problem is more difficult to solve than the monetary problem. For the monetary problem at a certain point it was clear that the solution was to set up the ECB with the power to issue the euro; the national currencies had to be abandoned, like a sinking ship. For fiscal power the problem is more complex: national governments can preserve a share of their fiscal power, but in the meantime they should give more of this power to the Union. How much? The answer to this question depends on the degree of fiscal solidarity accepted by the peoples of the Union. Here a crucial difference comes into sight in comparison with the existing federations. The European Union is a Union of national states, which within their domestic institutions have already built the main framework of solidarity among fellow citizens, the welfare state. As a matter of fact, the degree of solidarity among fellow citizens is higher than among citizens of different nation states. The European debate, at the very beginning of the sovereign debt crisis, between Germany, the virtuous country, and Greece, the spendthrift country, revealed that the Germans were not disposed to support a transfer union, i.e. to bailout Greece for its giant debt, 160 per cent of GDP. The different behaviour of the Germans, as German citizens and European citizens, is consistent: in the 1990s the German federal government accepted to bail out the land of Saarland and the city of Bremen. Moreover, the citizens of Western Germany accepted to bail out the six Länders of Eastern Germany. The behaviour of the German citizens as European citizens – who do not want to bail out Greece – is perfectly understandable and coherent with the behaviour of the other citizens of the Union: nobody will accept to pay the debts of another state.

The Greek problem cannot be solved by the method the American federation used in 1848 when the federal government decided to let the nine states in financial distress default. In the years of the gold and silver standard there was a clear-cut distinction between monetary and financial policy. The default of the nine states was not a problem for American and world monetary stability; only the credibility of the nine states and of the federal government in the world financial market were under discussion. Today, in Europe, this clear-cut distinction between monetary and fiscal policy has not yet been admitted nor established. Many economists (for instance De Grauwe, 2011; Bradford DeLong, 2011) and some governments think that the ECB should intervene in the market by buying national bonds under attack, fully playing its role of lender of last resort, like the other central banks in the US and UK. This claim is partly reasonable, because the Lisbon Treaty does not foresee the orderly default of a member state of the EMU and the only way, so they think, to save a defaulting state is for the ECB to act as a lender of last resort, buying an unlimited quantity of bonds issued by the states under stress. Indeed this explains why the international financial market does not attack the US and the UK, which are much more indebted than the EU. But the unwillingness and prudence of the ECB is based on solid ground. The Maastricht Treaty established two fundamental pillars for monetary policy: the ECB 'in the exercise of its powers and for its finances shall be independent'. Moreover, 'the purchase directly from member states by the ECB or national central banks of debt instruments' is prohibited. The Lisbon Treaty fully resumes these two principles. Therefore, when the ECB helped Greece, Italy and Spain to face up to the assaults of international finance, it infringed the Treaty: its behaviour was justified only in the name of the superior duty of rescuing the EMU from collapse. The financial crisis ruthlessly showed the original sin on which the EMU was built.

Now let's consider the different measures adopted by the EU to face the crisis, remembering that the above mentioned principles were considered a policy guideline not only by the ECB but also by the governments, especially the German government. In taking into account the measures adopted, we do not follow a chronological order; we only attempt to show their coherence.

Austerity Policy

Under the pressure of the German government a new set of rules was adopted in order to reinforce the SGP or, following the terminology of the EU Council, the European governance. First of all, during the 'European semester,' when the member states prepare their national budget, the European Commission organizes national budgetary coordination, taking into account not only the macroeconomic financial framework, but also the benchmarks of economic imbalances, such as trade deficit and surplus, competitiveness imbalances, the organization of the labour market, and pension schemes. The Commission proposes a 'structured surveillance' of national budgets being aware that some member countries have incurred in huge debts because of mismanagement of the real economy. Secondly, a legal framework for surveillance of national reform programmes has been established, increasing the power of the Commission, which can ask member states for more information, warn a member state to correct its budgetary policy, charge a fine of 0.2 per cent GDP to Eurozone members which supply fraudulent statistics and, finally, it can sanction them with an interest-bearing deposit of 0.1 per cent GDP if they fail to act on recommendations. The aim of these measures is to give more bite to the SGP, so as to control deficits and debt levels better. The Council can reject the Commission's recommendations only with a qualified majority (reverse qualified majority voting).

The third measure is the establishment of the European Financial Stability Facility (EFSF), a kind of European monetary fund, which the ECB considers 'a framework which could provide temporary financial support to euro area countries, with the aim of providing bridge funding for a period of time needed to implement a deep adjustment programme to correct imbalances and regain market access' (ECB, 2011: 72). The EFSF was set up as a provisional means to grant financial assistance to distressed countries: in 2012 it will be substituted by the European Stability Mechanism (ESM), with a total capital of €700 billion and a lending capacity of €500 billion. This lending capacity was originally conceived to provide aid to member countries such as Ireland, Portugal, Spain and Greece. After the Italian crisis, the Council tried to increase its lending capacity to €1 trillion or more by means of some financial schemes.

The EFSF can be considered a financial tool for European solidarity among Eurozone member states. Indeed it can provide limited and conditional assistance for a short period, as the IMF does for the global economy. Moreover, it is already a kind of Eurobond since its capital is made up of shares of national public finance. The rate of interest on the loans of the EFSF will be the funding cost plus a charge of 200 basis points. Therefore, the cost of the loans for a distressed country is a little higher than the best rate quoted on the financial market but considerably lower than the rate the country should pay for its debt. These are the positive aspects of the EFSF (and the future ESM), but there are also some negative facets. The EFSF has a limited capacity to help distressed countries; when international finance doubts the financial credibility of states like Italy or France, the EFSF becomes inappropriate for the simple reason that its lending capacity depends on the credibility of the national financial good health of the states that should be helped. Therefore, it cannot be considered a substitute for a lender of last resort (only the ECB can play the role of lender of last resort in the Eurozone) or a substitute for sound finances in member states. It can provide only limited solidarity for a short period of time: if the crisis cannot be stopped with the EFSF, the default of the distressed country becomes the inevitable final outcome.

Sovereign Debt Management

As already mentioned, the US and the UK have ratios of deficit and debt to GDP worse than those of the EU as a whole. But the Eurozone member states with high indebtedness, like Greece, Portugal and Italy, risk a default (for Ireland and Spain the main problem was a banking crisis). To some extent this is a liquidity problem, because Greece, Portugal and Italy are not able to renew their debt in the financial markets without paying high interest rates. And, when the interest rate is too high (more than the growth rate), sooner or later insolvency becomes inevitable. A solution to this problem is the issue of Eurobonds by a European agency with a joint guarantee of the Eurozone countries. At present Germany opposes this project saying that German bonds can be issued at a lower rate of interest. Meanwhile the European Commission (2011c) has revealed that a proposal for 'stability bonds' is under way. Here it is enough to say that the European Stability Mechanism (ESM) can easily evolve into a European Agency for issuing Eurobonds, by pooling together a share of the national sovereign debts. The German opposition is without grounds for two reasons. The first is that if only a precautionary share of debt to GDP is issued – say 60 per cent – by the European agency, every member state issuing more debts will probably be obliged to pay higher interest rates because of the higher risk the investors must bear in buying national bonds. Therefore national governments are pushed to reduce their indebtedness to the European average. The second reason is that the Eurobonds issue will create a financial market in Europe comparable to the US financial market, thus rendering the EU, with its currency and financial system, able to compete on a level playing field with the US and the dollar. Moreover, if the European monetary policy is really independent of fiscal policy, in the long run international financial investors, including the wealth sovereign funds, will certainly prefer the more stable monetary area. Eurobonds are not the average of national bonds: they are supranational bonds. With Eurobond the euro becomes a global money and the EU can take part, as an authoritative global player, in the new multipolar economic order.

Growth Policy and the EU Budget

Usually the budget of the EU is considered too small to play a meaningful role in European economic policy. In effect even during the European semester, the European Commission focuses its attention on national budgets without considering the relationship with the EU budget. However the EU budget, even though small – but later on we shall argue about it being increased – can be a powerful tool to spur the growth of European economy.

If compared with national budgets, which in the EU are 45 to 50 per cent of GDP, the EU budget is economically meaningless, but we should bear in mind that in practice all welfare and military expenses are included in national budgets and today, after the financial crisis and the new huge deficits, they are the main cause of national financial crises. On the contrary, the EU budget finances European public goods, which are becoming more and more strategic for the recovery and sustainable growth of the European economy. Let us consider the European Commission strategic plan 'Europe 2020'. Here we cannot give a full account of the plan. Suffice it to describe the main aim of the project Connecting Europe Facility (EC, 2011a), which is crucial for the completion of the single market and for the sustainable growth strategy. The sectors involved are transport connections, electricity grids and broadband networks; they are vital for a functioning, integrated economic area and for its social and territorial cohesion. The investments required and included in the next multi-annual financial framework for the period 2014–2020 are: €1 trillion for energy infrastructures; €500 billion for transport; €270 billion for telecommunication networks. These investments are European public goods because without them many national investments will not be made. The EU budget has therefore a strong multiplier effect, by facilitating and attracting other public and private financing projects.

How can the European Commission finance this ambitious plan of investments with the small EU budget at its disposal? The answer is in a further project called the Europe 2020 Project Bond Initiative. This initiative is based on the observation that the projects under discussion have a low or zero revenue but are nonetheless of great public interest. Therefore they need grants in all stages of their life.

> Public funds from the EU – says the European Commission – coupled with the participation of financial intermediaries, especially public development banks, can bring together the demand for long-term finance with private investors with long term orientation but low appetite for risk. The idea is to use appropriations from the EU budget to support projects to the extent required to enhance their credit rating, and thereby attract financing from other sources, including private capital market investors . . . The EU budget contribution will be capped ex ante . . . The support would be available during the lifetime of the project, including during the construction phase, which is usually the riskiest part of a project, but would not exceed 20% of the senior debt.
>
> (EC, 2011b)

This short review of the problems of the EU budget is inadequate to give a description of the main problems, especially the lack of efficiency and democracy, concerning EU budget policy. In a wide and well-grounded study three European members of the European Parliament, Haug, Lamassoure and Verhofstadt (2011: 3) state that: 'the European Parliament, while directly elected by European citizens, has no say in the decision on EU resources: according to the Treaty, the European Parliament and the Council of Ministers share the budgetary power . . . but only as regards spending.' The main problem of the EU budget is that of the so-called 'own resources,' of which more than 75 per cent are paid for by member states. These are the main cause of the pernicious practice of 'fair return' according to which every national government claims back the money it paid to the Union. In their study the three authors state: 'The financing system of the European Union is today on its legs. A radical change of its orientation is necessary if we want the EU budget to be reconciled with the solidarity role it should play, to prepare the ground for a strong economic recovery as well as to give the EU the means to properly address future challenges' (Haug et al, 2011). Indeed the aftermath of the financial crisis and the sovereign debt crisis have created a bulk of partial reforms, sometimes off the cuff, which today require a fully-fledged overhaul of the Lisbon Treaty. During the crisis Germany played the role of stabilizer. Indeed, Europe needs more than a stabilizer; it needs a federal government.

Finally, even if the European crisis is certainly not over, we can compare the European fiscal union under way with the existing federations. If we look to the US as a reference point, the main difference is that the EU implemented a kind of European Monetary Fund (the ESM), which does not exist in the US. This new institution is the key to understanding a more general problem. The EU is a Union of national peoples while the US is a nation of peoples organized on the basis of federal rules. It is likely that the degree of solidarity among the member states of the EU will remain at a lower level than that existing in the US, where every citizen shares national values. This means that the EU budget, even if it is increased, will never reach the amount of the US federal budget. If we include the military expenses, today financed by national budgets, and allow for more finance for expenses on research and sustainable development, we can reach the size of 3 to 4 per cent of GDP for the EU budget. In any case it is legitimate to say that the EU is a lean (or light) federation, very different from the existing federations. Moreover the relationship between monetary policy and fiscal policy in the EU is different from those present in existing federations. At Maastricht, as we said, the principle of independence of the ECB was agreed and stated in the Treaty. Today this principle is at risk because the ECB must buy national sovereign debts in the market to avoid the default of some member states and the collapse of the EMU. Nevertheless the determination of Germany to defend the principle that the ESM must have limited financial resources and that the ECB should maintain its commitment to the 'no bail out' clause is based on sound grounds. The central bank in a monetary union has the power to cause, with an inflationary policy, not only a vertical transfer of income – from different classes and ranks of the population – but also a horizontal transfer of income from one country to another. Country A with low or zero indebtedness is in principle damaged by an inflationary process; on the contrary, Country B with a great public debt welcomes the inflationary process, because it can turn financial repression to its advantage. But why should the citizens of Country A pay for Country B's excessive indebtedness? If the horizontal transfer of income is huge and manifest to all citizens, the monetary union will collapse sooner or later. Therefore the general rule is that the monetary policy should be independent of fiscal policy and the best guarantee of central bank independence is that fiscal policy should be independent from private finance. States and governments of course need some flexibility for their budget: to borrow money from their citizens is of course a legitimate and appropriate policy for long-term investments. But if they exceed some precautionary limits, which unfortunately are difficult to define in advance (see Cecchetti et al, 2011), they put their future and that of the Union at risk. To conclude, the model of fiscal union, which is under way in Europe, is institutionalizing the divorce between monetary policy and fiscal policy: the opposite direction of the historical coercion-extraction cycle described by Finer. The European Union is not only a lean federation; it is a new model[2] of a federal state; it is a supranational federal union.

6.5   A WORLD ECO-MONETARY UNION

The history of European integration and the drama of the sovereign debt crisis show how difficult it is for a group of national people to build their Union and keep it alive. Therefore a World Eco-Monetary Union (WEMU) can be considered a bold and even foolhardy project. But two good reasons prompt the sketching out what is today discussed under the general label of world governance in a more precise blueprint. The first reason is the urgent need to face the ecological crisis and to overcome the outrageous divide between the rich and the poor. The second reason is that the European supranational experience has already pointed the way and the dangers that should be avoided in order to build supranational institutions.[3]

Luckily, within the worldwide debate on sustainable development a general agreement exists concerning the need for a group of industrialized countries to take the lead for a big step forward. The WMU must precede the WEMU: a strong institutional link among a leading group of countries is the basis for the construction of a stronger union in which all the peoples of the world – with strong contrasting interests – must participate. An agreement is also emerging on the need to conceive a plan that integrates ecological sustainability with international justice, i.e. the fight against extreme poverty.

This perspective deserves a short historical remark. Underdevelopment was discussed after World War II as a problem concerning the so-called Third World. In 1964, in Geneva, during the United Nations Conference on Trade and Development (UNCTAD) the Group of 77 (now 131) developing countries launched a plan for a New International Economic Order (NIEO) to oppose the old economic order based on the GATT and IMF. After the end of the Cold War, a more cooperative order was possible, but the survival of the Group of 77 in the UN shows that the great divide between rich and poor countries is still unresolved. On the other hand, the environmental problem was not on the agenda of international politics during the first decades after World War II. Only in 1972 the UN Conference on Human Environment organized a meeting in Stockholm based on the report *Only One Earth*, thus opening a worldwide debate on the impact of human economic activities on natural resources. In 1987 the World Commission on Environment and Development, headed by Gro Harlem Brundtland, presented a report focused on the notion of sustainable development conceived as 'the development that meets the needs of the present without compromising the ability of future generations to meet their own needs.' This definition encloses the idea of the needs of poor people and the limits of environmental resources to satisfy present and future needs of human populations. After the Brundtland Report the way was open for a policy integrating the fight against extreme poverty and an eco-friendly economy but for at least two decades the two policies ran on different tracks.

Convergence towards a shared sustainable global policy was made easier by three factors. The first was public opinion's progressive support for the scientific findings, worked out mainly by the Intergovernmental Panel on Climate Change (IPCC), showing that human economic activities are the main cause of climate change and environmental degradation. There is now a consensus on the global goal of restricting rising global temperatures to not more than 2°C of the pre-industrial age. This goal will require the reduction of global emissions by at least half by 2050 from the 1990 levels. Initially, acceptance of this global goal fostered the proposal of absolute emissions reductions (of CO_2) in every country. This proposal opened a difficult but constructive debate among developed and developing countries. Brazil, China and other emerging economies raised the problem of the historical responsibility of industrialized countries, which for more than two centuries polluted the atmosphere and the entire planet. Therefore, and that is the second factor to consider – equity – the developing world should bear the greater part of the mitigation and adaptation costs: high-income countries must transfer funds to developing countries to provide assistance for mitigation and adaptation. The third factor is the development of a theoretical framework to integrate the notions of sustainability and equity: the human development index (HDI). According to the Human Development Report, 'Human development is the expansion of people's freedoms and capabilities to lead lives that they value and have reason to value. It is about expanding choices. Freedoms and capabilities are more expansive notions than basic needs' (UNDP, 2011: 1). This report remarks that environmental degradation will be especially harmful to poor people. Developed countries have more power and income available to face the damage. Degradation of productive lands and water, deforestation and desertification are a direct danger for developing countries. Therefore the burden of environmental degradation and climate change is likely to widen the gap in standards of living between the rich and the poor. If we consider environmental deprivation for cooking fuel, clean water and basic sanitation then 'these absolute deprivations are major violations of human rights' (UNDP, 2011: 5).

Until now the main global policy adopted by the UN is the Kyoto Protocol (1997). It came into force in 2005 and now includes 184 parties, but some very important polluters, such as the US, China and India, did not accept the Protocol. The target of the Kyoto Protocol was to reduce greenhouse gas emissions, by means of a system of cap and trade, to the levels of 1990 by the year 2000. Since developing countries did not accept an absolute cap to their carbon emissions, which would have hindered their development, a Clean Development Mechanism (CDM) was set up to allow developed countries to finance mitigation policies in developing countries: in order to lower global emissions the required investments can be made everywhere. Today everybody admits the failure of the Kyoto initiative. Greenhouse gas emissions have increased by 25 per cent since 1997 and the CDM has brought little improvement in the overall development strategies. A radical overhaul is now under way in the UN. Here, our task is not to consider the details of the issue, but simply to take into account the financial efforts at stake: how it is possible to provide and manage the resources required.

The IPCC calculates that the cost of cutting greenhouse gas emissions by half by 2050 is 1 to 3 per cent of GDP. This does not mean that all the cost should be borne by the public sector; on the contrary, the private sector should give a substantial contribution. According to the World Bank (2010: 257), in developing countries mitigation could cost $140–175 billion a year over the next 20 years and adaptation investments could cost $30–100 billion a year over the period 2010–2050. At present, says the report, funding for mitigation and adaptation are fully inadequate: they are less than 5 per cent of the projected needs. Also the UNDP provides some estimation of the total cost for mitigation and adaptation. The mitigation cost (the investment needed to reduce concentrations of greenhouse gases), is 0.2–1.2 per cent per year of GDP by 2030. The total annual mitigation and adaptation costs to address climate change by 2030 are $249 – 1,371 billion by 2030. The report remarks:

'The amounts needed are clearly large, if uncertain. But they are below current spending on defence, on recent financial sector bailouts and on perverse subsidies . . . In 2009 global military expenditure neared 3% of world GDP, while some countries spent much more, including the United States (4.7% of GDP) and the Russian Federation (4.3% of GDP). The bailouts in the wake of the recent financial crisis . . . [in USA and EU] . . . were about 6% of annual GDP in both cases'. (UNDP, 2011, 92)

How to finance this cost? The UNDP report suggests two ways. The first is the use of the IMF Special Drawing Rights. But this proposal is not in agreement with the main economic policy proposed here. The monetary financing of mitigation and adaptation costs will create a kind of soft world budget causing a potential clash among members with a different propensity to inflation. The cohesion of the World Monetary Union will be at risk if the agreed inflation target is not fulfilled. The second proposal is a currency transaction tax, which will be progressive as the countries with larger currency transactions tend to be more developed. A rate of 0.01–0.05 per cent could generate nearly €200 billion a year in the EU and $650 billion at the global level. The World Bank suggests two other fiscal resources: taxes on tradable permits and a global carbon tax. In both cases the amount needed can be attained, but these proposals run into serious political hostility. 'Proposals for a national administered but globally levied carbon tax have the appeal that the tax base would be broad and the revenue flow fairly secure' (World Bank, 2010: 270). Moreover a carbon tax will create a global price for carbon fuels, which is a crucial reference for spurring innovation in the alternative energy sector. Nevertheless, 'the main drawback is that an international coordinated tax could impinge on the tax authority of sovereign governments. Gaining international consensus for this option may thus be difficult' (WB, 2010: 270).

There is a straightforward way to overcome this difficulty: to provide the WEMU with a budget, the power to raise global taxes and to spend its own financial resources (a more ambitious alternative is to provide the UN with its own budget, widening the scope of the budget beyond the economic sphere). The failure of the Kyoto initiative should teach national governments a lesson. It is basically impossible to overcome the free rider problem without creating supranational institutions. The creation of a budget at the disposal of the WEMU by means of an international treaty is tantamount to entrust a world 'governance' with the financial tools necessary to face mitigation and adaptation costs. The size of this budget should be more or less that of the EU budget, that is 1 per cent of world GDP. The advantage of this decision is that every national government accepts, once and for all, to finance in advance the necessary global policies and that there is an administrative body (the Council of the WEMU) responsible and accountable for the implementation of the policies.

The prompt objection to this proposal is that no national government is ready to give up its fiscal sovereignty to a world organization. Nevertheless this objection only considers the formal aspect of the problem but not the gist of the issue at stake. Every national government should not forget the existence of a global integrated financial market. Vito Tanzi (2000 and 2011: 140) reminds us that some voracious fiscal termites are already at work lowering the capacity of national government to collect taxes significantly. The main global fiscal termites are multinational companies, which can easily manipulate transfer prices; off-shore financial centres and tax havens, which can lodge legal financial entities, as off-shore trusts, and illegal entities devoted to money laundering and tax evasion; economic activities conducted outside the countries of residence and fiscal competition among national governments which causes their growing inability and often unwillingness to tax financial capital and individual income with high tax rates. The fiscal termites are certainly at work, but it is difficult to quantify how great the damage is.

There is a lively debate on the effect of globalization on the fiscal revenues of states and income distribution. At present it is only possible to hypothesize some very general trends. In an interesting paper Hines and Summers assume that the future impact of globalization on national tax systems can be inquired by looking at the behaviour of small countries because 'globalization means that in some sense all countries are becoming smaller.' They find evidence showing that 'since the early 1980s, countries with less open economies (as measured by ratios of exports plus imports to GDP) have relied more heavily on income taxes than countries with more open economies.' As far as corporate taxes are concerned, the evidence is 'that smaller countries collect significantly less corporate tax revenue as fractions of total taxes' (Hines and Summers, 2009: 142). Their general conclusion is that 'governments of countries with smaller and more open economies rely less on personal and corporate income taxes, and more on expenditure and trade taxes, than other governments do.' The consequences on income distribution are straightforward: 'In practice many expenditure taxes are considerably less progressive than income tax alternatives, so movement away from income taxation and in the direction of greater expenditure taxation is typically associated with less equal after-tax distribution of income' (Hines and Summers, 2009: 151). This observation reinforces our findings from Chapter 3 on increasing global inequalities. If this trend is confirmed, one can expect the welfare system in developed countries to become subject to stress in the near future. At present (but on the basis of studies carried out before the financial crisis) the evidence is that in OECD countries the total tax revenues do not endanger the welfare system of developed countries even if, since 1980s, a clear decline in corporate tax rate is evident in OECD countries: 'Average corporate tax rates exceeded 40 per cent through the mid 1980s, at which point they began declining . . .reaching 33 per cent by 2002' (Hines, 2006: 337). But the share of corporate tax collections in OECD countries did not decline over the same decades because corporate tax bases increased, thanks to the increased volume of international investments. Since corporate taxes are only 3.96 per cent of tax revenues (as a share of GDP) in OECD countries the bulk of welfare expenditure is financed by personal income taxes and social insurance contributions. Therefore, even if tax competition eventually erodes the revenues from corporation taxes, other revenue sources will be available to compensate the falls. Nevertheless, the preservation of the welfare state becomes more difficult because of the shift of taxation towards indirect taxes, which are more regressive than personal taxes. Here a difference between European continental countries and liberal welfare countries is apparent. Poverty rates are twice as high in the UK and Canada as they are in Scandinavian countries and roughly three times as high in the US (Gatti and Glyn, 2006: 308). It is very difficult to preserve welfare expenses in developing countries (non-OECD), where corporate taxes are 2.54 per cent of GDP, personal income taxes only 1.21 per cent and expenses on social insurance contributions 3.15 per cent. In developing countries, where the welfare state is in its infancy, international fiscal competition[4] and the fall in corporate taxes are a hopeless plight. The conclusion is that the WEMU, endowed with the power to tax, will be a crucial tool to help developed countries to stop the work of fiscal termites, and it will also be a crucial tool to help developing countries to build their welfare state. In a global market the national power to tax is sentenced to dry up.

Ultimately, it may be useful to examine how the WEMU project can fit into the theory of public finance. As we have already said, the

WEMU can be considered an institutional tool to implement a world plan for sustainable development, taking away the free rider hindrance from international politics. The power to tax is crucial to implement its policies. Let's consider these World Bank remarks: 'stabilizing temperatures will require a global mitigation effort. At that point carbon will have a price worldwide and will be traded, taxed, or regulated in all countries.' A carbon tax is crucial to achieve this result, but it is not sufficient.

> 'Some activities, such as risky research and development or energy-efficiency improvements, are hindered by market or regulatory failures; others, such as urban planning, are not directly price sensitive. The forest and agriculture sectors present significant additional potential for emission reduction and sequestration in developing countries but are too complex, with intricate social issues, to rely exclusively on market incentives. Many climate actions will require complementary finance and policy interventions'.
>
> (WB, 2010: 271)

These remarks point out that a world supranational authority should not only have the power to tax but also to regulate many economic activities, which provoke negative externalities if regulated only at a national level. As far as the financial market is concerned, we already upheld the case (in Chapter 5) for a world supervisory authority, endowed with some financial power. But, as we noticed, sustainable development requires a larger regulatory scope. The experience of the European Union shows that European regulations, enforced by the European Court of Justice, were required to build the single European market and for a number of policies, especially for the protection of the environment. Indeed, some scholars maintain that the European Union is a regulating power or a regulating state (Majone, 1996). This task is new and its seriousness is increasing for all governments because of the development of modern technologies and world economic integration. All governments, at every level, and especially at world level, have the duty 'to protect citizens against an increasing number of risks and to assume more responsibilities. This battle has (directly) less to do with redistribution and much more to do with risk prevention,' says Vito Tanzi (2011: 325), who also remarks that the idea that the market system will provide all the information required by the citizens to protect their health and their welfare are no longer true, contrary to what Hayek assumed. The citizens should be properly informed about the unperceived or concealed risks concerning the environment, drugs, food, cars, travel, and many other goods, services and products. Asymmetries in information, ex ante, permeate the modern global market. In this world, 'free-rider problems are very important and the free riders may be whole nations. This is an area in which the absence of a world government, or at least a global institution with the power to require and enforce changes, makes the solution more difficult' (Tanzi, 2011: 327).

Now we have gathered all the elements required for a general assessment of the WEMU in the theory of public finance. Richard Musgrave (1998) provides a very useful classification of pairings of state and fiscal theory: the service state, the welfare state, the communal state and the flawed state. As far as our WEMU is concerned, we can discard the welfare state, which is a national institution for the redistribution of income among citizens. The communal state holds mainly a historical interest, since the German finance school conceived the state as an organic body and a positive force in itself, independent and above individuals. Finally, the flawed state is focused on public sector failure. Here we are interested in the service state, which Musgrave derives directly from Adam Smith, who observed that the market cannot provide public institutions, public works and even basic education for poor people. Therefore, the notion of the service state includes assistance for the deserving poor, which is one of the global public goods provided by the WEMU. Moreover, the WEMU should also have the power to regulate the global economy: it is therefore not only a service state but also a regulating state.

These remarks do not exhaust the topic. We should not forget that the WEMU is not a centralized world government; it is not a world Leviathan; it is only a supranational institution necessary to avoid the free rider problem, when national cooperation fails. The WEMU is a federal institution because it is the highest level of a world multi-level government system, the other levels are the nations or the regional unions, like the EU, and the sub-national governments, regions, provinces and municipalities. Federal institutions are necessary to provide a hard budget constraint at all government levels (and to solve Hamilton's Problem). Federalism is the bulwark against market fundamentalism and government activism (or statism). From this perspective, our efforts to shape the main institutional framework for monetary policy and fiscal policy yielded the economic backbone of a world cosmopolitan constitution. This achievement is important but certainly not sufficient to guarantee the future of humankind if it is not completed with political institutional reforms. Cosmopolitan institutions cannot work, in our age, without the support of people. In other words, a cosmopolitan democracy should become the ideal for anyone looking for a better human condition.

NOTES

1. The original meaning of the acronym EMU was 'Economic and Monetary Union' but, since the goal of the Economic Union was completely forgotten for many years in European politics, today everybody thinks that the meaning of EMU is simply 'European Monetary Union.'

2. The principle of independence of monetary policy from fiscal policy and vice versa is central to understanding the problems of bailout and hard budget constraints. The power of a federal central government to refuse to bail out a local government is of course reduced if the central government can oblige a central bank to finance its budget. In such a case we can say, as McKinnon rightly remarks, that the central government has a soft budget. Robert Inman discusses the problems of fiscal decentralization and the bailout strategy by means of the prisoner's dilemma game. Inman expounds a game in which 'the local elected representative chooses either to support the legislative action 'shift,' which provides benefits to its citizens while shifting a fraction of the costs of those benefits to the citizens of all other sub-national governments, or the legislative action 'no shift,' which provides the benefits without shifting any of the associated costs' (Inman 2003: 40). The strategy of the game is that the box 'no shift, no shift' – the cooperative solution – is not chosen. The outcome of the game is that all local governments adopt the cost-shifting strategy and receive the socially inefficient payoff.

   This picture describes why the existing federations, which adopt the national principle of centralizing monetary and fiscal power and therefore have a soft central budget constraint, face great difficulties in denying bailouts to local governments fairly well. But if, as in the European Union, the monetary and fiscal policies are independent both of central (federal) governments and of all other levels of government, the bailout becomes a cost clearly felt by the entire community, i.e. all member states. Since this cost should be shared among different countries with different degrees of indebtedness, the resistance of the not-indebted country to a bailout is strong and the indebted countries are, in the last resort, obliged to default. In such a case, to utilize the Inman example, the pay-offs of the game change. It could be easily shown that if the default becomes a realistic possibility, the pay-offs of the box 'shift, shift' can assume a negative value, and a new game can be built in which the box 'no-shift, no-shift' becomes the cooperative solution.

   These remarks are useful to clarify the principle of hard budget constraints. In order to have a sub-central government fully responsible for the revenues and expenses of its jurisdiction, it is necessary for all the other governments to be equally responsible. For instance, in the European Union every level of government – local, regional, national and European – should comply with the budgetary rule 'close to balance,' established in the Stability and Growth Pact. This means that the European federal government – after the reform of the Lisbon Treaty – should have the power, like every other government of the Union, to issue bonds and to have budget deficits, of course in compliance with the SGP.

3. Deep-rooted prejudices in political and academic quarters hinder a calm debate on these issues. For instance in a paper called *The Future of Fiscal Federalism*, Vito Tanzi observed that it was necessary to consider the theory of fiscal federalism not only as a technique to decentralize the financial policy of a central government but also as a means to build a supranational public finance for world institutions. He remarked: 'Some public goods, being global, require global rather than national financing. It is not too farfetched to assume that the globalizing world would need a global government (or a proxy for one) in the same way in which governments were needed in nations.' (Tanzi, 2008: 709). But Roland Vaubel harshly opposed this point of view arguing that 'a global government would be a world monopolist.' Vaubel thinks that a world government is nothing but a world Leviathan because 'the centralization of policy making undermines individual freedom, democracy and efficiency' (Vaubel, 2009).

4. It is necessary to distinguish between fiscal competition in a federal framework and fiscal competition in the global economy. As we said previously, in a federal closed

state or in a world federation, fiscal competition among different governments means horizontal competition and vertical competition among public powers: the outcome is hard budget constraints for all levels of government. In the global economy, without a federal constitution, the outcome of fiscal competition can be completely different: national governments simply lose their power to tax in favour of the market: wealthy individuals, multinational corporations and private financial institutions. Jeffry Sachs observes: 'When capital becomes international mobile, countries begin to compete for it. They do this by offering improved profitability compared with other countries, for example, by cutting corporate tax rates, easing regulations, tolerating pollution, or ignoring labor standards.' The final outcome is that: 'all countries lose in the end, since all end up losing the tax revenues and regulations needed to manage the economy. The biggest loser ends up being internationally immobile labor, which is likely to face higher taxation to compensate for the loss of taxation on capital' (Sachs, 2011: 94–5). On the contrary, in a federation, like the US, fiscal competition can be mitigated by the federal structure of the state. Tax collection may be more convenient at the federal level rather than at the state level. 'The fifty states are in competition with one another for businesses and wealthy citizens. . . The race to the bottom among the states can be obviated in part by unified federal tax collection that is then returned to the states so that they can implement programs that are tailored to each state's needs' (Sachs, 2011: 227).

References

Abbas, S. A., N. Belhocine, A. El Ganainy and M. Horton (2010), 'A historical public debt database', IMF working paper WP/10/245.

Adalet, M. and B. Eichengreen (2007), 'Current account reversal: always a problem?', in R. H. Clarida (ed.), *G7 Current Account Imbalances: Sustainability and Adjustment*, Chicago, IL: Chicago University Press.

Albertini, M. (1960), *Lo Stato Nazionale (The Nation State)*, Milan, Italy: Giuffré, reprinted in N. Mosconi (ed), *Mario Albertini: Tutti gli Scritti (Collected Writings)*, vol. III, Bologna, Italy: Il Mulino.

Alessandrini, P. and M. Fratianni (2009a), 'Dominant currencies, special drawing rights, and supernational bank money', *World Economics*, **10** (4), 45–67.

Alessandrini, P. and M. Fratianni (2009b), 'Resurrecting Keynes to stabilize the international monetary system', *Open Economy Review*, 339–58.

Alexander, S. S. (1952), 'Effects of a devaluation on a trade balance', *IMF Staff Papers*, **2** (2), 263–78.

Aliber, R. (1966), The Future of the Dollar as an International Currency, New York: Frederick Praeger.

Anderson, J. E. (1979), 'A theoretical foundation for the gravity equation', *American Economic Review*, **69** (1), 106–16.

Anderson, J. E. and E. Van Wincoop (2003), 'Gravity with gravitas: a solution to the border puzzle', *American Economic Review*, **93** (1), 170–92.

Archibugi, D. (2008), *The Global Commonwealth of Citizens: Toward Cosmopolitan Democracy*, Princeton, NJ: Princeton University Press.

Archibugi, D. and G. Montani (eds) (2011), *European Democracy and Cosmopolitan Democracy*, Ventotene, Italy: The Altiero Spinelli Institute for Federalist Studies.

ASEAN (2008), *ASEAN Economic Community Blueprint*, Jakarta: ASEAN.

Aslund, A. (2007), *Russia's Capitalist Revolution*, Washington, DC: Peterson Institute for International Economics.

Astley, M., J. Giese, M. Hume and C. Kubelec (2009), 'Global Imbalances and the Financial Crisis', *Bank of England Quarterly Bulletin*, **49** (3), 178–90.

Author, D. H., F. Levy and R. J. Murname (2001), 'The skills content of recent technological change: an empirical exploration', NBER working paper series (8837).

Bairoch, P. (1993), *Economics and World History: Myths and Paradoxes*, Harmondsworth: Penguin Books.

Balassa, B. (1967), 'Trade creation and trade diversion in the European common market', *Economic Journal*, **77**, 1–21.

Balassa, B. (1976), 'Types of economic integration', in F. Machlup (ed), *Economic Integration Worldwide, Regional, Sectoral*, London: Macmillan.

Barraclough, G. (1979), *An Introduction to Contemporary History*, Harmondsworth: Penguin Books.

Barrett, S. (2007), *Why Cooperate? The Incentive to Support Global Public Good*, Oxford: Oxford University Press.

Barroso, J. M. D. (2011), 'European renewal: state of the union address 2011', Speech given at Strasbourg, France, 28 September.

Barth, J., J. Tatom and G. Yago (2009), *China's Emerging Financial Markets: Challenges and Opportunities*, New York and London: Springer.

Berg, A. G. and J. D. Ostry (2011), 'Inequality and unsustainable growth: two sides of the same coin?', IMF staff discussion note, **11** (08), 1–20.

Bergh, A. and T. Nilsson (2010), 'Do liberalization and globalization increase world inequality?', *European Journal of Political Economy*, **26** (4), 488–505.

Bergsten, F. C. (2002), 'The euro vs the dollar: will there be a struggle for dominance?', *Journal of Policy Modeling*, **24**, 307–14.

Bergsten, F. C. (2009), 'The dollar and deficits: how Washington can prevent the next crisis', *Foreign Affairs*, **88** (6), 20–38.

Bergstrand, J. H. (1985), 'The gravity equation in international trade: some microeconomic foundations and empirical evidence', *The Review of Economic and Statistics*, **67** (3), 474–81.

Berkmen, S. P. (2011), 'The impact of fiscal consolidation and structural reforms on growth in Japan', IMF working paper WP/11/13.

Bernanke, B. S. (2005), 'The global saving glut and the U.S. current account deficit', *The Federal Reserve Board*, 10 March.

Bird, G. (2001), 'IMF programs: do they work? Can they be made to work better?', *World Development*, **29** (11), 1849–65.

Blanchard, O. and G. M. Milesi-Ferretti (2009), 'Global imbalances: in midstream?', *IMF Staff Position Note*, **29**.

Blanchard, O., F. Giavazzi and F. Sa (2005), 'The U.S. current account and the dollar', NBER working paper series 11137.

Blankenburg, S. and J. G. Palma (2009), 'Introduction: the global financial crisis', *Cambridge Journal of Economics*, **33**, 531–38.

Blejer, M. I. and T. Ter-Minassian (eds) (1997), *Macroeconomic Dimensions of Public Finance: Essays in Honor of Vito Tanzi*, London: Routledge.

Bobbio, N. (1985), *Stato, Governo, Società: Per una Teoria Generale della Politica (State, Government, Society: For a General Theory of Politics)*, Turin, Italy: Einaudi.

Bollè, P. (2008), 'Inequalities and financial globalization: a timely report', *International Labour Review*, **147** (4), 433–38.

Bordo, M. D. (1999), *The Gold Standard and Related Regimes: Collected Essays*, Cambridge: Cambridge University Press.

Bordo, M. D. (2000), 'The International Monetary Fund: its present role in historical perspective', NBER working paper series 7724.

Bordo, M. D. and H. James (2008), 'A long term perspective on the euro', NBER working paper series 13815, 1–34.

Bordo, M. D. and L. Jonung (1997), 'The history of monetary regimes including monetary unions: some lessons for Sweden and EMU', *Swedish Economic Policy Review*, **4** (2), 285–358.

Bordo, M. D. and C. M. Meissner (2005), 'The role of foreign currrency debt in financial crises', NBER working paper series 11897.

Bordo, M. D., C. M. Meissner and D. Stuckler (2009), 'Foreign currency debt, financial crises and economic growth: a long run view', NBER working paper series 15534, 1–48.

Bordo, M. D. and H. Rockoff (1999), 'The gold standard as a "Good Housekeeping seal of approval"', in M. D. Bordo (ed), *The Gold Standard and Related Regimes: Collected Essays*, Cambridge: Cambridge University Press, 318–63.

Bordo, M. D. and E. N. White (1999), 'A tale of two currencies: British and French finance during the Napoleonic wars', in M. D. Bordo (ed), *The Gold Standard and Related Regimes: Collected Essays*, Cambridge: Cambridge University Press, 367–81.

Bracke, T., M. Bussière, M. Fidora and R. Straub (2010), 'A framework for assessing global imbalances', *The World Economy*, **33** (9), 1140–74.

Bradford DeLong, J. (2011), 'The ECB battle against central banking', *Social Europe Journal*, 1 November.

Branstetter, L. and F. C. Foley (2010), 'Facts and fallacies about US FDI in China', in R. C. Feenstra and S.J. Wei (eds), *China's Growing Role in World Trade*, Chicago, IL: The University of Chicago Press, 591.

Brautigam, D. (2010), 'Looking East: Africa's newest investment partners', *Global Journal of Emerging Market Economy*, **2** (2), 173–88.

Bremmer, I. and N. Roubini (2011), 'A G-zero world: the new economic club will produce conflict, not cooperation', *Foreign Affairs*, **90** (2), 2–7.

Brooks, S. and W. C. Wohlforth (2011), 'Reshaping the world order: how Washington should reform international institutions', *Foreign Affairs*, **88** (2), 49–63.

Brown, G. W. and D. Held (eds) (2010), *The Cosmopolitan Reader*, Cambridge: Polity Press.

Bryan, K. A. and L. Martinez (2008), 'On the evolution of income inequality in the United States', *Economic Quarterly*, **94** (2), 97–120.

Buchanan, J. (1979), *What Should Economists Do?*, Indianapolis, IN: Liberty Press.

Buchanan, J. and G. Tullock (1965), *The Calculus of Consent: Logical Foundations of Constitutional Democracy*, Ann Arbor, MI: The University of Michigan Press.

Buchanan, J. and R. Wagner (1978), *Democracy in Deficit, The Political Legacy of Lord Keynes*, New York: Academic Press.

Caballero, J. R. and A. Krishnamurthly (2009), 'Global imbalances and financial fragility', *American Economic Review*, **99** (2), 584–8.

Caballero, R. J. (2010), 'The "other" imbalance and the financial crisis', NBER working paper series **15636**, 42.

Calleo, D. (2009), 'Twenty-first century geopolitics and the erosion of the dollar order', in E. Helleiner and J. Kirshner (eds), *The Future of the Dollar*, Ithaca, NY and London: Cornell University Press.

Cannan, E. (1912), *The Economic Outlook*, London: Fisher Unwin.

Cecchetti, S., M. S. Mohanty and F. Zampolli (2010), 'The future of public debt: prospects and implication', BIS working papers 300.

Cecchetti, S., M. Monhanty and F. Zampolli (2011), 'The real effects of debt', BIS working papers 352.

Celik, S. and U. Basdas (2010), 'How does globalization affect income inequality? A panel data analysis', *International Advances in Economic Research*, **16** (4), 358–70.

Cham, K. C., H. G. Fung and Q. W. Liu (2007), *China's Capital Markets: Introduction, Development and Challenges of Chinese Financial Markets*, Cheltenham, UK and Northampton, MA, USA: Edward Elgar.

Chamon, M. D. and E. S. Prasad (2010), 'Why are saving rates of urban households in China rising?', *American Economic Journal: Macroeconomics*, **2** (1), 93–130.

Chen, C. (ed) (2009), *China's Integration with the Global Economy*, Cheltenham, UK and Northampton, MA, USA: Edward Elgar.

Chen, J. and W. Liu (2007), 'An empirical study on the US-China trade deficit produced by FDI', *Frontiers of Economic in China*, **2** (3), 404–23.

Cheng, L. K. and Z. Ma (2010), 'China's outward foreign direct investments', in R. C. Feenstra and S. J. Wei (eds), *China's Growing Role in World Trade*, Chicago, IL: Chicago University Press, 545–78.

Chinn, M. D. and J. Frankel (2007), 'Will the euro eventually surpass the dollar as leading international reserve currency?', in *G7 Current Account Imbalances: Sustainability and Adjustment*, Chicago, IL: The University of Chicago Press.

Chinn, M. D. and J. A. Frankel (2009), 'The euro may over the next 15 years surpass the dollar as leading international currency', in A. S. Sisodya and J. N. Rao (eds), *The US Dollar: Dominance, Decline and Future*, Hyderabad, India: ICFAI University Press, 137–64.

Chinn, M. D. and H. Ito (2005), 'Current account balances, financial development and institutions: assaying the world "savings glut"', NBER working paper series 11761.

Clarida, R. (2005), 'Japan, China, and the U.S. current account deficit', *CATO Journal*, **25** (1).

Clarida, R. H. (ed) (2007), *G7 Current Account Imbalances: Sustainability and Adjustment*, Chicago, IL: The University of Chicago Press.

Clarida, R. H. and M. P. Taylor (2007), 'Are there thresholds of current account adjustment in the G7?', in R. H. Clarida (ed), *G7 Current Account Imbalances*, Chicago, IL: Chicago University Press.

Clower, R. W. (1967), 'A reconsideration of the microfoundations of monetary theory', *Western Economic Journal*, **6** (December), 1–8.

Cohen, B. (2009), 'Toward a leaderless currency system', in E. Helleiner and J. Kirshner (eds), *The Future of the Dollar*, Ithaca, NY and London: Cornell University Press.

Conceição, K. Le Goulven and R. U. Mendoza (eds), *Providing Global Public Goods. Managing Globalization*, New York: Oxford University Press.

Conceição, K. Le Goulven and R. U. Mendoza (2007), *Why Cooperate? The Incentive to Supply Global Public Good*, Oxford: Oxford University Press.

Cooke, J. E. (ed) (1964), *The Reports of Alexander Hamilton*, New York: Harper Torchbooks.

Corden, M. W. (2009), 'China's exchange rate policy, its current account surplus and the global imbalances', *The Economic Journal*, **119** (November), 430–41.

Cornia, A. G. (2003), 'The impact of liberalisation and globalisation on income inequality in developing and transitional economies', CESifo working paper 843.

Corsetti, G., P. Pesenti and N. Roubini (2005), 'What caused the Asian currency and financial crisis?', in N. Roubini and M. Uzan (eds), *New International Financial Architecture*, vol. I, Cheltenham, UK and Northampton, MA, USA: Edward Elgar, pp. 214–82.

Davidson, P. (1982), *International Money and the Real World*, London: Macmillan.

Davies, J. B., S. Sandstrom, A. Shorrocks and E. N. Wolf (2011), 'The level and distribution of global household wealth', *The Economic Journal*, **121** (March), 223–54.

De Boyer des Roches, J. and R. Solis Rosales (2011), 'R. G. Hawtrey on the national and international lender of last resort', *The European Journal of the History of Economic Thought*, **18** (2), 175–202.

De Fontanay, P. and G. M. Milesi-Ferretti (1997), 'The role of foreign currency debt in public debt management', in M. I. Blejer and T. Ter-Minassian (eds), *Macroeconomic Dimensions of Public Finance: Essays in Honor of Vito Tanzi*, London: Routledge.

De Grauwe, P. (2007), *The Economics of Monetary Union*, Oxford: Oxford University Press.

De Grauwe, P. (2009), 'The fragility of the Eurozone's institutions', *Open Economies Review*, **21** (1), 167–74.

De Grauwe, P. (2011), 'Europe needs the ECB to step up to the plate', *Financial Times*, 19 October.

De Gregorio, J. (2005), 'Global imbalances and exchange rate adjustment', in R. H. Clarida (ed), *G7 Current Account Imbalances*, Chicago, IL: Chicago University Press.

Deardoff, A. V. (1998), 'Determinants of bilateral trade: does gravity work in a neoclassical world?', in J. A. Frankel (ed), *The Regionalization of the World Economy*, Chicago, IL: Chicago University Press.

Delpla, J. and J. von Weizsacker (2010), 'The Blue Bond Proposal', *Bruegel Policy Brief*, **3**, 1–8.

Dettmann, G. (2011), 'A view on global imbalances and their contribution to the financial crisis', *Birkbeck Working Paper Series in Economics and Finance*, **1102**, 1–28.

Devroye, D. and R. B. Freeman (2001), 'Does inequality in skills explain inequality in earnings across advanced countries?', NBER working paper series 8140.

Dobson, W. and P. R. Masson (2009), 'Will the renminbi become a world currency?', *China Economic Review*, **20**, 124–35.

Dooley, M. P., D. Folkerts-Landau and P. Garber (2003), 'An essay on the revived Bretton Woods system', NBER working paper series 9971.

Dooley, M. P., D. Folkerts-Landau and P. Garber (2007), 'Direct investment: rising real wages and the absorption of excess labour in the perifery', in R. H. Clarida (ed), *G7 Current Account Imbalances*, Chicago, IL: Chicago University Press.

Dooley, M. P., D. Folkerts-Landau and P. M. Garber (2004), 'The US currrent account deficit and economic development: collateral for a total return swap', NBER working paper series 10727.

Dreher, A. and N. Gaston (2008), 'Has globalization increased inequality?', *Review of International Economics*, **16** (3), 516–36.

Driffil, J. and P. Subacchi (eds) (2010), *Beyond the Dollar: Rethinking the International Monetary System*, London: Chatamhouse.

Duncan, R. (2005), *The Dollar Crisis*, Singapore: John Wiley & Sons.

Dutta, M. (2005), 'The theory of optimum currency area revisited: lessons from the euro/dollar competitive currency regimes', *Journal of Asian Economics*, **16**, 352–75.

Dyan, K. E., J. Skinner and S. P. Zeldes (2004), 'Do the rich save more?', *Journal of Political Economy*, **112** (2), 397–444.

EC (2011a), *Green Paper on the Feasibility of Introducing Stability Bonds*, Brussels: COM (2011) 818 Final.

EC (2011b), *A Pilot for the Europe 2020 Project Bond Initiative*, Brussels: COM (2011) 660 final.

EC (2011c), *Proposal for a Regulation of the European Parliament and of the Council Establishing the Connecting Europe Facility*, Brussels: COM (2011) 665.

ECB (2010a), 'The ECB's response to the financial crisis', *Monthly Bulletin*, October, 59–74.

ECB (2010b), 'Euro area fiscal policies and the crisis', *Occasional Paper Series*, 109.

ECB (2011), *The International Role of the Euro*, Frankfurt am Main: European Central Bank.

Edwards, S. (2005a), 'The end of large current account deficits, 1970–2002: are there lessons for the United States?', NBER working paper series 11669.

Edwards, S. (2005b), 'Is the US current account deficit sustainable? And if not how costly is the adjustment likely to be?', NBER working paper series 11541.

Edwards, S. (2007), 'On current account surpluses and the correction of global imbalances', NBER working paper series 12904.

Eichengreen, B. (1992), *Golden Fetters*, Oxford: Oxford University Press.

Eichengreen, B. (1996), *Globalizing Capital: A History of the International Monetary System*, Princeton, NJ: Princeton University Press.

Eichengreen, B. (1997), *European Monetary Unification: Theory, Practice and Analysis*, Cambridge: MIT Press.

Eichengreen, B. (2007), *The European Economy Since 1945: Coordinated Capitalism and Beyond*, Princeton, NJ: Princeton University Press.

Eichengreen, B. (2011), *Exorbitant Privilege*, New York: Oxford University Press.

Eichengreen, B. and M. Flandreau (2008), 'The rise and the fall of the dollar (or when did the dollar replace sterling as the leading international currency?)', *European Review of Economic History*, **13** (3), 377–411.

Eilstrup-Sangiovanni (ed) (2006), *Debates on European Integration: A Reader*, London: Palgrave Macmillan.

Engel, C. and J. H. Rogers (2006), 'The US current account deficit and the expected share of world output', NBER working paper series 11921.

Evans, R. (2010), 'Tata's Outbound Strategy', *International Financial Law Review*, **29** (2), 30–51.

Feenstra, R. C. and S. J. Wei (eds) (2010), *China's Growing Role in World Trade*, Chicago, IL: The University of Chicago Press.

Feldstein, M. S. (2008), 'Resolving the global imbalance: the dollar and the U.S. saving rate', NBER working paper series 13952.

Feldstein, M. S. (2011), 'The role of currency realignments in eliminating the US and China current account imbalances', NBER working paper series 16674.

Ferguson, N. (2011), *Civilization: The West and the Rest*, London: Allen Lane.

Finer, S. E. (1993–99), *History of Government from the Earliest Times (3 volumes)*, Oxford: Oxford University Press.

Fiorentini, R. (2002), 'Current account deficit and seignorage in a two countries pure endowment monetary model with asymmetric liquidity constraints', *RISEC*, **1**, 81–95.

Fiorentini, R. (2005), 'The international role of the euro and the relationship between Europe and the International Monetary Fund', *Il Politico*, **LXX** (1), 35–55.

Fiorentini, R. and G. Montani (2010), 'Global imbalances and the transition to a symmetric world monetary system', *Perspective on Federalism*, **2** (1), 1–42.

Fischer, S. (2000), *On the Need for an International Lender of Last Resort*, Princeton, NJ: Princeton Essays in International Economics.

Florio, M. (2002), 'Economists, privatisation in Russia and the waning of the "Washington consensus"', *Review of International Political Economy*, **9** (2), 359–400.

Fonteyne, W., L. Cortavarria-Checkley, A. Giustiniani, A. Gullo, D. Hardy and S. Kerr (2010), 'Crisis management and resolution for a European banking system', IMF working paper WP/10/70.

Forbes, K. J. (2008), 'Why do foreigners invest in the United States?', NBER working paper series 13908.

Foreman-Peck, J. (1995), *A History of the World Economy: International Economic Relations Since 1850*, Hemel Hempstead: Harvester Wheatsheaf.

Frattianni, M. and F. Spinelli (1997), *A Monetary History of Italy*, New York: Cambridge University Press.

Fratzscher, M. and A. Mehel (2011), 'China's dominance hypothesis and the emergence of a tri-polar global currency system', ECB working paper series 1392 (October), 1–44.

Freund, C. and E. Ornelas (2010), 'Regional trade agreement', *Annual Review of Economics*, **2** (1), 139–66.

Fukao, K., T. Okubo and R. M. Stern (2003), 'Trade diversion under NAFTA', in R. M. Stern (ed), *World Scientific Studies in International Economics*, vol. 9, Hackensack, NJ and Singapore: Word Scientific, 303–42.

Fukuyama, F. (1992), *The End of History and the Last Man*, New York: The Free Press.

Gaddis, J. L. (1987), *The Long Peace: Inquiries into the History of the Cold-War*, New York and Oxford: Oxford University Press.

Galbraith, J. and L. Jiaqing (1999), 'Inequality and financial crisis: some early findings', UTIP working paper 9.

Gale, W. G. and J. Sabelhaus (1999), 'Perspectives on the household saving rate', *Brookings Papers on Economic Activity*, **1**, 181–224.

Gardner, R. N. (1969), *Sterling-Dollar Diplomacy*, New York: McGraw-Hill.

Gatti, D. and A. Glyn (2006), 'Welfare states in hard times', *Oxford Review of Economic Policy*, **22** (3), 301–12.

Gellner, E. (1983), *Nations and Nationalism*, Oxford: Basil Blackwell.

Gilpin, R. (2001), *Global Political Economy: Understanding the International Economic Order*, Princeton, NJ: Princeton University Press.

Golberg, L. S. and C. Tlle (2008), 'Macroeconomic interdependence and the international role of the dollar', NBER working paper series 13820.

Goldberg, L. (2010), 'Is the international role of the dollar changing?', *Federal Reserve Bank of New York Current Issues in Economics and Finance*, **16** (1), 1–7.

Goldberg, P. K. and N. Pavcnik (2007), 'Distributional effects of globalization in developing countries', *Journal of Economic Literature*, **45** (3), 39–82.

Gomes, L. (1990), *Neoclassical International Economics: An Historical Survey*, London: Macmillan.

Goodhart, C. A. E. (2010), 'The changing role of central banks', BIS working papers 326.

Gourinchas, P. and H. Rey (2005), 'From world banker to world venture capitalist: US external adjustment and the exorbitant privilege', NBER working paper series 11563.

Gu, J. (2009), 'China's private enterprises in Africa and the implications for African development', *European Journal of Development Research*, **21** (4), 570–87.

Guidolin, M. and E. A. La Jeunesse (2007), 'The decline in the US personal saving rate: is it real and is it a puzzle?', *Federal Reserve Bank of St. Louis Review*, **89** (6), 491–514.

Haass, R. (2008), 'The age of nonpolarity', *Foreign Affairs*, **87** (3), 44–56.

Hamada, K., B. Reszat and U. Voltz (2009), *Toward Monetary and Financial Integration in East Asia*, Cheltenham, UK and Northampton, MA, USA: Edward Elgar.

Hanson, P. (2004), 'Putin and Russia's economic transformation', *Eurasia Geography and Economics*, **45** (6), 421–28.

Haug, J., A. Lamassoure and G. Verhofstadt (2011), *Europe for Growth: for Radical Change in Financing the EU*, Brussels: Notre Europe, Paris, and the Centre for European Policy Studies.

Hayek, F. A. (1999), 'The denationalisation of money: an analysis of the theory and practice of concurrent currency', in S. Kresge (ed), *The Collected Works of F. A. Hayek, Good Money: The Standard*, vol. 6, part II, London: Routledge.

Held, D. (1995), *Democracy and the Global Order: from the Modern State to Cosmopolitan Governance*, London: Polity Press.

Helleiner, E. and J. Kirshner (2009), *The Future of the Dollar*, Ithaca, NY and London: Cornell University Press.

Hicks, J. (1969), *A Theory of Economic History*, Oxford: Oxford University Press.

Hines, J. R. (2006), 'Will social welfare expenditures survive tax competition?', *Oxford Review of Economic Policy*, **22** (3), 330–47.

Hines, J. R. and L. H. Summers (2009), 'How globalization affects tax design', in J. R. Brown (ed), *Tax Policy and the Economy*, Chicago, IL: University of Chicago Press, 123–57.

Hobsbawm, E. J. (1990), *Nations and Nationalism since 1780: Programme, Myth, Reality*, Cambridge: Cambridge University Press.

Hodgson, G. M. (1998), 'The approach of institutional economics', *Journal of Economic Literature*, **36** (1), 166–92.

Hodgson, G. M. and T. Knudsen (2006), 'Why we need a generalized Darwinism, and why generalized Darwinism is not enough', *Journal of Economic Behaviour & Organization*, **61** (1–61).

Hong, P. (2001), 'Global implications of the United States trade deficit adjustment', DESA discussion paper 17.

Hooper, P. and C. L. Mann (1989), 'The emergence and persistence of the US external imbalance, 1980–1987', *Princeton Studies in International Finance*, 65.

Hoshi, T. and A. K. Kashyap (2004), 'Japan's financial crisis and economic stagnation', *Journal of Economic Perspectives*, **18** (1), 3–26.

Huang, H. (2007), 'Chinese financial market no longer isolated from the world at large', *China Economist*, **10**, 130–55.

Ikenberry, G. J. (2001), 'The future of the liberal world order', *Foreign Affairs*, **90** (3), 56–68.

International Labour Organization (ILO) (2008), *World of Work Report 2008*, Geneva: ILO.

International Monetary Fund (IMF) (2010), *World Economic Outlook: Recovery, Risk and Rebalancing*, Washington: IMF.

IMF (2011a), *Enhancing International Monetary Stability: a role for the SDR*, Washington: IMF.

IMF (2011b), *Strengthening the International Monetary System: Taking Stock and Looking Ahead*, Washington: IMF.

Inman, R. P. (2003), 'Transfers and bailouts: enforcing local fiscal discipline with lessons from US federalism', in J. Rodden, G. S. Eskeland and J. Litvack (eds), *Fiscal Decentralization and the Challenge of Hard Budget Constraints*, Cambridge, MA and London: The MIT Press.

Issing, O. (2000), *Hayek, Currency Competition and European Monetary Union*, London: Institute of Economic Affairs.

Issing, O. (2008), *The Birth of the Euro*, Cambridge: Cambridge University Press.

James, H. (2010), 'Central banks: between internationalisation and domestic political control', BIS working paper 327.

Jauomotte, F., S. Lall and C. Papageorgiou (2008), 'Rising income inequality: technology or trade and financial globalization?', IMF working paper 185.

Jayakumar, V. and B. Weiss (2011), 'Global reserve currency system: why will the dollar standard give way to a tripolar currency order?', *Frontiers of Economics in China*, **6** (1), 92–130.

Jeanne, O. and C. Wyplosz (2001), 'The international lender of last resort: how large is large enough?', NBER working paper series 8381.

Jing, J. and H. F. Zou (2003), 'Soft-budget constraints and local government in China', in J. Rodden, G. S. Eskeland and J. Litvack (eds), *Fiscal Decentralization and the Challenge of Hard Budget Constraints*, Cambridge, MA and London: The MIT Press, 289–323.

Jordà, O., M. Schularick and A. M. Taylor (2010), 'Financial crisis, credit booms, and external imbalances: 140 years of lessons', NBER working paper series 16567.

Jorgenson, D. W. and K. Vu (2005), 'Information technology and the world economy', *Scandinavian Journal of Economics*, **107** (4), 631–50.

Kagan, R. (2008), *The Return of History and the End of Dreams*, New York: Alfred A. Knopf.

Kaminsky, G. L. and C. M. Reinhart (1999), 'The twin crisis: the causes of banking and balance-of-payments problems', *The American Economic Review*, **89** (3), 473–500.

Kaplan, R. D. (2009), 'Center stage for the twenty-first century: power plays in the Indian Ocean', *Foreign Affairs*, **88** (2), 17–32.

Kaul, I., P. Conceiçào, K. Le Goulven and R. U. Mendoza (eds) (2003), *Providing Global Public Goods: Managing Globalization*, New York: Oxford University Press.

Kaul, I., I. Grunberg and M. A. Stern (eds) (1990), *Global Public Goods: International Cooperation in the 21st Century*, New York: Oxford University Press.

Kelly, B. (2009), 'China's challenge to the international monetary system: incremental steps and long-term prospective for internationalization of the renminbi', *CSIS Issues and Insights*, **9** (11).

Kenen, P. (1995), *Economic and Monetary Union in Europe; Moving Beyond Maastricht*, London and New York: Cambridge University Press.

Kenen, P. and E. Meade (2008), *Regional Monetary Integration*, London and New York: Cambridge University Press.

Kennedy, P. (1988), *The Rise and Fall of the Great Powers: Economic Change and Military Conflict from 1500 to 2000*, London: Unwin Hyman.

Kenwood, A. G. and A. L. Lougheed (1983), *The Growth of the International Economy 1820–1980. An Introductory Text*, London: Allen & Unwin.

Keynes, J. M. (1933), 'National self-sufficiency', in D. Moggridge and A. Robinson (eds), *The Collected Writings of John Maynard Keynes. XXI Activities 1931–9: World Crisis and Policies in Britain and America*, Basingstoke: Macmillan and Cambridge University Press, 233–46.

Kindleberger, C. P. (1987), *The World in Depression 1929–1939*, Harmondsworth: Pelican Books.

Kindleberger, C. P. and R. Aliber (2005), *Manias, Panic and Crashes: A History of Financial Crisis*, 5th edn, London: Palgrave Macmillan.

Klein, L. and M. Pomer (2001), *The New Russia: Transition gone Awry*, Stanford: Stanford University Press.

Kouparitsas, M. (2005), 'Is the US current account sustainable?', *Chicago FED Letter*, 215.

Kraay, A. (2000), 'Household saving in China', World Bank policy research working paper 3633.

Kreinin, M. E. (1959), 'On the "trade-diversion" effect of trade-preference areas', *Journal of Political Economy*, **67**, 398–401.

Krugman, P. R. and R. E. Baldwin (1987), 'The persistence of the US trade deficit', *Brookings Papers on Economic Activity*, **1**, 1–55.

Krugman, P. R. and R. Wells (2010), 'The slump goes on: why?', *The New York Review of Books*, 30 September.

Kupchan, C. (2011), *The End of the American Era*, New York: Random House, Inc.

Ladeur, K. H. (2004), 'Globalization and conversion of democracy to polycentric networks: can democracy survive the end of the nation state?', in K. H. Ladeur (ed), *Public Governance in the Age of Globalization*, Aldershot: Ashgate.

Laibson, D. and J. Mollerstrom (2011), 'Capital flows, consumption booms and asset bubbles: a behavioural alternative to the saving glut hypothesis', NBER working paper series 15759.

Lardy, N. and P. Douglass (2011), 'Capital account liberalization and the role of the renminbi', *Peterson Institute for International Economics*, working paper 11–6.

Lawrence, R. Z. (2008), *Blue Collar Blues: Is Trade to Blame for Rising US Income Inequality?* Washington DC: Peterson Institute for International Economics.

Lee, J. and M. D. Chinn (2002), 'Current account and real exchange rate dynamics in the G-7 countries', IMF working paper WP/02/130.

Leightner, J. E. (2010), 'Are the forces that cause China's trade surplus with the USA good?', *Journal of Chinese Economic and Foreign Trade Studies*, **3** (1), 43–53.

Levine, R. (2010), 'The governance of financial regulation: reform lessons from the recent crisis', BIS working papers 329.

Lindert, P. H. and J. G. Williamson (2001), 'Does globalization make the world more unequal?', NBER working paper series 8228.

Lipsey, R. G. (1957), 'The theory of custom unions: trade diversion and welfare', *Economica*, **24**, 40–46.

Liu, C. Z. (2007), 'Lenovo: an example of globalization of Chinese enterprises', *Journal of International Business Studies*, **38** (4), 573–77.

Machlup, F. (ed) (1976), *Economic Integration Worldwide, Regional, Sectoral*, London: Macmillan.

Majone, G. (1996), *Regulating Europe*, London: Routledge.

Maki, D. M. and M. G. Palumbo (2001), 'Disentangling the wealth effect: a cohort analysis of household saving in the 1990s', Board of Governor of the Federal System finance and economics discussion series 21.

Malle, S. (2008), 'Economic transformation in Russia and China: how do we compare success?', *Eurasia Geography and Economics*, **49** (4), 410–44.

Marquis, M. (2002), 'What's behind the low US personal saving rate?', *Federal Reserve Bank of San Francisco Economic Letter*, **9**, 1–3.

Marshall, A. (1923), *Money, Credit and Commerce*, London: Macmillan.

Marshall, A. (1930), *The Pure Theory of Foreign Trade: The Pure Theory of Domestic Values*, London: The London School of Economics and Political Science.

Masson, P. and A. M. Taylor (1993), *Policy Issues in the Operation of Currency Unions*, New York: Cambridge University Press.

Matsushita, M. (2008), 'Proliferation of free trade agreements and development perspectives', *Law and Development Review*, **1** (1), 23–49.

Matsushita, M. (2010), 'Proliferation of free trade agreements and development perspectives', Law and Development Institute Inaugural Conference. Sydney, Australia, accessed at www.lawanddevelopment. net/img/matsushita.pdf.

McCallum, B. T. (1999), 'Theoretical issues pertaining to monetary unions', NBER working paper series, **7393**, 1–31.

McCarten, W. (2003), 'The challenge of fiscal discipline in the Indian states', in J. Rodden, G. S. Eskeland and J. Litvack (eds), *Fiscal Decentralization and the Challenge of Hard Budget Constraints*, Cambridge, MA and London: The MIT Press, 249–86.

McCormick (2008), *Understanding the European Union: A Concise Introduction*, London: Palgrave Macmillan.

McKinnon, R. I. (1997), 'Market-preserving fiscal federalism in the American monetary union', in M. I. Blejer and T. Ter-Minassian (eds), *Macroeconomic Dimensions of Public Finance: Essays in Honor of Vito Tanzi*, London: Routledge, 73–93.

McKinnon, R. I. (2004), 'Optimum currency areas: Mundell I versus Mundell II', *Journal of Common Market Studies*, **42** (4), 689–715.

Meier, G. (1982), *Problems of a World Monetary Order*, Oxford: Oxford University Press.

Milesi-Ferretti, G. M. and A. Razin (1996), 'Current account sustainability', *Princeton Studies in International Finance*, 81.

Milesi-Ferretti, G. M. and A. Razin (1997), 'Sharp reductions in current account deficit: an empirical analysis', NBER working paper series 6310.

Minsky, H. P. (1975), *John Maynard Keynes*, New York: Columbia University Press.

Moghadam, R. (2011), 'Strengthening the international monetary system: taking stock and looking ahead', *IMF*, 23 March.

Mohan, G. and M. Power (2008), 'New African choices? The politics of Chinese engagement', *Review of African Political Economy*, **35** (115), 23–42.

Montani, G. (1996), *L'economia Politica e il Mercato Mondiale [Political Economy and World Market]*, Bari, Italy: Laterza.

Montani, G. (2008), *L'economia Politica dell'integrazione Europea [The Political Economy of European Integration]*, Novara, Italy: UTET.

Montani, G. (2010), 'Lo stato sovranazionale: ordine cooperativo e ordine coercitivo nell'esperienza Europea' (The supranational state: cooperative order and coercive order in the European experience)', *Il Politico*, LXVV (May–August), 27–52.

Montani, G. (2011a), 'Money and finance as global public goods: contribution to a supranational macroeconomic theory', *SAGE Open*, I (11).

Montani, G. (2011b), 'The neo-Ricardian theory of economic integration', in R. Ciccone, C. Gehrke and G. Mongiovi (eds), *Sraffa and Modern Economics*, vol. II, London: Routledge, 229–39.

Montani, G. (2012), 'World trade and world money: A neoricardian outlook on global economy', *Bulletin of Political Economy*, 6 (1).

Mulhearn, C. and H. R. Vane (2008), *The Euro: Its Origin, Development and Prospects*, Cheltenham, UK and Northampton, MA, USA: Edward Elgar.

Mundell, R. (2005), 'The case for a world currency', *Journal of Policy Modelling*, 27, 465–75.

Murnane, R. J., J. B. Willet and F. Levy (1995), 'The growing importance of cognitive skills in wage determination', NBER working paper series 5076.

Musgrave, R. (1981), 'Leviathan cometh – or does he?', in H. Ladd and T. Tideman (eds), *Tax Expenditure Limitations*, Washington, DC: The Urban Institute Press.

Musgrave, R. (1998), 'The role of the state in fiscal theory', in P. Birch (ed), *Public Finance in a Changing World*, Houndmills: Macmillan, 35–50.

Nagel, T. (2010), 'The problem of global justice', in *Secular Philosophy and the Religious Temperament: Essays 2002–2008*, Oxford: Oxford University Press, 61–91.

Nye, J. S. (2010), 'The future of American power: dominance and decline in perspective', *Foreign Affairs*, 89 (6), 2–12.

Nye, J. S. (2011), 'Zakaria's world', in *Foreign Policy*, 8 March.

Oates W. E. (2008), 'On the theory and practice of fiscal decentralization', in A. J. Auerbach and D. N. Shaviro (eds), *Institutional Foundations of Public Finance: Economic and Legal Perspectives*, Cambridge, MA and London: Harvard University Press, 165–89.

Obstfeld, M. and K. Rogoff (1998), *Foundation of Intertemporal International Economics*, Cambridge, MA: MIT Press.

Obstfeld, M. (2005), 'America's deficit, the world problem', *Monetary and Economic Studies* (special edition).

Obstfeld, M. (2009), 'International finance and growth in developping countries: what have we learned?', *IMF Staff Papers*, **56** (1), 63–111.

Obstfeld, M. and K. Rogoff (2007), 'The unsustainable US current account position revisited', in R. H. Clarida (ed), *G7 Current Account Imbalances*, Chicago, IL: Chicago University Press.

Organisation for Economic Co-operation and Development (OECD) (2008), *Growing Unequal? Income Distribution and Poverty in OECD Countries*, Paris: OECD.

OECD (2010), *Factbook 2010: Economic, Environmental and Social Statistics*, Paris: OECD.

OECD (2011a), *Divided We Stand: Why Inequality Keeps Rising*, Paris: OECD.

OECD (2011b), *Growing Income Inequality in OECD Countries: What Drives It and How Can Policy Tackle It?*, Paris: OECD.

Padoa-Schioppa, T. (1992), *L'Europa Verso L'unione Monetaria: Dallo SME al Trattato di Maastricht*, Turin, Italy: Einaudi. English translation, with minor changes (1994): *The Road to Monetary Union in Europe: The Emperor, the Kings, and the Genies*, Oxford: Clarendon Press.

Pakko, M. P. (1999), 'The US trade deficit and the new economy', *Federal Reserve Bank of St. Louis Review*, September/October.

Palais-Royal Initiative (2011), *Reform of the International Monetary System: A Cooperative Approach for the Twenty First Century*, a group convened by M. Camdessus, A. Lamfalussy and T. Padoa Schioppa, Paris.

Palma, J. G. (2006), 'Globalizing inequality: "centrifugal" and "centripetal" forces at work', DESA working paper **35**, 1–23.

Palma, J. G. (2009a), 'The revenge of the market on the rentiers: why neo-liberal reports of the end of the history turned out to be premature', *Cambridge Journal of Economics*, **33** (4), 829–66.

Palma, J. G. (2009b), 'The revenge of the market on the rentiers: why neo-liberal reports of the end of the history turned out to be premature', Cambridge working papers in economics 0927 (June).

Parker, G. (1974), 'The emergence of modern finance in Europe', in C. M. Cipolla (ed), *The Fontana Economic History of Europe: The Sixteenth and Seventeenth Centuries*, Glasgow: William Collins & Co.

Parker, J. (1999), 'Spendthrift in America? On two decades of decline in the US saving rate', in, *NBER Macroecomics Annual*, 317–69.

Plummer, M. G. and R. W. Click (2009), 'The ASEAN economic community and the European experience', in *Toward Monetary and Financial Integration in East Asia*, Cheltenham, UK and Northampton, MA, USA: Edward Elgar.

Pogatsa, Z. (2011), *Heterodox International Political Economy*, Sopron, Hungary: University of West Hungary Press.

Pogge, T. (2010), *Politics as Usual: What Lies Behind the Pro-Poor Rhetoric*, Cambridge: Polity Press.

Przesworski, A. and J. R. Wreeland (2002), 'The effects of IMF programs on economic growth', *Journal of Development Economics*, **62**, 384–421.

Quadrio Curzio, A. and V. Miceli (2010), *Sovereign Wealth Funds: A Complete Guide to State-Owned Investment Funds*, Petersfield: Harriman House Publishing.

Qureshi, M. S. and G. Wan (2008), 'Distributional consequences of globalization: empirical evidence from panel data', *Journal of Development Studies*, **44** (10), 1424–49.

Rajan, R. G. (2010), *Fault Lines: How Hidden Fractures Still Threaten the World Economy*, Princeton, NJ and Oxford: Princeton University Press.

Redish, A. (2000), *Bimetallism: An Economic and Historical Analysis*, New York: Cambridge University Press.

Reich, R. B. (2010), *Aftershock*, New York: Alfred A. Knopf.

Reinhard, W. (1999), *Geschicthe der Staatgewalt (History of State Power)*, Munich, Germany: Verlag C. H. Beck.

Reinhart, C. M. and K. Rogoff (2008), 'This time is different: a panoramic view of eight centuries of financial crisis', NBER working paper series 13882.

Reinhart, C. M. and K. S. Rogoff (2009), *This Time is Different*, Princeton, NJ: Princeton University Press.

Reinhart, C. M. and M. B. Sbrancia (2011), 'The liquidation of government debt', *Peterson Institute for International Economics*, 11–10.

Ricardo, D. (1951a), 'On the principles of political economy and taxation', in P. Sraffa and M. Dobb (eds), *The Works and Correspondence of David Ricardo*, vol. I, Cambridge: Cambridge University Press.

Ricardo, D. (1951b), 'Pamphlets and Papers 1815–1823', in P. Sraffa and M. Dobb (eds), *The Works and Correspondence of David Ricardo*, vol. IV, Cambridge: Cambridge University Press.

Robbins, L. (1937), *Economic Planning and International Order*, London: Macmillan.

Robbins, L. (1952), *The Theory of Economic Policy in English Classical Political Economy*, London: Macmillan.

Rodden, J. A. (2006), *Hamilton's Paradox: The Promise and Peril of Fiscal Federalism*, Cambridge: Cambridge University Press.

Rodden, J. A., G. S. Eskeland and J. Litvack (eds) (2003), *Fiscal Decentralization and the Challenge of Hard Budget Constraints*, Cambridge, MA and London: The MIT Press.

Rodrik, D. and A. Subramanian (2009), 'Why did financial globalization disappoint?', *IMF Staff Papers*, **56** (1), 112–38.

Rossi, E. and A. Spinelli (1941), 'The Ventotene manifesto', accessed at www.altierospinelli.org.

Ruding, H. O. (2010), 'From national to European regulation: towards European financial supervisory authorities', *CEPS Policy Brief*, **209** (May).

Saccomani, F. (2008), *Managing International Financial Instability: National Tames versus Global Tigers*, Cheltenham, UK and Northampton, MA, USA: Edward Elgar.

Sachs, J. (2008), *Common Wealth: Economics for a Crowded Planet*, New York: Penguin Press.

Sachs, J. (2011), *The Price of Civilization: Reawakening American Virtue and Prosperity*, New York: Random House.

Salvatore, D. (2000), 'The euro, the dollar, and the international monetary system', *Journal of Policy Modelling*, **22** (3), 407–15.

Schinasi, G. J. (2003), 'Responsibility of central banks for stability in financial markets', IMF working paper WP/03/121.

Searle, J. R. (1995), *The Construction of Social Reality*, New York: Free Press.

Searle, J. R. (2005), 'What is an institution?', *Journal of Institutional Economics*, **1** (1), 1–22.

Searle, J. R. (2010), *Making the Social World: The Structure of Human Civilization*, Oxford: Oxford University Press.

Shusong, B. and S. Shanshan (2010), 'Research on China's export structure to the US: analysis based on the US economic growth and exchange rate', *Frontiers of Economics in China*, **5** (3), 339–55.

Sing, A. (2011), 'Reviving the animal spirits: a strategy for promoting growth in Japan', IMF and Nihon Keizai Shimbun, 31 January.

Singer, P. (2002), *One World. The Ethics of Globalization*, New Haven, CT and London: Yale University Press.

Smith, V. C. (1990), *The Rationale of Central Banking and the Free Banking Alternative*, Indianapolis, IN: Liberty Press.

Stiglitz, J. E. (2002), *Globalization and Its Discontents*, W.W. Norton and Company.

Stiglitz, J. E. (2006), *Making Globalization Work*, New York: W. W. Norton and Company.

Stiglitz, J. E. (2010), *Freefall: America, Free Markets, and the Sinking of the World Economy*, New York and London: W. W. Norton and Company.

Stiglitz, J. E. and A. Charlton (2005), *Fair Trade for All*, Oxford: Oxford University Press.

Strange, S. (2002), 'Finance in politics: an epilogue to mad money, 1998', in B. J. Cohen (ed), *International Monetary Relations in the New Global Economy*, vol. II, Cheltenham, UK and Northampton, MA, USA: Edward Elgar, 429–47.

Strauss, J. C. and M. Saavedra (2009), 'Introduction: China, Africa and internationalization', *China Quarterly*, **0** (199), 551–62.

Summers, L. and C. Carroll (1987), 'Why is US national saving so low?', *Brookings Papers on Economic Activity*, **1987** (2), 607–42.

Tanzi, V. (2000), 'Globalization, technological development, and the work of fiscal termites', IMF working paper WP/00/181.

Tanzi, V. (2011), *Government versus Markets: The Changing Economic Role of the State*, Cambridge and New York: Cambridge University Press.

Tanzi, V. and L. Schuknecht (2000), *Public Spending in the 20th Century: A Global Perspective*, Cambridge: Cambridge University Press.

Taylor, A. (2011), 'Tata takes on the world building an auto empire in India', *Fortune*, **163** (6), 86–92.

Taylor, J. B. (2009), *Getting Off Track: How Government Actions and Interventions Cause, Prolonged, and Worsened the Financial Crisis*, Stanford, CA: Hoover Institution Press.

The Economist (2011a), 'Taming Leviathan: a special report on the future of the state', 19 March.

The Economist (2011b), 'To rip asunder', 17 September.

The New York Times (2011), 'Executive pay', 8 September.

Thomson, D. (1972), *Europe Since Napoleon*, Harmondsworth: Penguin Book.

Toulemon, R. (2007), *Aimer l'Europe [Love Europe]*, Paris: Lignes de Repère.

Trichet J-C. (2011), 'Tomorrow and the day after tomorow: a vision for Europe', Humbold University, Berlin, accessed at www.ecb.int/press/key/date/2011/html/sp111024.en.html.

Triffin, R. (1960), *Gold and the Dollar Crisis: The Future of Convertibility*, New Haven, CT: Yale University Press.

Triffin, R. (1968), *Our International Monetary System: Yesterday, Today and Tomorrow*, New York: Random House.

Triffin, R. (1981), 'An economist's career: What? Why? How?', *Banca Nazionale del Lavoro – Quarterly Review*, **138**, 239–59.

Triffin, R. (1992), 'The IMS (International Monetary System . . . or scandal?) and the EMS (European Monetary System . . . or success?)', *Banca Nazionale del Lavoro – Quarterly Review*, special issue (June).

Ulubasoglu, M. A. (2004), 'Globalisation and inequality', *The Australian Economic Review*, **37** (1), 116–22.

United Nations Conference on Trade and Development (UNCTAD) (2011), *Trade and Development Report*, New York and Geneva: UNCTAD.

United Nations Development Programme (UNDP) (2011), *Human Development Report 2011: Sustainability and Equity: A Better Future for All*, Basingstoke and New York: Palgrave Macmillan.

Vaubel, R. (2009), 'The future of fiscal federalism and the need for global government: a response to Vito Tanzi', *European Journal of Political Economy*, **25**, 133–36.

Wang, J. Y. (2007), 'What drives China's growing role in Africa?', IMF working papers **07** (211), 30.

Weingast, B. R. (1995), 'The economic role of political institutions: market-preserving federalism and economic development', *The Journal of Law, Economics, and Organization*, **11** (1), 1–31.

Wheare, K. C. (1967), *Federal Government*, Oxford: Oxford University Press.

Whitaker, J. K. (1975), *The Early Economic Writings of Alfred Marshall*, vol. 2, London: Macmillan.

Wildasin, D. E. (2004), 'The institutions of federalism: toward an analytical framework', *National Tax Journal*, **LVII** (2, Part 1), 247–72.

William and Lovet (1988), 'Solving the US trade deficit and competitiveness problem', *Journal of Economic Issues*, **22** (2), 459–67.

Williamson, J. (ed) (1990), *Latin America Adjustment: How Much Has Happened?*, Washington, DC: Peterson Institute for International Economics.

Williamson, O. E. (2000), 'The new institutional economics: taking stock, looking ahead', *Journal of Economic Literature*, **38**, 595–613.

Wolf, M. (2008), *Fixing Global Finance*, New Haven, CT and London: Yale University Press.

Wolff, E. (2010), 'Recent trends in household wealth in the United States: rising debt and the middle-class squeeze – an update to 2007', Levy Economic Institute working papers 589.

Wood, A. (1999), 'Openess and wage inequality in developing countries: the Latin America challenge to East Asian conventional wisdom', in R. Baldwin, D. Cohen and A. Sapir (eds), *Market Integration, Regionalism and the Global Economy*, New York and Melbourne: Cambridge University Press, 153–81.

World Bank (2001), *World Development Report*, Washington DC: The World Bank.

World Bank (2010), *World Development Report: Development and Climate Change*, Washington, DC: The World Bank.

World Bank (2011a), *Multipolarity: the New Global Economy*, Washington: The World Bank.

World Bank (2011b), *World Development Report: Conflict, Security, and Development*, Washington: The World Bank.

Xinhua, H. and C. Yongfu (2007), 'Understanding high saving rates in China', *China & World Economy*, **15** (1), 1–13.

Yang, D. T., J. Zhang and S. Zhou (2011), 'Why are saving rates so high in China?', NBER working paper series **16771**, 1–45.

Yang, L. and C. Liao (2007), 'US FDI in China has widened China-US trade surplus', *China Economist*, May, 83–9.

Zakaria, F. (2009), 'Are America's best days behind us?', Time.

Zakaria, F. (2011), *The Post-American World: Release 2.0*, New York: W.W. Norton and Company.

Zhou, X. (2009a), *Reform the International Monetary System*, Beijing: People's Bank of China.

Zhou, X. (2009b), 'On saving ratio', Speech at The People's Bank of China, Beijing: People's Bank of China.

Index